Cross the Water Blues

CROSS the
WATER
BLUES

||||||||||||||||||||||||||||||||||||||||||||||||||

AFRICAN AMERICAN
MUSIC IN EUROPE

Edited by NEIL A. WYNN

UNIVERSITY PRESS OF MISSISSIPPI / JACKSON

www.upress.state.ms.us

The University Press of Mississippi is a member
of the Association of American University Presses.

First Edition 2007

∞

Library of Congress Cataloging-in-Publication Data
Cross the water blues : African American music in Europe / edited by Neil A. Wynn.
—1st ed.
    p. cm. — (American made music series)
Includes bibliographical references and index.

ISBN-13: 978-1-60473-546-8   1. African Americans—Europe—
Music—History and criticism.   2. African Americans—Music—Influence.
3. Popular music—Europe—History and criticism.   I. Wynn, Neil A.
    ML3488.C76 2007
    780.89'9607304—dc22   2007004256

British Library Cataloging-in-Publication Data available

Contents

Preface

The centenary celebrations of W. C. Handy's "discovery" of the blues in 2003[1] included considerable recognition of the influence of the classic African American music beyond America's shores. Much attention was given particularly to the inspirational effects of the blues on British popular music, both in the official Year of the Blues website[2] and in film documentaries such as *Red, White and Blues*, directed by Mike Figgis as one of the seven-part series *Martin Scorsese Presents the Blues*, broadcast on national television in the United States and in the United Kingdom.[3] While the links between the blues and popular music in Europe are probably well-known in the United States, there is often little appreciation of the wider impact of black music. It is clear that African American musical influences were not just limited to those of the blues on popular music of the 1960s, nor just to Britain. From the time of slavery onwards, black music in one form or another, from minstrelsy, through to gospel song and jazz, was performed and heard across many parts of Europe—and beyond. In turn people of African and/or Afro-Caribbean origin often took music back across the Atlantic to the United States. It was in recognition of this significant transatlantic cultural exchange that a conference entitled "'Overseas Blues': European Perspectives on African American Music" was held at the University of Gloucestershire, supported by the European Blues Association, in July 2004.[4]

The speakers at the conference, from the United Kingdom, the United States, the Netherlands, and Germany, included some of the major writers on the subject, such as Paul Oliver, Bob Groom, Rainer Lotz, Guido van Rijn, as well as younger scholars exploring the subject from a more contemporary perspective. Although the focus of the papers was essentially on Britain, France, Germany, and the Netherlands, they ranged across disciplines, offering interpretations that were historical, musical, social, and philosophical. Together they covered the influence of black music, chronologically from the late nineteenth century through to the present, examining the European reception of the variety of musical forms, and considering the nature of the appeal of black music to European collectors, audiences, and musicians. Some (but not all) of the papers from the conference have been rewritten and expanded for this volume. While the central focus is on the blues, some chapters deal with other forms of black music, particularly jazz; and because the subject offered more than "European perspectives" and focused on more than a one-way flow of music, the title for the book has been changed to *Cross the Water Blues: African American Music in Europe.*

The collection begins with my own broad overview of the subject raising some of the issues and concerns to be addressed in more detail by other contributors from a personal historical perspective. The personal point of view continues with Paul Oliver's insight into the appeal of the blues to British audiences of his generation. As one of the earliest writers on the topic, and now one of the world's leading authorities on the subject of African American music, Oliver is a prime example not only of the way in which black American culture took hold in Europe, but also how it became part of transatlantic culture. His influence is reflected in this collection in a variety of different ways—but especially in the endnote references in almost every chapter.

Broad, general (one might say, universal) questions about the blues are explored by David Webster looking at the appeal of African American music, particularly the blues, for a white (European) audience in broad, philosophical terms. Points raised in these early chapters inform most of the remainder which deal with particular historical and geographical locations: Jeffrey Green challenges the assumption that people of African origin were only active in non–concert hall or "classical" music making, and looks at black composers who also went to the United States from Britain in the late nineteenth and early twentieth centuries; Rainer Lotz provides an examination of, and begins to document, the largely unresearched subject of the impact of black music in early recordings both in the United States and in Europe, particularly Germany, and of German interest in black music prior to the First World War, while Catherine Parsonage looks at the mixed responses to jazz in Britain. In her consideration of African American influences in interwar Paris, Iris Schmeisser, like Parsonage, suggests that in their emphasis on the exotic, European responses showed both the acceptance and rejection of black music as the "other" in a "mixture of fascination, fear, and even envy." Sean Creighton, on the other hand, offers a survey of Paul Robeson's visits to Britain that emphasize the wide appeal and success of that talented performer.

In turning to postwar developments Roberta Schwartz examines in detail the work of the "evangelists" (including Paul Oliver) who brought the blues to a wider audience, while Bob Groom looks at how the blues were popularized as part of the British "skiffle" boom and also raises wider questions about the origins and authorship of specific songs. The often controversial questions of authorship and the incorporation of black music into white "pop" are taken further in Rupert Till's examination of the blues in the work of three of the major British bands, the Beatles, Rolling Stones, and especially Led Zeppelin. Also taking the influence of the blues on British performers in the 1960s as his starting point, Leighton Grist looks at the blues as a product of modernism in an approach that might be described broadly as cultural studies.

The final three chapters return to the wider European context. Guido van Rijn's chapter charts the black American cultural presence in the Netherlands from the late nineteenth century on before focusing on the appeal of the blues to modern Dutch audiences. Special emphasis is given to the detail of Bill Broonzy's connections with the Netherlands. In looking at the blues in France, Robert Springer provides a concise overview of the subject and offers some possible explanations for the appeal of black American music for non-English speakers. Finally, Christopher Bakriges explores the attraction of Europe for the black avant-garde and demonstrates once more how musical forms have evolved to transcend geographical, national, and possibly even racial boundaries. Thus, in one way or another the various contributors to this volume point up the importance not only of African American music to the wider world, but also something of the influence and significance of European writers and musicians on this subject which has "crossed the water" back and forth for almost two centuries and become part of our common cultural heritage.

I am, of course, grateful to all the contributors to the conference from which these papers originated, but I am especially grateful to those who then contributed to this volume. They have been enormously patient over a two-year period and have unfailingly taken on board whatever suggestions were made to them by myself, editors, and readers. Anonymous readers made helpful comments in the early stages of production; David Evans read the whole manuscript in draft and provided extremely helpful feedback. Craig Gill was very encouraging from the start and showed enormous perseverance, and Valerie Jones dealt with the many errors I missed. The volume is better as a result of all their comments, although I may have chosen to ignore a few—sometimes at the insistence of the particular contributor! Special thanks are due to Paul Oliver who has always been supportive and whose influence on blues writing is evident in almost every chapter of this book. Paul not only suggested the title, but his own work is the greatest proof that African American music did indeed "Cross the Water."

—Neil A. Wynn
UNIVERSITY OF GLOUCESTERSHIRE
2006

NOTES

Most references in this book appear in the endnotes of respective chapters; where there are either few or no notes, references have been provided in separate bibliographies, and, where appropriate, discographies are also provided. U.S. spelling is used except in quotations from British or non-U.S. sources.

1. Apparently there is some degree of uncertainty about the date of Handy's "discovery" — although Handy claimed to have first heard the blues at a station in Tutwiler, Mississippi, he also printed a blues song that he heard around 1890 and referred to hearing a tune called "East St. Louis" in 1892. See David Evans, *Big Road Blues: Tradition and Creativity in the Folk Blues* (Berkeley: University of California Press, 1982), 33.

2. http://www.yearoftheblues.org

3. PBS, *Martin Scorsese Presents the Blues: A Musical Journey*, Vulcan Road Movies, 2003.

4. The conference was supported by grants from the British Academy and the Cultural Affairs Office of the U.S. Embassy, London.

Cross the Water Blues

1

"Why I Sing the Blues"

AFRICAN AMERICAN CULTURE IN THE TRANSATLANTIC WORLD[1]

—NEIL A. WYNN

As everyone knows, blues, and then rhythm & blues, provided the inspiration not just for early rock 'n' roll in the 1950s, but later for much of the explosion of British popular music in the 1960s and its spread to the European continent. The impact African American music had on specifically British popular culture was celebrated in the widely shown television documentary *Red, White and Blues*, directed by Mike Figgis as one of the seven-part series *Martin Scorsese Presents the Blues* made to celebrate the "centenary" of the blues in 2003.[2] In the course of the documentary well-known British performers including Eric Clapton, Van Morrison, Georgie Fame, Eric Burdon, Tom Jones, and others reflected upon the influence that black American music had on their own development. So much has the blues become a part of British musical culture that the *Observer* Sunday newspaper could run an ad as the lead up to its monthly edition on music marking "100 years of the Blues" (or as it described it, "Celebrating a century of sorrow") inviting readers to fill in missing lyrics with the lines which began, of course, "I woke up this morning. . . ."[3]

Although little mention was made of wider European interest in the blues in Scorsese's documentary series and accompanying publication, African American music and culture has long had an audience beyond the English Channel.[4] Even today, European interest in the blues remains high—it is reported that 70 percent of blues record sales are in Europe, and there are several companies on the continent producing recordings of jazz and blues; and many programs and series devoted to the blues are regularly aired on radio stations.[5] Blues performers are often to be found touring in Europe from Sweden to Croatia, Russia to Spain, and beyond, and the many blues magazines and web sites attest to the wide range of interest in black music in all its forms across the continent.[6]

Europeans did not just listen to or play black music—they were among some of the first to write scholarly works dealing with it. According to one of the leading authorities on the blues, the Englishman Paul Oliver, the first jazz critic in the world was probably the Belgian writer Robert Goffin, who published reviews in 1920 and established the first jazz magazine, *Music*, in 1921.[7] Another Belgian, Yannick Bruynoghe, was one of the earliest biographers of the bluesman Big Bill Broonzy (and the biography was illustrated by Paul Oliver[8]); Bruynoghe, Oliver, George Adins, Jacques Demêtre, Marcel Chauvard, and Albert McCarthy all engaged in field trips to the United States that led to the "discovery" of unknown black blues artists in the 1950s and 1960s. A Frenchman Serge Tonneau published *R & B Panorama*, described by one writer as "The first blues periodical in Europe (and probably in the world) . . ." in 1960.[9] Academic interest remains as strong as ever. "Europe's largest public research archive on jazz" can be found at the Jazz-Institut in Darmstadt, Germany, another large jazz/blues archive exists in Eisenach, Germany, and a further significant resource is housed at the Institute of Jazz Research in Graz, Austria. Not only did the University of Gloucestershire host the conference in 2004 which produced this book, but in 2006 the university signed an agreement with the European Blues Association (based in Cheltenham) to act as custodian to a major part of the Paul Oliver Collection of African American Music and Related Traditions for use in teaching and research.[10]

The conference held in Gloucestershire made me think about the subject of the blues, and reminded me of the reasons I had become interested in American, and especially African American, history and culture in the first place. By way of introduction to this collection I want to use my personal perspective to examine some of the reasons for the spread and influence of African American culture in western Europe particularly in the 1950s and 1960s, but also in the twentieth century as a whole. Firstly, I want to look at the way I was influenced by African American music and culture as a teenager. Secondly, in doing this I want to locate my journey in a broader context and briefly consider the well-known story of the way in which African American culture became part not just of British popular culture, but also of a wider transatlantic culture. Although I will focus on the post–World War II period, I will also try to provide a broader historical overview of this interaction. Thirdly, in the process I want also to look at how this "history" was also part of an ongoing and continuing discourse on race.

Like many British teenagers in the 1960s I was influenced by black American music. For about two years between the ages of sixteen and eighteen (although suffering from impaired hearing and possessing little musical ability!), remarkably I was a member of a group called Tiny and the Titans. The play list for our first paid appearance in Edinburgh in 1965 is very revealing. The song titles were:

"Route 66"—Chuck Berry
"You Can't Judge a Book"—a Willie Dixon song, recorded by
    Bo Diddley and the Yardbirds
"You Really Got Me"—the Kinks
"Blueberry Hill"—Fats Domino
"House of the Rising Sun"—Georgia Turner/Bert Martin—and the
    Animals
"Reelin' & Rockin'"—Chuck Berry
"Hi Heel Sneakers"—R. Higginbotham a.k.a. Tommy Tucker
"Money"—a Beatles song originally by Barrett Strong
"Walking the Dog"—Rufus Thomas—and the Rolling Stones
"I Just Wanna Make Love to You"—Willie Dixon for Muddy Waters
"Talking about You"—Chuck Berry
"Shout"—Isley Brothers—and Lulu (who, perhaps surprisingly given
    her association generally with more popular music, appears in the
    Figgis documentary)
"It's All Over Now"—Womack Brothers—and the Rolling Stones

With the exception of the Kinks' song all of these were of African American origin and might be classed as rhythm & blues, the music that in many ways inspired the development of white rock 'n' roll from the mid-1950s. It was in part the re-discovery of the original black rhythm & blues by British performers that helped to bring about the sudden explosion of popular music in the 1960s.

Again, like many other people at the time, I was drawn back from modern versions to the original songs and their antecedents—and in doing so followed exactly in the footsteps of the new leading groups of the day—the Beatles and Rolling Stones. Both were heavily influenced by black American music. Almost half of the titles on the first Beatles album *Please, Please Me* in 1962 were covers of black ballads and soul songs by groups like the Marvelettes, the Miracles, Smokey Robinson, and the Drifters—only "Twist and Shout" might be described as rhythm & blues. This mixture continued through several of their early albums, and Chuck Berry numbers were a regular Beatles' feature on long play and extended play records. However, my favorite of the two groups, the Rolling Stones were, recalled their bass player Bill Wyman, "totally obsessed by the blues."[11] The Stones, of course, took their name from a Muddy Waters song; Keith Richards and Mick Jagger became friends when Richards noted Jagger carrying Chuck Berry and Muddy Waters albums. Drummer Charlie Watts had played (and still plays) in a jazz band. The Stones' early records were dominated by versions of black songs, from the "pure" blues of Robert Johnson, through to the Chicago blues of Muddy Waters, and rhythm & blues of Chuck Berry and Bo Diddley.

What the Stones and other British groups did was take this music, reinterpret it, and play it louder and faster than the originals had. As the black American bluesman Little Walter remarked in 1964, "they were playing the hell out of the blues."[12] The Stones were soon joined by a catalogue of British blues/rhythm & blues bands—the Animals, Yardbirds (including Eric Clapton), John Mayall's Blues breakers, Manfred Mann, Spencer Davis, Georgie Fame, Them (with Van Morrison)—and of course Tiny and the Titans—to name just a few. By 1965 visiting black singer Nina Simone could recall that all the kids in London were "singing Negro rhythm and blues." More than this she noted, "they give credit and respect where it is due, something they don't do too much at home."[13] In fact, these groups often cut their

musical teeth providing the backing for visiting African American performers such as Muddy Waters, Howlin' Wolf, and Sonny Boy Williamson.

These black musicians had begun to visit Britain first of all in the 1950s,
partly as a result of a revival in folk music, and partly as a result of growing
interest in jazz. Another factor was certainly the programs sponsored by the
U.S. government to encourage the spread of American culture and influence
after the war: as one writer said of jazz, musicians became "counterrevolution-
ary agents and cultural ambassadors" during the Cold War.[14] According to his
biographer, Josh White became "the first blues guitarist" to visit the United
Kingdom when he arrived in 1950 following a goodwill tour of Scandinavia
where he had performed before the Swedish royal family; he also performed
before royalty in Denmark and Britain.[15] White was very successful and
toured again in 1951, but by then he was eclipsed by the "less sophisticated"
Big Bill Broonzy (described in adverts as "'last of the country bluesmen'").[16]
Broonzy spent time in Europe, especially France, in the early 1950s, and,
as Guido van Rijn reveals, established especially strong connections in the
Netherlands where he had a long-term relationship that produced a son.[17]
He first toured the United Kingdom in 1951 following a stint organized by
the Hot Club de France in Paris. A few years later, in 1953 to be exact, Lonnie
Donegan, the Glasgow-born banjo player with Chris Barber's jazz band
began to play guitar and sing versions of American folk and blues songs
during the band's intermission. One of these songs, "Rock Island Line,"
originally recorded by Leadbelly (although as Bob Groom points out, he had
heard it first from prisoners in Arkansas), was so popular it was released as
a record in 1956, sold three million copies, and became a hit on both sides of
the Atlantic. The skiffle craze was launched. This, combined with the emergence of rock 'n' roll in the United States, encouraged many young British
teenagers to take up guitars and form groups. By 1957 there were estimated
to be more than five thousand skiffle bands in Britain; one of these, the
Quarrymen, eventually became the Beatles.[18]

The popular reception of the blues songs encouraged Chris Barber to
bring over the Chicago bluesmen Muddy Waters and Otis Spann to tour
with him in 1958. This was not without its problems: as Waters said, "They
thought I was Big Bill Broonzy. . . ."[19] In fact, Waters had moved from the
older, acoustic country blues style when he traveled to Chicago in 1943 following the many African Americans who migrated north during and after

World War II. His new amplified sound was more suitable to city clubs and bars, and it reflected the mood of the growing northern urban black populations. It was to have an enormous impact in Britain. Although he promised to learn some of the old blues numbers before he returned, by the time Waters toured again in 1962, the city blues had caught on in Britain.

The spread of the blues in Britain was due in part to the "evangelistic" journalism and writing of record collectors and blues devotees described by Roberta Schwartz.[20] But it was also the result of equally evangelistic musicians. The intermission performances in the jazz sessions had become full evening blues sessions; Barber's guitarist Alexis Korner soon left to open his own blues club and form Blues Incorporated, and very quickly there was a proliferation of blues clubs in and around London in the "Thames Valley cottonfields" of Richmond, Windsor, and beyond.[21] By then Waters, Sonny Boy Williamson, John Lee Hooker, and Howlin' Wolf—treated like heroes in Europe, but practically ignored and unknown to white audiences in the United States—had become regular visitors to these shores. Some, like several jazz players before and after them, made their homes on this side of the Atlantic: Champion Jack Dupree moved first to Switzerland, then Sweden before marrying and settling in Halifax, England; Memphis Slim became established in Paris where he organized blues tours. Sonny Boy Williamson spent all of 1964 in the United Kingdom, and he adopted an English tailor, wore a bowler hat, and carried an umbrella! Others joined him in the American Folk Blues Festival that toured the United Kingdom/Europe from 1963 to 1971.[22]

Why had this African American music, and jazz before it, become so popular in Britain and Europe? Firstly, it was new, different, American. Some British listeners said they did not initially realize the music was performed by African Americans or that it was of African American origin; they were attracted just because it was American. A ban by the British Musicians' Union from 1935 until 1956 had limited the opportunities for American musicians to perform live in the United Kingdom, and the war and postwar austerity had also limited access to records. Nonetheless, there was already an audience in Britain that had heard American music on the radio, on the American Forces stations, or on imported records from U.S. servicemen or merchant seamen. Paul Oliver recalled that he overheard African American servicemen in Suffolk in 1942—"It was the strangest, most compelling singing I'd ever heard."[23]

Similarly the British jazz singer, journalist, and raconteur George Melly became addicted when he chanced to hear a Bessie Smith record. He later captured the sense of novelty when he commented on going to hear Big Bill Broonzy in 1951, that "the idea of hearing an American Negro singing the blues was almost unbearably exciting."[24]

The blues, of course, was often associated with jazz, and the influence of jazz in Britain, and elsewhere in Europe, predated the 1960s. Jazz had come to Europe during and immediately after the First World War, and so by the 1950s already had a long-established following, but also, as Catherine Parsonage makes clear, had provoked some less than favorable responses.[25] The early reactions to jazz by supporters and opponents were echoed later in some of the responses to the blues. "Jazz provoked controversy all around Europe."[26] Jazz and blues were often seen as immoral, suggestive, primitive, and subversive. Jazz particularly was even questioned in terms of its musical value. In Britain a reporter in the *Times*, January 14, 1919, described jazz as "one of those American peculiarities which threaten to make life a nightmare. The object of a jazz band, apparently, is to provide as much noise as possible. . . ." One critic in Sweden suggested in 1921 that any musician who played jazz for any length of time would lose their musical ability and eventually become an idiot! A later Swedish reviewer of a concert by Louis Armstrong said jazz was hardly music at all, merely "an irritating rhythmic throbbing, which in its grotesque ugliness and eccentricity can never be enjoyable and hardly·ever fun to hear."[27]

Elsewhere moral and musical issues were raised. In Paris, where jazz was "everywhere" by 1920, the new music was particularly associated with the red-light district of Montmartre and was viewed by some as a threat to the traditional "chanson." For a time it was banned by the Parisian police; jazz dancing was also banned in Italy in 1926.[28]

Jazz and blues had a long, but complicated, history in the then Soviet Union. "Introduced" to the country by the avant-garde poet Valentin Parnakh following his visit to Paris in 1922 rather than by visiting Americans, "dzhaz" was accepted initially both as revolutionary and, with blues, associated with the (black) proletariat. The oldest jazz orchestra in continuous existence, the Russian State-Chamber Orchestra of Jazz, had its origins in the orchestra started by Oleg Lundstrem in 1934 while he was in Shanghai. Apparently it was not until 1926 when Sam Wooding's band appeared with the thirty-five singers and dancers in "The Chocolate Kiddies" in Moscow that the first black American jazz performers arrived in the Soviet Union. However, the Soviet authorities later tried to prohibit jazz as "bourgeois," and the Russian author Maxim Gorky in his 1928 essay "The Music of the Gros" in *Pravda*, described it as ". . . rumblings, wails, and howls like the smarting of a metal peg, the shriek of a donkey, or the amorous croaking of a monstrous frog . . . ," an "insulting chaos of insanity. . . ." For a while, even the playing of a saxophone was prohibited in the USSR.[29] After becoming acceptable once more in the late 1930s and early 1940s, jazz fell out of favor again during the Cold War as bourgeois, decadent, American music—Oleg Lundstrem was banished and Edward Rosner, the Russian trumpeter known as "the white Louis Armstrong," spent seven years in the penal camps.[30]

According to one recent study, "Blues in Russia is a post-communist phenomenon."[31] Apparently little of the music was heard other than in jazz or by jazz performers. Urban suggests that blues reached the USSR largely through the records of white British bands like the Rolling Stones and Yardbirds, and it was not until 1979 with tours by B.B. King and Gatemouth Brown that Russian audiences really encountered authentic live blues. However, a further period of cultural repression held back the development of blues until after Perestroika in 1985. Thus blues and jazz were linked very much to internal political developments.

If not always seen in such political terms, throughout Europe in the interwar years many people spoke explicitly of jazz in moral, religious, and racial terms, casting black secular music as the "Devil's music": a Canon Drummond of Maidenhead, England, condemned jazz dancing as, "one of the most degrading symptoms of the present day. . . . The dance of low niggers in America, with every conceivable crude instrument, not to make music but to make a noise."[32] In 1927 the *Melody Maker* quoted the rector of Exeter College, Oxford, urging his congregation not to take their music "from America or from niggers, take it from God, the source of all good music."[33] As late as April 1939 a reviewer in the *Times* could still describe jazz as "the immediate choice of the undiscriminating masses," but by then broadcasts on the "History of Jazz" had already become a regular feature of the BBC National Home Radio broadcasts, although blues tended not to be included.[34]

While jazz and blues were often regarded critically in moral, musical, and racial terms, black church music, gospel songs, and spirituals, on the other hand, were equally seen in terms of stereotypes, but of a more acceptable nature. Black musicians had visited Europe right through the nineteenth century—Major Dumbledon's Ethiopian Serenaders came in 1848, the Georgia minstrels toured in 1866, and most famously the Fisk Jubilee Singers performed before Queen Victoria and attracted crowds in their thousands in the 1870s in Britain and elsewhere in Europe.[35] But as other writers in this volume make clear, even the Fisks were seen as something of an oddity, and not just in the color of their skin. A reviewer of their performance on February 21, 1899, given in St. James Hall, London, for "the benefit of the YMCA and the Factory Helpers' Union," said that: following an introduction by the Countess of Portsmouth, the ten singers "proceeded to sing the curious programme of sacred and secular songs which created so much interest in them in days long gone by. The effect of their singing is almost indescribable. Obviously the singing cannot be measured with the ordinary yard-stick of criticism. It is not ordinary. It is not even singing in the ordinary sense. It is an agglomeration of the most weird musical sounds, the most unordinary rhythmical nuances."[36]

The writer concluded, however, that the performers' "absolute sincerity carries all before it." The connection with later black music is made explicitly by a writer describing the "Negro" in the theatrical journal *Performer* in 1918. He traced the line of development in a telling fashion:

First he brings his slave ditties
Then he charms us with his coon songs,
Now he's sending us barmy with Jazz
What's his next stunt?[37]

The minstrel tradition, of white performers in blackface singing the songs of the old South and presenting stereotyped images of happy, carefree, simple slaves, was also long established in the British music-hall (at least since the Ethiopian Serenaders in 1848[38]) and survived into the twentieth century. One of the ironies of my own experience was to observe the pleasure with which my parents, who railed against the "jungle music" of Elvis Presley, watched the George Mitchell *Black and White Minstrel Show* that ran on British television from 1958 until 1978 and won the Golden Rose of Montreux award in 1961.[39]

As Rainer Lotz makes clear, the music of the minstrels, if not the style of presentation, had been recorded in Europe in different forms as early as the late nineteenth century.[40] In the 1930s and 1940s the African American actor and singer Paul Robeson also had enormous success in Europe and seemed to appeal to a diverse audience, across class and national boundaries. In part, as Sean Creighton demonstrates, this was due to the enormous range of his talent, from Shakespearean theater and movie actor through to classical music performer, but it was also due to the fact that his performances were often set within conventional (white) forms.[41] Even his role in the film *The Proud Valley* (1940) where he appeared working among Welsh miners was particularly unthreatening, and in some of his earlier film roles Robeson was perhaps closer to established stereotypes than he later became. Possibly, too, his rendition of spirituals, the music of survival and hope for an oppressed race, had a particular appeal to audiences experiencing the worst effects of the Depression.

Clearly, some black performers and musical styles did not divide their European audiences in the way that jazz, or later blues, did. In fact, of course, both critics and fans of black music shared some similar ground. It was precisely because jazz and blues were new, loud, often discordant, and questioning of established values with their use of the double entendres and open sexual references that they seemed attractive to young people in the "jazz age" of the 1920s and again to teenagers in the 1950s. In Britain George Melly could recall how his prep school headmaster in the 1930s would switch off any jazz discovered accidentally on the radio screaming "filthy jazz." Melly noted he would "mentally add jazz to Bolshevism and the lower classes . . . as things he was in favour of."[42] Poet and jazz critic Philip Larkin (who apparently wrote a number of unpublished blues lyrics) also came to jazz in the 1930s—he described it as a "fugitive minority interest" that provided the "unique private excitement that youth seems to demand."[43] It was because jazz was synonymous with the avant-garde and with decadence in interwar Germany that Himmler instructed that its followers should be put in the camps, whipped, and given hard labor. Nonetheless, jazz, in the form of "swing," survived and indeed became a form of rebellion against the authoritarian regime.[44] Later, as Berndt Ostendorf and Ralph Willett have shown, young people in

Germany after World War II associated jazz with liberation and democracy, and some thirty to eighty million people behind the Iron Curtain listened to jazz on "Music USA" broadcast by the Voice of America.[45]

In France, jazz and the avant-garde went hand in hand, most famously in Paris with the *Revue Nègre* at the Théâtre du Champs Élysées from 1925 and Le Carnaval Noir from 1927 where Josephine Baker from St. Louis, Missouri, experienced personal freedom and artistic liberation. Baker rose to stardom demonstrating the "unbridled sexuality, frenzy" and "primitivism" that captured the white audiences.[46] A number of American jazz musicians, black and white, found France particularly receptive to jazz and made their homes in Paris for some time during the interwar years. Among them was trumpeter Arthur Briggs who spent ten years in Europe and was put in a concentration camp by the Nazis during World War II. He pointedly remarked that the attraction of Paris was not just the "life-style," although that was clearly important—"we had wonderful contracts as well."[47]

Not surprisingly, perhaps, it was in Paris that native musicians developed exciting new forms of jazz. Surely one of the most significant jazz guitarists ever was Django Reinhardt, the Belgian-born musician who converted to jazz after hearing Ellington and Armstrong on record in 1930. Together with violinist Stephan Grapelli, Reinhardt made the Hot Club de France a draw for many American musicians in the 1930s.[48]

It was not just French music that was affected by jazz: several writers, most notably Colin Nettelbeck and here my colleague David Webster, have pointed to the importance attached to jazz by the existentialist writer and philosopher Jean-Paul Sartre. For Sartre, jazz represented "notre temps" (our times) with its "strange rhythms, abrupt phrases, and heavy voluptuous songs." It is the black jazz singer in *Nausea* (1938) and the song "Some of These Days" (although ironically a song written by a black Canadian and sung by a white woman, Sophie Tucker), that give Sartre's character Roquentin some hope.[49] However, Aimé Césaire commented on the appropriation of black music and the black body by white audiences as he left France to return to his native Martinique in 1939:

> They simply love us so much!
> Gaily obscene, doudou about jazz in the excess of their boredom,
> I can do tracking, the Lindy-hop and tap dance.[50]

For Sartre and others in pre– and post–World War II Europe, black music was attractive also because it was a "vehicle of the dynamism of American culture in all its immediacy and uncompromising energy."[51] In the post–World War II austerity that affected Britain and much of Europe to an even greater extent, jazz offered a release from the drab hardships and spoke of another world. At the same time, ironically, in its liberation and identification with the African American minority, it was a mode of protest. Thus it was that jazz bands frequently led the Campaign for Nuclear Disarmament (CND) demonstrations against American nuclear might and the presence of U.S. ships and aircraft in Britain in the 1950s and 1960s; indeed, one CND campaigner could claim "the jazz revival and the rise of CND were more than coincidental: they were almost two sides of the same coin. Similar social attitudes and positivist humanist values informed them both."[52] But above all, for many Europeans, as the British writer of the counterculture Jeff Nuttall wrote, echoing the naivety and stereotyping of Americans Jack Kerouac and Norman Mailer, jazz was the music of the "American Negro, criminal, proletariat."[53] While Val Wilmer recalled that early British listeners craved a "fantasy version of the South," the historian Brian Ward pointed out whites who identified with the bluesmen as rebels expressing a rootless, emotional, primitive, sexual view of life filled with hard drinking, loose women, and even looser men, not only often romanticized the black experience, but also (just like the critics and opponents of black music) made the mistake in seeing the music as representative of the totality of black life.[54] Black performers not only captured the tension between modern and modernism referred to by Leighton Grist, but also W. E. B. Du Bois's famous sense of "two-ness."[55]

Although modern in the sense they came to a larger white audience from 1912 with the first publication of sheet music, and in 1920 with the first blues recording, jazz and blues were seen by both detractors and devotees as music of an earlier simpler, pre-industrial age.[56] It was always "primal," said Stones guitarist Keith Richards. Blues and jazz both could trace their origins back to the music of black slaves and could (as several scholars including Paul Oliver have shown) trace their roots back to Africa, if only indirectly. Recognizing the links with slavery, Larkin recalled being hooked on the rhythm "that had made the slaves shuffle in Congo square."[57] Although sometimes born in southern cities, the legendary classic bluesmen—Blind Lemon Jefferson, Charley Patton, Robert Johnson—and blues women, Bessie

Smith and Gertrude "Ma" Rainey—not only represented a predominantly rural southern community, they did so in the years before the mechanization of the cotton industry in the 1940s. Their songs reflected a bygone era for most white audiences, a pre-modern era with an oral tradition and references to mojos, black cat bones, and John the Conqueror; they also reflected a life of hardship and suffering.

For some British converts to black music, there was a sense of identification with the socio-economic hardships of African Americans. Indeed, Leighton Grist suggests that the music had a particular class-based appeal.[58] "Geordie" (i.e., Newcastle-born) Eric Burdon of the Animals recalled that he heard Muddy Waters in Newcastle, and later John Lee Hooker, and related to what they were singing directly—"it was happening to men on my block." (In a neat reversal Hooker, who performed in Newcastle, once asked a friend if he had ever heard of it; the friend racked his brain and asked "'Newcastle, Mississippi?'" Hooker replied "'No, Newcastle, Britain'" and commented on playing there, "'that was rough.'"[59]

Future Stones' bass player Bill Wyman also suggested an element of empathy in his introduction to the excellent *Blues Odyssey* when he wrote, "I was born in south-east London just prior to the outbreak of World War II. Although my father worked, we were far from well off, life was a struggle. Years later I found that many black musicians grew up in the Southern States of the USA in difficult circumstances, something of a shared experience."

It is doubtful that Wyman's childhood really stood comparison with growing up black in the American South as he properly acknowledged when he indicated that he did not experience the "awfulness of segregation and the problems of being treated as a second-class citizen."[60] It would be convenient to claim that I came from a poverty-stricken family and that growing up in the predominantly working-class area of Oxgangs in Edinburgh, Scotland, represented a deprived background, but happily for me this was not the case. My family was lower, but aspiring, middle class, I went to a good school, and was fortunate enough to have a grant to support me through university. Most of the members of the British blues bands seemed to come, with some exceptions, from similarly comfortable backgrounds; many like Mick Jagger, Keith Richards, and Eric Burdon were university or art college students.

This seemed true too of earlier generations of British lovers of African American music. Historian Eric Hobsbawm, while describing jazz as the "music of protest and rebellion," was introduced to it by his cousin who "conformed exactly to the type of the 1930s British jazz fan"—"the intelligent, self-educated young man from the lower middle classes, preferably a little bohemian."[61] Alexis Korner's biographer, Harry Shapiro, also suggested that black music "mainly attracted the offspring of the middle classes whose parents had supported socialism and communism in the wake of the 1914–18 war...."[62] In the 1950s, recalled author and leading figure in American Studies in Britain Malcolm Bradbury, jazz was part of the rejection of traditionalism and "the intellectual's music."[63] Many of the British "Angry Young Men" postwar school of writers, like Kingsley Amis, were jazz aficionados. At the same time not surprisingly, writers who were presenting gritty, northern working-class realism, together with politically left-wing inclined members of the middle class, could easily identify with what they saw as "'the music of the proletariat.'"[64]

Of course what attracted many young British people to the blues regardless of their class or politics was the music itself and its apparent simplicity. Several of my colleagues have recalled that they were captivated first by hearing someone play a harmonica or guitar (although one also associated it with a teenage broken heart!). In the 1950s and 1960s music became much more accessible with the growing popularity of the guitar. My sixth-year class in Boroughmuir senior secondary school in Edinburgh in 1964–65 included at least four guitarists and two drummers, none, to my knowledge, with any formal music training. Time and time again people like Eric Clapton recall hearing various blues artists, and although "feeling empathy with the underdog," also became obsessed more with trying to master the guitar techniques they heard. Clapton recalled "I realized I could play guitar when I mastered this bit of Muddy Waters' 'Honey Bee.'"[65] Their success was evident in the blues explosion of the 1960s.

Ironically the blues was "rediscovered" and reintroduced to white American audiences at the very moment that many African Americans were disassociating themselves from what they saw as down-home, old-fashioned, and even Uncle Tom music. B.B. King reported playing in a key venue in 1963 before audiences that were 95 percent black; by 1968 the audience was 95 percent white.[66] The music of the civil rights movement that grew to dominate the headlines in the United States and here from 1955 on was increasingly soul, or more directly relevant, the music of protest.

With the rise of civil rights came the "discovery" of black history. While this was especially true in the United States with the growth of Black Studies programs, it was also the case in British institutions. At my university in Edinburgh in 1965 there already was a well-established department of African Studies and the history department offered not just courses in American history, but also unusually, one in black history.[67] Many of us (and the class was full) took courses in American history precisely because it was still unusual in many traditional British university history departments— America was modern, it was different—it also meant we avoided anything involving Latin or a European language. At the same time African American history was part of the developing revisionist critique of the superpower by then heavily involved in the war in Vietnam. American race relations was also something the wider public were made increasingly aware of—black civil rights leaders like Martin Luther King and Malcolm X were both visitors to Britain and other parts of Europe, as were writers like James Baldwin, and sports personalities, most notably Muhammad Ali.

One of the attractions for me was the sense of an "alternative" history. I remember as a student first reading Paul Oliver's now-classic book, *Blues Fell This Morning*, published in 1960. Although I didn't realize it at the time, here was a very early (but I think not widely recognized as such among the historical profession) example of the emerging new social history. This history came from below and looked less at the dominant narrative of historical fact, the meta-narrative of the white hierarchy, but the lived experience of a people for whom the major dramas of national history often had little real significance. In writing of these often unknown performers and their songs, people like Paul Oliver, and LeRoi Jones in *Blues People* (1963), "rescued them from the enormous condescension of posterity," as the British Marxist historian and jazz writer Eric Hobsbawm noted, using the words of E. P. Thompson and the *Making of the English Working Class*, itself a seminal work of the period.[68]

More than this, the blues, rather than being the music of accommodation as some Africans Americans in the 1960s suggested, could be read as a form of protest. Black historian Robin Kelley has suggested that blues songs offer a "hidden transcript" for a people, many of whom could neither read nor write, and reveal the "infra politics" of segregated life in which black popular culture, if not directly oppositional, offered an alternative view of life.[69] What could be seen as resignation or acceptance, might also be read as defiance—

> Down so long
> Down don't worry me
> I've been down so long, now,
> Down don't worry me.[70]

As the writer Ralph Ellison suggested, the blues express "both the agony of life and the possibility of conquering it through sheer toughness of spirit."[71]

Despite this universal aspect of the music, with Black Power came increasing criticism of what was seen by some as the "colonization" of black cultural forms by whites. African Americans no longer wished to see their campaigns, their history, nor their culture appropriated by whites, no matter how liberal or well-meaning they might be. (I discovered this myself when I was asked to leave the Black Studies class I was auditing at SUNY in Buffalo in 1970.) As Paul Garon and others have argued, what makes the blues unique is "a system of reference based upon a shared experience in the past and the present," and this is the black experience, the experience of race prejudice.[72] When it is said that "you can't sing the blues until you have paid your dues," and that white people cannot sing the blues, the reference is historical, not racial or biological. B.B. King's song, that provided me with my title "Why I Sing the Blues," locates him overtly and specifically in a history that stretches from slavery to urban ghetto.[73] That history is, however, a shared history, one in which Europeans played all too often a crucial role—and besides, surely no one is restricted to write only their own history, or play only their "own" music. But more than this, as Paul Gilroy and others have clearly demonstrated, African American culture was also a transatlantic culture: while Chris Bakriges shows how through transatlantic migration jazz became more than just an American music, John Cowley has also demonstrated the varied links between Afro-Caribbean, Afro-American, and British Caribbean music.[74]

At the same time European audiences often proved more receptive to African American music than did Americans—as Bill Moody noted of jazz, "In Paris, Stockholm, Copenhagen, London, and Amsterdam, American jazz musicians found appreciation, acceptance, and acclaim. Black musicians found in addition a far less hostile racial atmosphere." "Jazz," said saxo-phonist Bud Freeman, "has moved to Europe."[75] European musicians from England to the Soviet Union also adopted and adapted and recorded jazz—and of course, as several contributors here make clear, the blues. Thus, in the discovery and rediscovery of black music, and in the varied responses to it, Europeans have often revealed not only the universal appeal of the music, but also a constant element in the discourse on race and the transatlantic relationship. They too, share a part in African American history.

NOTES

1. I first gave a version of this paper at my Inaugural Address, University of Gloucestershire, April 20, 2004. A different version appeared as "Freedom and the Blues: African American Culture and Liberal Democracy in the Transatlantic World," in D. Silander and C. Wallin, eds., *Democracy and Culture in the Transatlantic World* (Växjö, Sweden: Växjö University Press, 2005).

2. PBS, *Martin Scorsese Presents the Blues: A Musical Journey*, Vulcan Road Movies, 2003.

3. *The Observer*, November 16, 2003.

4. Peter Guralnick, Robert Santelli, et al., eds., *Martin Scorsese Presents the Blues: A Musical Journey* (New York: Amistad, 2003).

5. Thomas "Tomcat" Colvin (2004), "The Blues: Calling for a Response," http://www.thebluehighway.com/manila.html, 2004: 1. Radio programs in Britain in 2004, for example, included George Melly, *Memories of the Blues*, BBC Radio 2, Euon Griffith, *True Blues*, Radio Wales, and *Deep Blue*, featuring Michael Roach, on Radio 4. The oldest extant independent jazz label in Europe is "Storyville," established by Karl Emil Knudsen (1929–2003) in Copenhagen in 1950.

6. See, for example, *Back to the Roots* (Belgium), *Blues News* (Germany and Norway), *Il Blues* (Italy), *Blues Magazine* (France), and *Blues & Rhythm*, and *Juke Blues* (United Kingdom); web sites include, http://www.swedishblues.com; http://www.blues-germany.de/; http://www.terra.es/personal3/spainblues/i/index.htm; http://www.mary4music.com/FestsEurope.html; http://www.europejazz.net/; http://www.jazzinternet.com/europe.htm.

7. Paul Oliver, "Jazz is where you find it," in C. W. E. Bigsby, ed., *Superculture: American Popular Culture and Europe* (London: Paul Elek, 1975).

8. *Big Bill Blues: William Broonzy's Story as told to Yannick Brunoghe* (London: Cassell, 1955).

9. Bob Groom, *The Blues Revival* (London: Studio Vista, 1971), 88–94.

10. http://www.darmstadt.de/kultur/musik/jazz/us.htm; http://www.kug.ac.at/ijf/website_directory/institute/overview.html; http://www.euroblues.org/.

11. Wyman, *Blues Odyssey: A Journey to Music's Heart and Soul* (London: Dorling Kindersley, 2001), 322.

12. Quoted in *Melody Maker*, October 3, 1964.

13. Brian Ward, *Just My Soul Responding: Rhythm and Blues, Black Consciousness and Race Relations* (London: UCL Press, 1998), 175.

14. E. Taylor Atkins, "Toward a Global History of Jazz," in Atkins, ed., *Jazz Planet* (Jackson: University Press of Mississippi, 2003), xvii.

15. Elijah Wald, *Josh White: Society Blues* (New York and London: Routledge, 2002), 172–74. The first country bluesman to visit Europe was probably Huddie Ledbetter (Leadbelly), who played in Paris in 1949 shortly before his death.

16. Wald, *Josh White,* 174, 220–21.

17. See van Rijn, "Lowland Blues."

18. Harry Shapiro, *Alexis Korner: The Biography* (London: Bloomsbury, 1996), 79–80; see here Groom, "Whose 'Rock Island Line'?" The origins of the term *skiffle* are outlined in Roberta Schwartz's chapter, "Preaching the Gospel of the Blues: Blues Evangelists in Britain."

19. Robert Gordon, *Can't Be Satisfied: The Life and Times of Muddy Waters* (London: Pimlico, 2003), 158–59.

20. Roberta Schwartz, "Preaching the Gospel of the Blues."

21. The phrase was used by George Melly, *Revolt into Style: The Pop Arts in Britain* (Harmondsworth: Penguin, 1972), 88. Korner's crusading work is outlined by Shapiro, in *Alexis Korner: The Biography.*

22. Robert Palmer, *Deep Blues: A Musical and Cultural History* (New York: Penguin, 1982), 261.

23. Paul Oliver, *Blues Off the Record* (Tunbridge Wells: The Baton Press, 1984), 3.

24. George Melly, *Owning Up* (Harmondsworth: Penguin, 1965), 11.

25. Catherine Parsonage, "Responses to Early Jazz in Britain."

26. Jeffrey H. Jackson, *Making Jazz French: Music and Modern Life in Interwar Paris* (Durham and London: Duke University Press, 2003), 71.

27. Johan Fornäs, "Swinging Differences: Reconstructed Identities in the Early Swedish Jazz Age," in Atkins, ed., *Jazz Planet,* 210, 211.

28. Jackson, *Making Jazz French,* 1, 56–57; Macdonald Smith Moore, *Yankee Blues: Musical Culture and American Identity* (Bloomington: Indiana University Press, 1985), 111.

29. Simon Weil, "Degenerate Music," *All About Jazz,* http://www.allaboutjazz.com/articles/artio801 (April 27, 2004), 6.

30. The story of jazz in the USSR is outlined in S. Frederick Starr, *Red and Hot: the Fate of Jazz in the Soviet Union, 1917–1980* (New York: Oxford University Press, 1983). See also Sam Solecki, *Talkin' Moscow Blues* (New York: The Echo Press, 1988). Sam Wooding probably merits a chapter on his own in a book like this. A tenor horn player in the army during World War I, Wooding and his band joined "The Chocolate Kiddies" revue on a tour that began in 1925 in Germany where Wooding's became the "first jazz ensemble to record in Europe." The revue went on to tour Russia, Turkey, England, and Italy. Wooding returned to the United States in 1927. See article by Susan C. Cook in *American National Biography Online,* http://www.anb.org/articles/18/18-02631.html, February 2000.

31. Michael Urban with Andrei Evdokimov, *Russia Gets the Blues: Music, Culture, and Community in Unsettled Times* (Ithaca and London: Cornell University Press, 2004), 1.

32. *Times,* March 15, 1919.

33. Jen Wilson, "Black Soul, Welsh Hwyl: Black Music in Wales, 1870–1935," paper, "'Overseas Blues': European Perspectives on African American Music," University of Gloucestershire, July 23–26, 2004.

34. *Times,* April 8, 1939, and see issues for 1937 detailing radio broadcasts.

35. David Boulton, *Jazz in Britain* (London: W. H. Allen, 1958), 92. The visits to Europe of these early black performers are described here by Lotz, "Black Music Prior to the First World

War: American Origins and German Perspectives," van Rijn, "Lowland Blues," and Green, "Spirituals to (Nearly) Swing."

36. *Times*, February 22, 1899.

37. In Jim Godbolt, *A History of Jazz in Britain 1919–50* (London: Paladin, 1986), 7.

38. The Ethiopian Serenaders, described in the London *Illustrated News* as "negroes," were apparently whites in blackface. A black group, the Ethiopian American Serenaders performed in Europe in the 1890s. (I am grateful to Rainer Lotz for this information.)

39. For the Black and White Minstrels see: http://www.museum.tv/archives/etv/B/htmlB/blackandwhim/blackandwhim.htm.

40. Lotz, "Black Music Prior to the First World War."

41. Sean Creighton, "Paul Robeson's British Journey."

42. Melly, *Owning Up*, 10.

43. Philip Larkin, *All What Jazz: A Record Diary* (London: Faber & Faber, 1985), 15.

44. See Mike Zwerin, *Swing Under the Nazis: Jazz as Metaphor for Freedom* (New York: Cooper Square Press, 2000); Rainer Lotz, *Hitler's Air Waves: The Inside Story of Nazi Radio Broadcasting and Propaganda Swing* (New Haven: Yale University Press, 1997); Eric Vogel, "Jazz in a Nazi Concentration Camp," and Josef Škvorecký, "Red Music," in James Campbell, ed., *The Picador Book of Blues and Jazz* (London: Picador, 1996), 211–39.

45. Berndt Ostendorf, "Subversive Re-education?: Jazz as a Liberating Force in Germany and Europe," *Revue Francaise d'Etudes Américaines*, December 2001, 14; Ralph Willett, *The Americanization of Germany, 1945–1949* (London: Routledge, 1989), 86–87; E. Taylor Atkins, "Towards a Global History of Jazz," in Atkins, ed., *Jazz Planet*, xviii.

46. Iris Schmeisser, "Paris and the Primitivist Reception of Jazz in the 1920s"; David Macey, "Frantz Fanon, or the Difficulty of Being Martinician," *History Workshop Journal* 58 (Autumn 2004): 213. Baker was one of few jazz performers to abandon American citizenship in favor of their new country of residence. However, several shared the sentiments of Sidney Bechet when he remarked, "every man has two countries, his own and France." Quoted in Bill Moody, *The Jazz Exiles: American Musicians Abroad* (Reno/Las Vegas/London: University of Nevada Press, 1993), xv.

47. Quoted in Moody, *The Jazz Exiles*, 17.

48. On Reinhardt, see Michael Dregni, *Django: The Life and Music of a Gypsy Legend* (New York: Oxford University Press, 2004).

49. Colin Nettelbeck, "Jean Paul Sartre, Simone de Beauvoir and the Paris Jazz Scene," *Modern and Contemporary France*, vol. 9, no. 2 (May 2001): 173–75; Webster, "Even Philosophers Get the Blues."

50. Quoted in Macey, "Frantz Fanon, or the Difficulty of Being Martinician," 211.

51. Nettelbeck, "Jean Paul Sartre, Simone de Beauvoir and the Paris Jazz Scene," 172.

52. Ian Campbell, "Music Against the Bomb," in John Minnion and Philip Bolsover, ed., *The CND Story: The First 25 Years of CND* (London: Allison & Busby, 1983), 115.

53. Jeff Nuttall, *Bomb Culture* (London: Paladin, 1970), 11.

54. Val Wilmer, *Mama Said There'd Be Days Like This: My Life in the Jazz World* (Aylesbury, Bucks.: Women's Press, 1991), 33; Ward, *Just My Soul Responding*, 12.

55. Grist, "The Blues Is the Truth: The Blues, Modernity, and the British Blues Boom." The location of the black performer within the modernist movement is also the subject of Christopher Bakriges, "Cultural Displacement, Cultural Creation: African American Jazz

Musicians in Europe From Bechet to Braxton." See also Paul Gilroy, *The Black Atlantic: Modernity and Double Consciousness* (London: Verson, 1993).

56. It is interesting to note here that it is probably no coincidence that Paul Oliver's other (some might say, main) area of expertise is in vernacular architecture on which he is a leading world authority.

57. Larkin, *All What Jazz*, 160.

58. Leighton Grist, "The Blues Is the Truth."

59. Charles Shaar Murray, *Boogie Man: The Adventures of John Lee Hooker on the American Twentieth Century* (New York: St. Martin's Press, 2000), 262; "The Birth of the British Blues," at The Year of the Blues, http://www.yearoftheblues.org, "The British Blues" (February 9, 2004), 1.

60. Wyman, *Blues Odyssey*, 9.

61. Eric Hobsbawm (as Frances Newton), *The Jazz Scene* (New York: Pantheon, 1993), xiv.

62. Shapiro, *Alexis Korner*, 38.

63. Malcolm Bradbury, "How I Invented America," *Journal of American Studies*, vol. 14, no. 1 (April 1980): 119–20.

64. Kevin Morgan, "King Street Blues: Jazz and the Left in Britain in the 1930s–1940s," in Andy Croft, ed., *A Weapon in the Struggle: The Cultural History of the Communist Party in Britain* (London: Pluto Press, 1998), 123.

65. Quoted in Gordon, *Can't Be Satisfied*, 163, and in *Uncut*, May 2004, 48–49.

66. Michael Haralambos, *Right On: From Blues to Soul in Black America* (London: Edison Press, 1974), 90.

67. The African American history course was taught by George "Sam" Shepperson, a Marxist historian whose writings included several works on W. E. B. Du Bois and aspects of the African diaspora.

68. Eric Hobsbawm, *Uncommon People: Resistance, Rebellion and Jazz* (London: Weidenfeld & Nicolson, 1998), vii; Paul Oliver, *Blues Fell This Morning: Meaning in the Blues* (London: Cassell, 1960, second ed. Cambridge University Press, 1990).

69. Robin D. G. Kelley, "We Are Not What We Seem: Opposition in the Jim Crow South," *Journal of American History*, vol. 80, no. 1 (June 1993): 76–77.

70. Ishman Bracey, 1928, quoted in Haralambos, *Right On: From Blues to Soul in Black America*, 77.

71. Ralph Ellison, *Shadow and Act* (New York: Signet Books, 1966), 104.

72. Paul Garon, *Blues and the Poetic Spirit* (San Francisco: City Lights, 1966), 193.

73. "Why I Sing the Blues," on *B.B. King: King of the Blues*, vol. 2, 1966–69, MCA Records, 1992, originally Bluesway single, 61024.

74. Gilroy, *The Black Atlantic: Modernity and Double Consciousness*; Bakriges, "Cultural Displacement, Cultural Creation: African American Jazz Musicians in Europe From Bechet to Braxton," and Cowley, "Black Music Traditions: Bridging the West Indies, the United States and Europe: An Historical Perspective," paper given at "'Overseas Blues'" conference, July 25, 2004. Also see Heike Raphael-Hernandez, ed., *Blackening Europe: the African American Presence* (New York: Routledge, 2004).

75. Quoted in Moody, *Jazz Exiles*, 7; see also 4–5.

2

Taking the Measure of the Blues

— PAUL OLIVER

Our band is the cat's nuts—
Banjo jazz, with a nickel-plated amplifier,
To soothe the savage breast . . .

That's how I remember the beginning of a poem with which I, and my friend
Jimmy Gribble, opened our first recital of jazz and blues at Harrow College
of Art, close on six decades ago. Some of our fellow students were amused,
a few were shocked, many were puzzled, but we used it to draw attention to
the originality of a contemporary American poet, William Carlos Williams,
as well as to the mistakes, misconceptions, and stereotypes which the poem
conveyed, if it were taken literally. Nostalgically, I even thought of using it
to open my talk at the conference in Gloucestershire, but I felt that maybe
it wouldn't be appropriate. Jimmy and I gave a few such recitals illustrated
with 78 rpm records from our respective growing jazz and blues collections,
until the principal of the College, John Platt, went berserk in threatening us
with expulsion, if we played "such muck" again.

For us it was a period of discovery in art and music; particularly for me, one of excitement as I explored African tribal art, and the music of African American blues. In his introduction Neil Wynn mentioned that it was the unique and spine-chilling experience of hearing the singing of black servicemen on "fatigues" who were "digging in" an American military base at Stoke-by-Clare in Suffolk, which stimulated a lifetime passion. "They're singing a *blues*," my fellow harvest camp worker, Stan Higham, told me. He had fifty or so blues records kept in an orange box, and it was hearing these that started my collecting. I've often been asked how, during World War II and the lean years after, it was possible to find blues records, and what items were among them. Some have inquired how I, and presumably, other collectors, developed our taste in the music and our understanding of it. How was it, I would be asked, that some of the earliest and most informed writing on blues, including the first large-format blues magazine, was published in Britain, when a blues singer had not even visited the country, let alone sang to the enthusiasts? How, using a phrase current at the time, did we "take the measure of the blues"?

As the term is one which implies evaluation and assessment of the quality of blues in our experience, it really requires an assessment of the criteria that were applied, and the standards by which the performances were assessed. But it goes deeper than that, for the issue that it raises is one which is fundamental: what attracted us to blues in the first place, and how did we meet it or adjust to it? To put it more simply: what was the appeal of the blues? I cannot give an answer to these queries on behalf of all who were excited by the music, because we each came to it by different routes and were engaged in it for different reasons. I must therefore speak for myself, although I am aware that a number of other enthusiasts came to the blues from a position which, to some extent we shared: that of the enjoyment of folk music.

Of course, one could ask the identical questions in relation to the appeal of folk music and song, but the story is somewhat different. For me, and others of my generation, folk music and folk dancing were actually part of our education—they were an element in school life. Many practices that are now regarded with nostalgia or with patronizing curiosity were customary experiences: Maypole dances or Morris dancing, for instance. Bargees still sang the songs of the sailing barges; there were fiddlers, singers, and string players in innumerable villages, and veterans who still recalled the sea shanties of their youth. It was fun, it was interesting, and I was a folk music enthusiast. Yet there were aspects that many of my contemporaries did not appreciate. For example, the melodies of folk music often appeared simple, and were frequently "arranged" for concert presentation—satisfying some, and infuriating me. It was their beauty in simplicity that meant much to me. On the other hand, the singers had their repertoires, and many seldom extended beyond them, so to avoid repetitiveness one had to travel to other parts of the country to meet other folk performers and hear other kinds of music.

My encounter with the blues was by chance, as I have explained. But the next singers that I heard, the next guitar players and pianists, whether live or on record, were different. What thrilled me was the individuality of each blues singer and his or her place within the idiom. No two singers were alike; most often, the blues they sang and played, although having similar underlying structures, were wholly personal and invented. I was exhilarated by the richness and inflections of the voices, the inventiveness of the guitar and harmonica playing, the originality of the themes and the poetry of the verses. This was a *living* folk music; one which was produced by an underprivileged but significant sector of the population in the United States. I had to learn as much as I could about it, and to hear as much of the music as I could—which led to correspondence with many who shared similar enthusiasm across the Atlantic. From a young age, for some reason, I always wanted to know the *reality* about whatever I was interested in—whether it was American Indians, or how windmills worked. I collected books on all my interests, becoming a familiar customer in a number of second-hand bookshops—a passion that has never died.

Of course, I had to learn to identify the blues in its many forms and traditions, and it soon became apparent that everything that was so termed (like, for instance, "The Limehouse Blues") was not blues. For me, and for a slowly widening circle of friends and contacts who shared my fascination with the music, this had to be an exploration, for there were virtually no guides to the subject. As an art student in Harrow, I spent time such time as I could spare in the "Communist Bookshop." It was there that I found in the mid-'40s a little fifty-page paperback booklet, *Background of the Blues* by Iain Laing, published by the Workers' Music Association at the price of one shilling (1/20 of a pound). Although it was intended as a summary of jazz history, the *Background* included some transcriptions of blues, uncredited to their singers with the exception of Bessie Smith. It was a nonetheless a useful guide to jazz and its origins, but for Laing, who was a foreign (but not U.S.) correspondent of the *Times*, "blues is not the whole of jazz, but the whole of blues is jazz. It has no existence apart from this idiom." This statement annoyed me, for I was already aware that while blues may well have been an influence on jazz, it had a separate tradition of its own. My listening was informing me that all blues singers had approaches to playing an instrument, singing blues, and conveying their feelings and messages, that were uniquely their own. In part, the problem that confronted me, and my circle of friends who were interested in the blues, was the need to hear the blues, to have information about it and its singers, and, in trying to understand and evaluate what we could hear, we needed to develop criteria. Far removed from the culture that had created blues and was still producing it, we had to focus our attention on the genre as a whole, insofar as we could define it, and also on its recorded exponents and the blues that they sang. With no blues singers visiting Britain we had to depend on 78 rpm records as our principal source. When we started obtaining them we had no idea how many blues records there might be, let alone who was on them, what they sang, where they came from, whether the singers were still living, or indeed, how old or extensive the blues tradition was.

So, how did we hear and obtain blues records? Well, though it is seldom recognized now, there had been a number of blues issues on 78s in the prewar years, and some were still in the catalogues. Prominent among them were the performances of boogie-woogie pianists like Albert Ammons, Pete Johnson, and Meade Lux Lewis, who were riding on the Swing tide. Lewis's "Honky Tonk Train Blues" was a *tour de force*, but more subtle were the four titles by Clarence "Pinetop" Smith, including "Pinetop's Blues" and "I'm Sober Now," as well as his historic item which gave the name to "boogie woogie." Tragically, Pinetop was shot and killed shortly after, in March 1929, during a fracas at a club where he was playing. With Big Joe Toe Turner taking the vocals, backed by Pete Johnson, on "Roll 'Em Pete" and "Cherry Red," we were introduced to Kansas City blues shouting, which was in contrast with the jazz-inflected style of the so-called "Classic" blues singers. Of these, Bessie Smith was the most celebrated and the most accomplished. Her "In the House Blues" backed, unexpectedly, by the Seven Gallon Jug Band playing "Wipe

'Em Off," had been issued on black-label Parlophone in England, many years before. Her last recording session before her tragic death was in 1933, was instigated especially for the British market, and included her raucous "Gimme a Pigfoot." Afterwards, some sixteen titles were issued on Parlophone in its "Rhythm Style" series as the *Bessie Smith Memorial Album.*

Bessie's range in her singing and her richly inflected vocal quality made her work the standard by which other women blues singers were judged. Later, in the 1950s, I wrote a small book on her, paradoxically in a series called "Kings of Jazz." Occasionally though, I found some of her records to be a bit too self-conscious. I welcomed the more direct approach of Ida Cox, whose "Hard Time Blues" and "Death Letter Blues" were issued during the War years. Another of the "Classic Blues" singers (the term was introduced in the 1940s by the jazz historian Rudi Blesh) was the young Trixie Smith, whose voice had a distinct edge to it, evident on her "Freight Train Blues," issued on Brunswick. On this she was accompanied by the exceptional New Orleans soprano sax and clarinet-player, Sidney Bechet. Reputed to have been, in 1920, the first blues singer to record, Mamie Smith appealed less, though she was clearly at her best on her lively "Jenny's Ball." Issued on Parlophone, it was backed by Lonnie Johnson and Eddie Lang's fine guitar duet, "Two Tone Stomp." Lonnie Johnson's unrivalled mastery of the guitar had been brilliantly demonstrated on his "Playing with the Strings," issued in Britain in the 1930s in what was termed "The Parlophone Race Series: The Negro and His Music." Also issued at this time was his duet with the Texas singer Victoria Spivey, "Toothache Blues," with its amusing and suggestive exchange of lines.

By the outbreak of War in 1939, many items had ceased to appear in the catalogs and were no longer available, but if one was persistent and lucky, single items could be found in junk-shops and street market stalls. Junk-shops scarcely exist now, or have been elevated to the status of "antique shops," but in their crowded mélange of discarded objects and artifacts they generally had a few piles of 78s. Along with second-hand bookshops they became my happy hunting grounds. One of my first discoveries was the Dixieland Jug Blowers' "Skip Skat Doodle Do" played by a Louisville string band, with a jug blown to provide the bass; it was backed on the old HMV disc with "Washboard Cut-Out," by the harmonica player Bobbie Leecan and his "Need-More" Band with its washboard rhythms. The issue of 78s with quite different couplings was not uncommon, so it was always advisable to turn over the record in case an item might be missed. For instance, "Down Hearted Blues," performed by Noble Sissle with the Harlem "stride" pianist Eubie Blake, was backed by a splendid "You're Always Messin' Round with My Man" sung by the New Orleans vaudeville singer Lizzie Miles. Other early issues in the "classic blues" genre that I found included Miss Margaret Johnson singing "If I Let You Get Away with It" on an old red-label Parlophone, and Rosa Henderson's "I've Got Somebody Now," on Oriole. Recordings by some of the early singers were issued by smaller companies under pseudonyms, and in the 1940s two collectors, John Rowe and Red Watson, worked on a *Junkshopper's Discography*, which was published in 1945. While mostly devoted to jazz records, their research revealed, for example, that the names of Lila Vivian and Daisy Cliff on Guardsman records hid the identities of Edna Hicks and Rosa Henderson.

Many of the items that I obtained drew my attention to aspects of blues and blues-related music that were quite unfamiliar to me, or they raised issues about them. My heart leaped when I found and played "K.C. Moan" and "Kansas City Blues" by the Memphis Jug Band, on Regal-Zonophone; it's still one of my favorite records. Another surprise was the fierce, but soul-stirring preaching of the Reverend Nix on his two-part "Black Diamond Express to Hell" which had been issued on Decca. Other records posed problems: W. C. Handy was reputedly the "father of the blues," but could "The Snaky Blues" played by Handy's Orchestra be seriously regarded as blues, or even as jazz? Or again, ragtime was believed to have been influenced by traditional banjo playing, and the guitar to have replaced the banjo at an early stage in blues evolution. Where did "Darktown Dandies," a banjo solo by Olly Oakley on HMV, or Vess Ossman's "Smoky Mokes" banjo piece on an old Imperial 78 fit in the picture? And were they Black, or were they White, and were their roots in minstrelsy or in a nineteenth-century folk tradition? Every record seemed to bring new experiences, if not always new delights, and presented us with problems, by which some of us were challenged. But then, who were "us"?

What is certain is that none of "us" were black, we were not even American, we had not visited the United States, and we had no instruction in the music and song that we were hearing. Some were close friends, like Roy Ansell and Pat Hawes; others we got to know through the "Rhythm Clubs" that were becoming popular in the late forties and early fifties, which gave us the opportunity to discuss "our" music with similar collectors. We encountered many difficulties as we endeavored to define what could be considered to be blues, or was closely associated with blues, and what lay outside the idiom. A similar problem posed by some of the records, was where, and in what category, let alone at what level of ability or quality, did every singer and musician that we had discovered, actually fit? Although we weren't aware of it at the time, in semiotic terms we were trying to establish the *langue*, or the characteristics, the extent, and the limitations of the music that we termed "blues," and the *parole* of each artist's creativity.

The latter involved the exercise of his or her expressive capabilities and the relationship of the content of their blues, both textual and musical, to their feelings and to what they were motivated to convey. Semiotically, this might be distinguished and examined as blues at the plane of content, and blues at the plane of expression. In fact, I would like to discuss the subject from a semiotic (study of signs) position, but that must wait until another more appropriate occasion or publication. Not that we were engaged in an academic discussion of these issues which were, nonetheless, very important to me. From recordings by Blind Lemon Jefferson or Blind Willie McTell we began to gain a sense of quality in the blues but we were continually trying to "place" a performer, such as Papa Charlie Jackson or Johnny Temple, Joe Pullem, or the "Yas Yas Girl." One or two of these singers we were inclined to regard as "minor," though it was by no means easy to identify our criteria in coming to that conclusion. Blues by these singers had not been issued on British labels, but after the war was over, American servicemen returned to the United States, and many sold off their records and other items before they left. I found a shop in Bournemouth which dealt with them; on my first visit I bought Kokomo Arnold's "Milk Cow Blues" on American Decca and a battered copy of the first book by an author of the Harlem Renaissance, Claude McKay's *Home to Harlem*. Some collectors acted as dealers, such as Mike Wyler, who was slowly compiling a discography, or complete listing, of the Paramount label. In the process he obtained many other records which he was prepared to sell. At a bar in the West End (London) several collectors would gather at intervals, to trade, exchange, or buy the records that appealed to us. I was particularly attracted by the subjects implied in the titles, whether it was "Highway 61" or "St. Louis Cyclone Blues," even though at that date I hadn't heard of blues singers Jack Kelly or Elzadie Robinson. Label preferences were notable among some collectors: Gerry Grounsell favored American Columbias for their high sound quality, while Jack Parsons preferred Deccas and John Mastaka (a Lithuanian, living in London) sought Vocalions as well as obscure minority labels.

A few dealers established connections with collectors in the United States, trading records by English dance bands such as Harry Roy's, for 78s that we sought from the lists provided by our American counterparts. Selection was a gamble, as we had no way of hearing them first, so we had to make guesses. If the singers had curious names we believed that they might be more "authentic," so we'd choose a Peg Leg Howell or a Peetie Wheatstraw rather than a Smith or (we regretted later!) a Johnson. We were helped in this by a somewhat racist policy among the recording companies, who issued items that were directed to Whites on certain numerical series, and reserved other number series for "Race records"—issues intended for the Afro-American "race." So, for instance, the 8000 Race series issued by Okeh Records was directed to the Black market, as were Paramount 12000s, Decca 7000s, the Victor V-38500s, and so on. There was a problem as to where the singers came from, and where they were recorded. It was a collector friend, Gerry Grounsell, who opened this issue for me. I asked him what kind of blues he liked, and he said "Texas blues." I'd never heard a specific regional interest like this before, but "discographers" were making this possible. Most recordings were made in the North, in New York, in Chicago, or at a company location in say, Richmond, Indiana, or Grafton in Wisconsin. But a number of companies in the 1920s and '30s sent out field units at intervals to Southern locations, such as Birmingham, Alabama, or Jackson, Mississippi, and Shreveport, Louisiana, among others. I was particularly interested in Columbia's regular field trips to Memphis, Tennessee, Dallas, Texas, Georgia, and New Orleans, so I began to rival Gerry for Columbias made on location. I was greatly assisted in this by chance: a collector, Claude Lipscomb, discovered a cache of Columbias in mint condition in the store-room of a Bond Street record dealer; they had been sent in the late 1920s and had never been put on sale, so a score of years later Claude bought them and sold items to fellow collectors like myself.

In attempting to "take the measure" of jazz and blues releases, discographers were seeking to list every record by a given artist, including the accompaniments and instrumentation, and were trying to ascertain the dates on which they were recorded. This was something that European collectors, who were far from the scene of the music, could do. Most collectors contributed the information on record labels, noting not only the issue numbers but the "matrix" numbers too; these were assigned by the companies for each item, at each session. Comparison revealed possible associations and accompanying musicians, while locations were ascertained, in some instances, by discographers gaining access to company files. It wasn't easy. A couple of duplicated periodicals, *Matrix* and *Discophile*, were initiated so that collectors could share information and contribute to listings. The sheer scale of the "Race" catalogues was now being recognized, and we felt that there was no hope that we would ever hear, let alone possess, all the blues on disc.

Despite wartime shortages, and restrictions on the use of shellac, throughout the war years hundreds of jazz and swing records were on sale to the public, although the number of copies of a specific issue could be limited. Collectors telephoned each other with the news if a sought-after item appeared in a local shop, and most were prepared to accept the difficult traveling conditions of the day in order to obtain their copies. A professional discographer, Edgar Jackson, compiled in the 1940s, for Parlophone, HMV, and the Decca-Brunswick-Vocalion consortium, complete listings of their records, with full personnel and approximate recording dates. Blues records represented only a minute percentage of the issues. Nevertheless, enthusiasts were making an impression on the "majors," the large record companies, with the "Jazz Appreciation Society" sponsoring the issue on Brunswick of "Drop Down Mama" by Sleepy John Estes, featuring the singer's wheezing vocal and Hammie Nixon's harmonica accompaniment. Among other releases were the powerful piano and strong, growling vocal of Jesse James's "Southern Casey Jones," and "Streamline Train," sung by Red Nelson to Cripple Clarence Lofton's boogie-styled piano. The backing side of each item was a twelve-bar, three-line blues of conventional type, but the verse structures of the cited titles appeared to relate to ballad and other song forms—raising further questions.

Even with these releases, blues was inadequately covered, but a few collectors took advantage of postwar opportunities and started their own record companies, reissuing titles from Paramount and other defunct labels. Most were largely jazz-oriented, but included blues items in their lists. So the white-labeled Jazz Collector, initiated by Colin Pomeroy of West Kensington, reissued such titles as "South Side Stomp" by the Dixie Four, with pianist Jimmy Blythe, and Lucille Bogan's "Down in Boogie Alley." Its contemporary label, Tempo, of Piccadilly Arcade, reissued Rambling Thomas's "Hard Dallas Blues" and "Brownskin Mama Blues" by Blind Blake, together with many others by, for instance, Blind Lemon Jefferson and Charlie Jackson. For the first of its short-lived series, Jazz Reissues made Ma Rainey's "Stack O'Lee Blues" available, also in association with the Jazz Appreciation Society, which gave its address as Newark, Nottinghamshire.

Nottingham was where Pete Russell operated his Hot Record Store for many years, before moving it to Plymouth. Specialist record shops opened to serve the jazz, blues, and sometimes also, folk collectors. Admittedly, most of the shops were in London. Among the most well-known was Doug Dobell's at 77 Charing Cross Road. Like Colin Pomeroy, James Asman, and other shop proprietors, he let collectors thumb through the fragile records, many of them considerable rarities, until they found what they wanted to purchase. The records were placed in orange boxes, which were literally that: wooden boxes in which oranges, each separately wrapped in decorative paper (which became collector's items also), were shipped from Spain to Britain. The internal width was 25cm, permitting the stacking on end of ten-inch records in card sleeves. As the length of the box, with a central wooden partition, was twice the width, this allowed eighty or more records to be placed in it. Many a dealer, like Dave Carey at the Swing Shop, Streatham, had literally dozens of orange boxes filled with 78s.

Sales of jazz and blues records increased markedly at this time. During and after the War, one or two small magazines were published, most notably *Jazz Music* edited by Max Jones and Albert McCarthy. They had to pretend to some academic credentials, for instance, as members of the "Jazz Sociological Society," in order to meet wartime requirements on the use of paper. This enabled them to publish Ernest Borneman's *A Critic Looks At Jazz*, among the most authoritative works published on the origins of jazz and the role of blues. Other books on jazz, written in Britain, were now appearing, some being published by Poetry London. Albert McCarthy edited *The PL Yearbook of Jazz, 1946*, which contained a thirty-five-page chapter "On Blues" by Max Jones, which was quite the best feature on the subject to have been published anywhere at that time. Three years later, *Shining Trumpets*, a history of jazz by Rudi Blesh was published, with two chapters on "The Blues," in which he proposed a classification. "Archaic blues" included Blind Lemon Jefferson, Mama Yancey, the pianist Montana Taylor, and Robert Johnson; the "Classic Blues" was represented by Ma Rainey and Bessie Smith, but also by Jelly-Roll Morton, Bertha "Chippie" Hill, and Sippie Wallace. Roosevelt Sykes was the first to be named in the "Post-Classic Blues" category, in which Jazz Gillum typified the pornographic, Josh White the pleasant "but scarcely deep and vital," and Billie Holiday, the sophisticated—"not a real blues singer but a smart entertainer." Although Max Jones's chapter was far more perceptive, Blesh defined the blues for many listeners, especially his category of the "Classic Blues," which still persists.

With the greater availability of paper, in 1947 Sinclair Traill founded *Jazz Journal*, a monthly illustrated magazine, for which Derrick Stewart-Baxter wrote his "Blues and Views" page for some thirty-five years. Derrick owned the first Robert Johnson that I had heard; visiting him was only marred for me by his incessant pipe smoking while he held court above a little record shop in Britain. I also wrote my first articles for the *Journal*, before joining the team of *Music Mirror*, for which I commenced a regular monthly series of articles on "Sources of Afro-American Music." Soon after, in the late 1950s, Albert McCarthy commenced the publication of *Jazz Monthly*, in which Mike Wyler serialized his listing of the Paramount Race label and initiated what was soon to become a feature of blues writing and discography: the reproduction of record labels, which were photographed (mainly from his own collection) by Gerry Grounsell. McCarthy invited me to review blues records and to contribute articles. This I did for several years and was happy to see the blues audience slowly increase. It raises the question: why were we interested in blues, and what was the appeal of the music?

As is the case with every art form the appeal is both general and specific. Regrettably, there was no blues magazine available, and it was to be some fifteen years before one was introduced in Britain. In the meantime, the opportunity to hear live blues arose. In 1949 the Paris Jazz Fair was held, with a concert of the Fondation des Etats Unis at which the famous songster and "King of the Twelve-string Guitar," Huddie Ledbetter, known to the folk and blues world as "Leadbelly," was booked. Curiously, only a dozen or so people turned up for the concert, but Leadbelly was evidently ill and not in good form. He did not tour, but returned to the United States, where he died a few months later of lateral sclerosis. Josh White, who had sung at Leadbelly's funeral, was the first of the singers to come to Britain. His visit was anticipated with enthusiasm by those who knew his records on the ARC labels, like Melotone and Perfect. He played the Kingsway Hall in London in 1951, but Josh had been playing too long for American urban "folk club" audiences, and though his voice still had its unique "catch" and his guitar-playing had much of his former dexterity, Rudi Blesh's perception was all-too accurate. His interpretations of "The House of the Rising Sun" and "One Meat-Ball" won him little applause. Soon after, Lonnie Johnson came to England, but he too, had underestimated his audience and songs such as "I Left My Heart in San Francisco" were too sentimental. It seemed as if the blues was finished, and when the visit of Big Bill Broonzy was announced in September 1951, Gerry Grounsell refused to see him, rather than be disappointed by a singer whose records he so admired. He needn't have worried.

Big Bill was introduced at the Kingsway Hall by Alan Lomax, who took up half the time available. But when Bill stepped in and began to play, the relatively small audience was captivated. He had a great repertoire, playing and singing blues with feeling and power, but also drawing upon the ballads and songs of his youth. The remarkable rhythm of his guitar on "John Henry" contrasted with his moving "Blues in 1890" or his protest song, "Black, Brown and White." A profound influence on many of his contemporary singers and musicians, Big Bill was exceptional in every respect. I was honored to draw a number of illustrations for his autobiography, *Big Bill Blues*, edited by Yannick Bruynogue and published in 1955. He showed little sign of decline during his frequent visits in the 1950s, but he died of throat cancer in 1958. I learned a lot from Big Bill; if our collecting and research had enabled us to take the measure of the blues in its diversity and distribution, it was Broonzy who gave an insight of its depth.

During the 1950s I visited Paris frequently with my wife, Val, to hear and talk with such visiting musicians as Sammy Price, Bill Coleman, and permanent residents like Sidney Bechet and Mezz Mezzrow. I met up with the African American author Richard Wright and many of his expatriate friends, who helped me a lot with their observations and their background experiences, which brought to life the information I was gathering in my ever-growing library of Afro-American history and culture. At this time I was invited to broadcast about blues on *Jazz Club*, a regular BBC program.

I didn't succeed in persuading the BBC to start a "Blues Club" but I did a few programs each year, mainly on themes which I'd explored for my *Music Mirror* articles and for a book that I was planning to do.

With the death of Big Bill it seemed as if we would be denied any future contacts with blues singers, but Chris Barber's idea of inviting blues singers as "intermission" and "variety" artists got round the Musician's Union ban on American musicians playing in Britain. Brownie McGhee and Sonny Terry came over frequently, and like Champion Jack Dupree and others, visited Val and me as house guests, as had Big Bill and Brother John Sellers a year or two before. They also provided me with details, explanations, and confirmation of many of the transcriptions that I was making of blues records. This was my personal focus—the meaning of, and in, the blues. My talks with them— they were hardly formal "interviews"—led to articles and sleeve-notes, some of which were collected later in *Blues Off the Record*. Sleeve-notes were the essays that appeared on the backs of the card covers for issues in the 1950s of ten-inch long-playing records. For me they were a boon, as I also had the opportunity to design the covers of many sleeves. Among the first, to my delight, was *Backwoods Blues* with 1920s recordings of Bobby Grant, Buddy Boy Hawkins, King Solomon Hill, and Big Bill Johnson (who was Big Bill Broonzy). Other sleeve designs were for compilations of Jimmy Blythe, Will Ezell, Blind Lemon Jefferson, Cripple Clarence Lofton, and many more. People have asked me whether I ever played blues—well, yes, a little guitar, but Val was a better guitarist than me, and she also played piano. I played some harmonica, and I got particularly interested in playing the mandolin. But, unlike many of my contemporaries, I did not wish to encroach on the blues singers' ground, so I deliberately gave up, once I'd attempted to "take the measure" of their work and had gained some understanding of what the guitarists and harp players were doing as they played the blues.

This has become autobiographical, and that in a sense is the way it was. We had reached the end of the 1950s, and the audience for blues, includ- ing "Rhythm and Blues," had grown considerably, with "skiffle" provid- ing opportunities for playing and the forming of small bands. "We" took our own directions as each felt, consciously or subconsciously, that they had acquired a fair understanding of the measure of the blues. Cassell pub- lished my book *Blues Fell This Morning: The meaning of the blues* in 1960, and within three years Horst Lippman and Fritz Rau had commenced their ground-breaking "American Folk Blues Festivals" which introduced the blues of veterans and contemporary blues singers to most countries in Europe. In 1963 the first edition of the monumental discography *Blues and Gospel Records 1902–1942* by Robert M. W. Dixon and John Godrich appeared, and a team which included Simon Napier, Mike Ledbetter, and John Broven produced the first English-language magazine on the subject, *Blues Unlimited.* Much of the blues had indeed been "measured," but there was much more to be studied, reported, and recorded; and that is still the case, as this book, and the conference that produced it, doubtless indicate.

REFERENCES

Recordings Cited

The following is a list of recordings cited in the text, with due acknowledgments to the Fourth Edition of *Blues and Gospel Records 1890–1943* by Robert M. W. Dixon, the late John Godrich, and Howard Rye, which should be consulted for full personnel and other data. The artist and his or her vocal or instrument, the recording location and dates are listed. Instruments are given as banjo: bjo; guitar: gtr; piano: pno; violin: vln. The matrix number and the song title precede the original USA issue label and number, which is cited first, followed by the British release label and number. Labels are Brunswick: Brun; Decca: Dec; His Masters Voice: HMV; Jazz Collector: JC; Paramount: Para; Parlophone: Parlo; Perfect: Per; Tempo: Tem; Victor: Vic; Voc: Vocalion; Vogue: Vog. Others label names are given in full.

Arnold, Kokomo, vo, gtr. Chicago, Sept. 10, 1934. C-9428pB. "Milk Cow Blues," Dec 7026.
Blake, Blind, vo, gtr. Chicago, c. Oct. 1927. 20106-2. "Brownskin Mama Blues," Para 12606, Tem R23.
Bogan, Lucille, vo acc Walter Roland, pno. New York, August 1, 1934. 15508-2. "Down in Boogie Alley," Per 0298, JC L90.
Broonzy, Big Bill, vo, gtr. Paris, Sept. 20–21, 1951. 51V-4100. "Black Brown and White," Vog 134.
———. 51V-4106. "Blues in 1890," Vog 131.
———. 51V-4110. "John Henry," Fog 2074.
Cox, Ida, vo acc All-Star Band. New York, Oct. 31, 1939. 26241. "Hard Times Blues," Voc 05298, Parlo R2948.
———. 25510. "Death Letter Blues," Voc 05336, Parlo R2974.
Dixie Four, Jimmy Blythe, and trio. Chicago, June 1928. 20659-2. "South Side Stomp," Para 12674, JC L67.
Dixieland Jug Blowers, Clifford Hayes vln, and quintet. Chicago, Dec. 10, 1926. 37224-2. "Skip, Skat, Doodle Do," Vic 20649, HMV B5398.
Estes, Sleepy John, vo, gtr. Chicago, July 9, 1935. 90176A. "Drop Down Mama," Dec 1289, Brun 03562.

Handy's Orchestra (W. C. Handy and twelve-piece orch). New York, Sept. 21, 1917. "The Snaky Blues," Columbia 2190.

Henderson, Rosa, vo, acc. New York, June 5, 1928. E3195. "I've Got Somebody Now," Voc 1025, Oriole 1001.

James, Jesse, vo, pno. Chicago, June 3, 1936. 90761-A. "Southern Casey Jones," Dec 7213, Voc V1037.

Johnson, Lonnie, vo, gtr. Memphis, Feb. 21, 1928. 400277-B. "Playing With the Strings," Okeh 8558, Parlo R2259.

Johnson, L. with Blind Willie Dunn (Eddie Lang) gtr. New York, Nov. 17, 1928. 401338-B. "Two Tone Stomp," Okeh 8637, Parlo R1195.

Johnson, Margaret, vo, acc Clarence Williams Blue Five. New York, Oct. 19, 1923. 71972-B. "If I Let You Get Away with It," Okeh 8107, Parlo E5187.

Kelly, Jack, vo, gtr acc His South Memphis Jug Band. New York, Aug. 1, 1933. 13712-1. "Highway No 61. Blues," Per 0254.

Leecan, Bobby, Need-More Band, R. Leecan bjo. Camden, NJ, Apr. 5, 1927. 38434-1. "Washboard Cut-Out," Vic 20660, HMV B5398.

Lewis, Meade Lux, pno. Chicago, May 7, 1936. 06301-1. "Honky Tonk Train Blues," Vic 25541, HMV B8579.

Miles, Lizzie, vo, acc Clarence Johnson, pno. New York, May 23, 1923. 28025-3. "You're Always Messin' Round with My Man," Vic 19083, HMV B1703.

Nelson, Red, vo, acc Cripple Clarence Lofton. Chicago, Feb. 4, 1936. 90598-B. "Streamline Train," Dec 7171, Brun 03508.

Nix, Reverend, vo, sermon, acc Congregation. Chicago, Apr. 23, 1927. C-810/11/12. "Black Diamond Express to Hell," Voc 1098, Dec F3850.

Oakley, Ollie, bjo, Landon Ronald pno. London, Mar. 12, 1903. 3274, "Whistling Rufus," HMV B-138.

Ossman, Vess, bjo acc unknown pno. New York, c. 1906. 7070. "Smoky Mokes," Imperial 45221.

Rainey, Gertrude Ma, vo acc Her Georgia Band. Chicago, c. Aug. 1925. 2376-2. "Stack O'Lee Blues," Para 12357, Jazz 5001.

Robinson, Elzadie, vo, acc Bob Call, pno. Chicago c. Nov. 1927. 20192-2. "St. Louis Cyclone Blues," Para 12573, Tem R33.

Seven Gallon Jug Band, Clarence Williams, jug and quintet. New York, Jan. 3, 1903. 149690-6. "Wipe 'Em Off," Columbia 2087D, Parlo R2329.

Smith, Clarence "Pine Top," vo, pno. Chicago, Dec. 29, 1928. C-2726. "Pine Top Blues," Voc 1245, Brun 03600.

————, vo, pno. Chicago, Jan. 14, 1929. C-2797-C. "I'm Sober Now," Voc 1266, Brun 04426.

Spivey, Victoria, vo, Lonnie Johnson vo, gtr. New York, Oct. 17, 1928. 401247-A. "Toothache Blues," Okeh 8744, Parlo 8744.

Thomas, Ramblin', vo, gtr. Chicago, c. Nov. 1928. 210182-2. "Hard Dallas Blues," Para 12708, Tem R51.

Turner, Joe, vo, acc Pete Johnson, pno. New York, Dec. 30, 1938. 23892-1, "Roll 'Em Pete," Voc 4607, Parlo R2672.

————, with Pete Johnson and Boogie Woogie Boys. New York, June 30, 1939. 25023-1. "Cherry Red," Voc 4997, Parlo R2717.

White, Josh, vo, gtr. New York, c. 1942. KJW11. "House of the Rising Sun," Keynote K542.

Reissues on 10″ Long-Play Records (London "Origins of Jazz")

Note that "London" in this list refers to the Decca subsidiary label.

Ma Rainey, 1927; Ida Cox, 1928; Bessie Smith, 1929; and Bertha "Chippie" Hill, 1946. *The Great Blues Singers.* London 3530, Sept. 1954.

Blythe, Jimmy. *South Side Blues Piano.* London AL3527, July 1954.

Blythe, Jimmy, State Street Ramblers. *South Side Chicago Jazz.* London AL3529.

Ezell, Will. *Will Ezell's Gin Mill Jazz.* London AL3539, Mar. 1955.

Grant, Bobby, 1927; Buddy Boy Hawkins, 1927; King Solomon Hill, 1931; Big Bill Johnson, 1932. *Backwoods Blues.* London AL3535, Dec. 1954.

Lofton, Cripple Clarence. *Lost Recording Date (1939).* London AL3531, Sept. 1954.

White, Josh. *Josh White Sings.* London H-APB 1032, Nov. 1954.

Books

Blesh, Rudi. *Shining Trumpets. A History of Jazz.* London: Cassell & Co., 1949.

Borneman, Ernest. *A Critic Looks at Jazz.* London: Jazz Music Books, 1946.

Broonzy, Big Bill, as told to Yannick Bruynoghe. *Big Bill Blues.* London: Cassell, 1955.

Dixon, R. M. W., and John Godrich. *Blues and Gospel Records.* Hatch End, London: Brian Rust, 1963.

Jackson, Edgar. *Swing Music and Hot Rhythm Records.* His Masters Voice, 1941.

———. *Parlophone Rhythm Style.* Parlophone, 1946.

———, with Leonard Hibbs. *Encyclopedia of Swing.* Decca Record Co., 1941.

Jones, Max. "On Blues" in Albert McCarthy, ed., *PL Yearbook of Jazz.* London: Poetry, 1946.

Laing, Iain. *Background of the Blues.* Workers Music Association. n.d. (c. 1943).

McCarthy, Albert, ed. *PL Yearbook of Jazz.* London: Poetry, 1946.

Oliver, Paul. *Bessie Smith.* London: Cassell & Co., 1959.

———. *Blues Fell This Morning.* London: Cassell & Co., 1960.

———. *Blues Off the Record.* Tunbridge Wells: The Baton Press, 1984.

Rowe, John, and Ted Watson. *Junkshopper's Discography.* Jazz Tempo, Pub. 1945.

3

Even Philosophers
Get the Blues

FEELING BAD FOR NO REASON

— DAVID WEBSTER

. . . the most astonishing aspect of the blues is that, though replete with a sense
of defeat and down-heartedness, they are not intrinsically pessimistic: their burden
of woe and melancholy is dialectically redeemed through sheer force of sensual-
ity, into an almost exultant affirmation of life, of love, of sex, of movement, of
hope. No matter how repressive was the American environment, the Negro never
lost faith in or doubted his deeply endemic capacity to live. All blues are a lusty,
lyrical realism charged with taut sensibility.

—Richard Wright[1]

Introduction

Let me begin with a disclaimer: I am not a specialist in music, never mind
the blues. I have very limited knowledge of the blues, but do enjoy listening to them. My background is as a philosopher—usually in a religious context. However, here I want to consider why it is that the blues can seem to

speak across such vast chasms of time and space. I want to investigate the seeming ability of the blues to transcend those very features which make it so distinctive.

When I woke up this morning, my woman hadn't gone and left me. I still got two legs, two arms, my sight, and my hearing. I'm not poor, I ain't got to work in the fields till the sun goes down, and I sure as hell ain't leaving town on the morning train. Given all this—why aren't I happy? Why, given that my life varies so much from the archetypical bluesman, do I feel something deep inside me move when Lightnin' Hopkins tells me he's got to pick cotton come the morning? If I cry, I know deep down that I don't cry for him—when we cry we always cry for ourselves: but what the hell have I got to bawl over?

The blues self-consciously arises out of conditions of misery and suffering and, arguably, the need to give an account of this—even at great cost. In a 1968 interview with the *Los Angeles Times* Sam "Lightnin'" Hopkins said, when discussing how his music came from the depths of his soul, "I'm killin' myself to tell them how it is."[2] This might give us a clue here about how the blues seeks to articulate something more than just a response to particular times of hardship, but how it uncovers a level of what we might call fundamental human unhappiness—an existential angst. This paper seeks to explore how music initially forged on the anvil of human suffering comes to represent, even for the more socio-economically advantaged, a means of engaging with our inner-most dis-ease and anxiety.

Further to this, we might suggest that appreciation of the blues has a political edge. For white listeners it can be a distancing of ourselves from the crimes of the slave-owner and the overseer. That is, a conscious siding with the oppressed. Identification with the blues can form a symbolic component of our response to the key political question: "which side are you on?"

While the blues might enable us to engage with our dis-ease, and situate ourselves socio-politically, lingering doubts remain as to claims (too numerous to mention—but see the white Bluesmen in Scorsese's Blues documentary for starters) that "it is nothing to do with race or color, it's just about feeling the blues."[3] As I hope to suggest, where and who you are is critical to the blues. From the notion that "to play the blues, you gotta pay your dues," to debates (that I have no intention of getting into here) about whether "white men can sing the blues"[4]—context matters in the blues. Even if you believe the blues can address universal themes, they are still addressed by someone—someplace—and the listener is a specific person in a specific place: these provide a landscape for the meaning of blues.

Damn, I Feel Guilty Enough Already

So—we have a roll call of specific ills that ail the bluesman. Poverty, oppression—but more than anything the pains of the heart in the face of love denied. While we may not suffer from most of these, I would imagine that any of us with a pulse would feel ourselves as able to recognize something in songs about romantic abandonment, jealousy, passion, and love. Even acknowledging this, the troubles of the blues are not really identical with mine. We might even say that unhappiness is never shared—citing what we might call the *Anna Karenina* principle. The opening line of Tolstoy's novel being: "All happy families are happy alike, all unhappy families are unhappy in their own way."

How, though, can we move from this to a sense of the blues as expressing something like a kind of generic dis-ease within our lives? I will return to this idea shortly. But first I want to briefly explore the tension that can often exist (especially, but not only, in white Europeans such as myself) in appreciation of the blues.

One approach, which I do not see as tenable, but which deserves a moment's attention, is the accusation that the white, European appreciator of the blues is in the grip of some type of false consciousness: that what they derive their real underlying pleasure from is a variant form of racist *Schadenfreude.* This would not be at a conscious level, not a form of "Phew—I'm sure glad it isn't me whose gotta live like that." Rather, one might suggest that it is an internalized process, a kind of rather patronizing enjoyment of the pleasures of the primitive.

This reminds me of a story from the American satirical newspaper, the *Onion,* entitled: "Affluent White Man Enjoys, Causes the Blues."[5] The piece mocks white affluent blues fans—as the man in question demonstrates an incredible level of patronizing idiocy, ending with the lines: "'Blues music is all about pain: It's about losing your job, your dog dying, and your woman leaving you for another man,' he continued. 'Listening to the blues, I can almost imagine what it would be like to experience one of those things.'"

I am not going to follow it up here, but many critics of the phenomenon of "world music" see such a process very much at work in that somewhat constructed genre—the name itself as implying a "catch-all" term for non-Western music—lumping it all together and ignoring its internal differences and, indeed, tensions. I may be doing a little of that generalizing myself with respect to the blues, but I shall try to keep it to a minimum.

I do not want to suggest that this is what lies behind my, or anyone else's, appreciation of the blues, but maybe we can use such a reflection as the starting point for some thoughts on how we partake of suffering when we hear (or sing) the blues. Perhaps we could suggest that some *jouissance* is found at the heart of the other's misery—a nugget of real, true-to-life suffering that seems juicy and authentic, in contrast to our own constructed, synthetic lives.

The Real Thing

This might be equated with what Slavoj Žižek describes (although he tends to use it in a somewhat technical, Lacanian, sense) as a "passion for the real"—the notion that in much of the developed West, we feel that somehow our lives are not properly real.[6] Alienated from our bodies by mind-only computer work-lives, softened from the externalities of war by our wealth, we crave the real. In response to coffee without caffeine, beer without alcohol, we are after something that is genuine and real. Whether in reality TV, "amateur" pornography, the rise of "extreme" sports, or the ethos of the movie *Fight Club*, we are desperate to *feel* something. The blues singer seems to have misery to spare—authentic, grounded, down-home, handmade suffering—and for our palates, used to artificial stimulation, a little of this misery can go a long way.

So, the first serious point here is that the blues may stand, particularly for the European listener, as a type of symbolic authenticity—it is "the real thing." The blues is not the bleating of the bourgeoisie, but a genuine cry from the depths of the human heart—irreducible, unmediated by over-analysis, and "genuine."

Now, I want to move on shortly but there is something vaguely disturbing—to me at least—about this idea of the "genuine." All musical genres have their purists, but blues purists seem more pure than average. I am tempted to mention John Fahey here and his view (accurate or not) that by releasing his blues music, partly, under the name of "Blind Joe Death" rather than his own name he would gain more success. The idea here is, perhaps, that to sing the blues, you gotta know them. To know them, you gotta have lived them (I will return shortly to the notion of authenticity).

This point would be even more sustainable were there no successful white, European, non-poor blues artists. We might suggest that such performers are acceptable primarily because they free us of any possible guilt that might undermine our pleasure—but I think that this, although containing a slight nugget of truth in certain cases—is probably unfair as a general rule. The reason that I could, had I any musical talent that is, sing the blues is because, when it comes down to it—and this is a return to my opening concern—we all know the blues, because our own lives—no matter how comfortable—are touched by blues.

Suffering and Redemption

I've got plenty of food on the table—still gonna die; you've got a nice car— still gonna get old; I've got a good woman waiting at home—still gonna get ill, get old and die, thus deriving all my comfort, wealth, and superficial pleasure of their shine—of their meaning. Hell, I'm feeling blue already. But I think we ignore something rather essential about the blues if we take ourselves too far down this rather dark and miserable pathway. To some extent it may be fair to read the blues as an existential howl, the human spirit crying out in the face of a cold, heartless, and purposeless universe, but there is surely more.

As the opening quote of the paper indicates, the blues often celebrate life as much as they bemoan its vicissitudes. While acknowledging this point, I shall leave others to concentrate on the joyous—as I want to consider the blues as an engagement with suffering, but in a way that is more than purely a cry of anguish.

There are at least two possible approaches here. We could consider in some sense the blues as a means of redemption—and I will come to that shortly. However, I first want to consider blues in religious context. Often we have a tacit recognition of the religious—god/devil exists—but the singer has chosen the devil—not just at the crossroads, but at the bar and the bedroom door.

While we can appreciate the potential redemptive power of the blues (whether or not this emerges from the actual suffering itself is an interesting question) as a transport to salvific liberation from the limits and shortcomings of this mortal world (whether via religion or not), we can also hear in the blues the cry of the damned. This cry is one whose misery has led him/her to reject God's covenant—to see those two paths and choose the one lined with bars and brothels.

Now, what could we read into this choice? Why might the archetypal bluesman choose the path of the damned? Maybe they are just bad: "*Bad to the bone*" (although this phrase was popularized by white blues artist, George Thorogood). This is a powerful and evocative phrase. It gives a sense of existing outside the borders of redemptive possibility—and ties in with all the usual outsider motifs that run through blues music. A second reading might be that of the rejection of an uncaring God. When we see the early blues we see it arise out of a people made abject by slavery—by people who have undergone trauma that is, mercifully, hard for us to imagine—beyond our borders of experience. Having seen what they have seen, known what they know, lost what they have lost—alone, penniless, and homeless, what indeed can they be said to owe God who has paid them out so badly?

But perhaps we ought to be wary of going too far down this route; the blues is, at least not most of the time, not a variety of bleak theological critique. Nonetheless the blues is often situated within a theological context. Given what I have said here, how are we to read the theologically ambivalent—although humanly direct and moving—cry of "Lord, have mercy." The obvious parallel is with the crucified Christ—crying out as to why he has been abandoned—like the African American slave left alone by God in his hour of need.

So, there are a number of ways of reading the blues as a response to suffering—but how does it reach across the Atlantic to touch me in the way it does?

Maybe we come to a view, then, that our appreciation of the blues is a process that exoticizes the universal (and mundane, in a sense) phenomena of suffering—of mortality? This could be seen to occur such that the specific hardships of the blues performer come to stand for universal human problems—those categorized by Buddhist thought as aging, sickness, and death? We might argue that the blues is a displaced form of reflection on mortality. Perhaps "reflection" is the wrong word—we might see it more as a range of complex responses to finitude—a finitude we all share.

Blues and Justification

I want to move on from this notion though to look at the idea of how the blues might be seen as a means of justifying experience. One, I imagine relatively standard, way to read the blues is as an alienated community, or members thereof, justifying their existence. This would be to say that by giving voice to experience, it finds a means of validating that experience and seeking to come to terms with it. However, we can broaden this notion. In *Nausea*, Sartre's anti-hero Antoine Roquentin finds his last hope in his existential distress in the voice of a jazz-blues record.[7] Listening to the record, he muses:

> The negress[8] sings. So you can justify your existence? Just a little? I feel
> extraordinarily intimidated. It isn't that I have much hope. But I am like a man
> who is completely frozen after a journey through the snow and who suddenly
> comes into a warm room. I imagine he would remain motionless near the door,
> still feeling cold, and that slow shivers would run over the whole of his body.
>
> Some of these days
> You'll miss me honey (251–52)

After this he makes a resolution to write—to find his own way to justify his existence. To abandon his historical project as, "an existent can never justify the existence of another existent" (252), and find a means of self-expression that allows him to accept his own being. To understand how he comes to this, I will quote just one more section—that preceding the one a moment ago—that leads him to the view that you can, somehow, justify your existence:

> She sings. That makes two people that are saved: the Jew and the Negress.
> Saved. Perhaps they thought they were lost right until the very end, drowned

in existence *[like Roquentin feels—when he suffers the nausea, looking at the tree root whose very being threatens to overwhelm him—DW]*. Yet nobody could think about me as I think about them, with this gentle feeling. Nobody, not even Anny. For me they are a little like dead people, a little like heroes of novels; they have cleansed themselves of the sin of existing. Not completely, of course—but as much as any man can. This idea suddenly bowls me over, because I didn't even hope for that any more. I feel something timidly brushing against me and I dare not move because I am afraid it might go away. Something I didn't know any more: a sort of joy. (251)

This discovery is not only a moment of great poignancy in the novel, but for me encapsulates something of the blues—and leads me closer to an understanding of why the blues moves me like it does. Previously in the novel, Roquentin was struck down by the "nausea"—paralyzed by the pointlessness and contingency of existence at the counter of the cafe. This reverie of overwhelmed sensation is only escaped from by music—by the same record—which "snaps him out of it."

We could read this as a form of existential grounding. In light of the existentialist slogan that "existence precedes essence," we can see the blues as a form of raw being—musically as a form which is often spartan or basic, and in communion with raw emotion. Whether the simplicity of the blues form contributes directly to its ability to commune, without the mediation of complexity, with something deep and almost primal within us is a question for musicologists. However, the simple frame might be seen as contributing to the way in which a listener is transported across a world of boundaries to a place where a man (or woman) stands alone—at the crossroads—not doing, but just being.

Return to Reality

Be it stripped down bare, or lush, the blues seems to stand—both for aficionados and in the general culture—as a symbol of genuine human emotions. The blues can be seen as connecting us to something deeper than what we do, wear, buy, or, even, think. This returns us to the aforementioned notion of the blues as the expression of a passion for the real or authentic. It is not just the authentic product, but the authentic experience—authentic being. Is much of what passes for "the blues," however, not a false real—not the constructed real of the reality TV show? What does it mean to make a distinction between "authentic" and somehow contrived or manufactured blues? That this is a recurrent issue in many types of music is interesting.

People often complain that modern groups (for example "boy bands") are "manufactured," and that they haven't earned the right to their success. The issue of authenticity is both a common concern and lyrical pre-occupation in hip-hop.[9] Indeed, hip-hop—with its sometime[10] focus on poverty, exploitation, and oppression, and self-conscious understanding of the genre as a response to these circumstances—has exported the notion of "keeping it real" into the wider culture. Internally the genre still has an ongoing concern with the fake from the authentic, genuine, and—thereby—valid performers. There are many significant differences between the blues and hip-hop, but it is notable that both genres of predominantly black music are surrounded by questions of authenticity and a desire, often by non-black appreciators, to ensure that they get "the real thing."

Further, there are concerns over the way the blues has, in the eyes of some, been "domesticated"—and we could even import, a little out of context, Max Weber's notion (from the sociology of religion) of the "routinization of charisma" here—leading to a notion that the further the blues moves from its roots of oppression the more formulaic it becomes and hence its authenticity diminishes. Weber's view that as a religious or other radical or revolutionary leader dies, organizations or movements seek, often structural, ways of maintaining their momentum and agenda, might find a home here in the notion that there is a danger that as the blues moves forward it becomes ·"just another genre"—another choice in the lifestyle supermarket of choice and branding. Do I really like the blues just because it is consistent with my personal brand-identity profile?

Given this worry, can there be new blues? Is it not better to cede it as a historical genre? I like to believe not. The claim that context is critical, in finding meaning in the blues, should not lead us to believe that new performers are somehow inherently inauthentic. If we find work that is really a copy of the older forms—with themes that ape the past, surely we should eschew it for work that seeks to engage with contemporary contexts, with the things that make us blue today. Some of these are perennial, others more subject to the season—but, maybe sadly, there will never be a shortage of reasons to be blue.

Some might argue that older material is as relevant today as ever (in that it deals with "timeless" themes such as the search for satisfaction, self-expression, and human dignity)—and much of it is. Nonetheless, many of us might prefer a blues that speaks to the age from which it originates—that treats the genre not as a museum piece, but as an active engagement with the contemporary context. The blues is indeed steeped in tradition, but is not a key thread of that tradition acting as a living commentary on the time of its composition, and of, to steal an old Quaker phrase, "speaking the Truth to Power"?

Now, I do not want to suggest that people seek oppression just for the sake of their art. To do so, just so as to feel one's voice to be "authentic" would be absurd. Surely such a practice is somewhat self-indulgent and may itself be deeply patronizing. In an idea stolen from the realms of theodicy,[11] we might learn from suffering—but it is not there to teach us things—and we should not seek it for educational purposes!

The Spirit of Blues

So, to continue: Yes, the blues has become many things, and I am neither qualified nor inclined to comment in detail on issues of commercialism, exploitation, and purity, but to me there seems to be an element of blues music that runs like a thread through time and tradition. From those early bluesmen—people like Son House and Lightnin' Hopkins—to the white teenager I saw playing blues outside Bristol train station last week, an ineffable trace of the same spirit remains. This is not to say that this "spirit" is other-worldly, or that it is ever comprehensible other than via its concrete context. Rather I use the term to denote a person in whose performance we see a genuine attempt to engage with elements of their own nature as limited, mortal, imperfect, and suffering being who recognizes these facts about themselves. The blues can capture, in a moment via a phrase or picked string, a moment of self-insight that—mediated by context—has the potential to stir our own (often dormant) introspective apparatus.

Of course, we need—before I get too philosophical—to remember that normally we listen to the blues not as historical record, agit-prop, or seeking a trace of the divine, but because we enjoy it in a way that does not require or usually invite further speculation. However, seeing as we have started with the speculation. . . .

To return to the Sartre again, Paul Vincent Spade concentrates, in an article on the record in *Nausea*, on how the recording of the sound—unlike its transcription—has a certain power to immortalize: but he goes on to find something particular in the record: "The singer's wail really does express an 'exemplary' suffering. It is the suffering of redemption. She is singing that we must take up our cross and follow her, that we too must suffer in rhythm."[12] But, as we know, not all blues is suffering. Some is joyous or rowdy, or crude or any of the shades of human emotion. But when it moves me, at least, the most is when it captures (even when not trapped in the grooves of a record or the data of a CD—but live) this suffering in rhythm. While on the surface it may sometimes seem to do so, the blues is not a wallowing in misery, and because of the connection with our universal imperfection, it may feel as though it goes beyond the justification of a specific experience of a certain people in a particular place and time, and moves towards something truly sublime. As I have already indicated, this does not mean we can strip it of context without loss. To say that there is a "pure blues"[13] which is an essentialist essence transcending race, ethnicity, and class is too naïve, rather it is through seeing the context that we see the way it can connect with us. For the blues, any universal is buried deep within the particular.

I have mentioned the notion of the blues as redemptive. What does this mean? It is not meant in the sense that blues music can save us from our sins. Rather I mean it in the sense of "redeeming" or validating elements of our existing. When somebody sings the blues, when they sing them like they're dying just to tell you how it is, they exist at the frontiers of emotional experience in such a way as to open up the possibility of a self-redeeming, self-justifying being. At its best, the blues faces up to suffering without sentimentality, without self-pity, and in such a way that it becomes something which is not an escape from life, but rather something which affirms life. And anything life-affirming enriches us all.

Despite the misery, the suffering, and the heartache, the blues can bring us towards more than just an acceptance of our finite, mortal selves—it can even bring us close to that thing that Sartre's character is so timidly aware of: joy.

NOTES

1. Richard Wright in the Foreword to Paul Oliver, *Blues Fell This Morning* (Cambridge: Cambridge University Press, rev. ed. 1990, first pub. 1960), xv.

2. http://www.houstonculture.org/cr/lightnin.html.

3. My paraphrasing of this oft-repeated assertion.

4. Paul Garon has addressed this in some detail, both in his 1975 book *Blues and the Poetic Spirit*, and in 1993 when he wrote for *Living Blues Magazine*. He is a strong advocate of the view that "race matters," and that to pretend that it is just about some transcendent spirit of pure music is, frankly, naïve and—I would contend—potentially rather offensive. The topic is one of widespread concern, even finding satirical musical expression in the Bonzo Dog Doo-Dah Band's track *Can Blue Men Sing the Whites*.

5. *The Onion,* February 23, 2000.

6. Slavoj Žižek, *Welcome to the Desert of the Real* (London: Verso Books, 2002). Jacques Lacan was a French psychoanalyst whose work in the 1950s marked a return to Freud and whose emphasis on the "unconscious" helped shape "post-structuralism."

7. The record in the book is what Paul Vincent Spade calls "a mixture of fact and literary licence." See Paul Vincent Spade, *For Sapphire Needle: An Essay on Suffering in Rhythm.* http://indiana.edu/~pvsclass/SapphireNeedle.html. As early as 1949, Vladimir Nabokov identifies the song, writing in his (typically argumentative) *New York Times Book Review* piece: "I have ascertained that in reality the song is a Sophie Tucker one written by the Canadian Shelton Brooks." What is noteworthy, perhaps, is that Tucker was not a "negress" at all, but a Russian Jew, who grew up in Connecticut. Nonetheless, due to the style of music she performed, she had been required to wear "blackface" make-up early in her career. You can hear her remarkable voice on a wax cylinder recording from 1910 at http://www.tinfoil.com/cm-9706.htm#e10449. Shelton Brooks was a black Afro-Canadian, born in Ontario.

8. This is not a term still in current usage—with its strong associations with racist attitudes, I retain only out of concern for the "authenticity" of the original words.

9. For an exploration of related themes with regard to hip-hop, see Patrick Neate, *Where You're At: Notes from the Frontline of a Hip Hop Planet* (London: Bloomsbury, 2003).

10. Arguably less now than at any point in its previous, brief history. Some feel slightly disillusioned that a genre once producing social comment from the likes of Public Enemy, KRS-One and even (to some degree) NWA—is now dominated by "bling" and bragging.

11. In theology, a theodicy is an attempt to solve the Problem of Evil, which maintains God's Omnipotence, Omniscience, and Omnibenevolence. For a detailed attempt to address Theodicy and the Blues more directly, see Michael Spencer's *Blues and Evil* (Knoxville, Tenn.: University of Tennessee Press, 1993).

12. Paul Vincent Spade, *For Sapphire Needle: An Essay on Suffering in Rhythm.* http://indiana.edu/~pvsclass/SapphireNeedle.html.

13. As I indicated earlier, if you watch the recent Martin Scorsese blues documentaries, it is notable that a number of middle-aged white blues performers make exactly this claim.

4

Spirituals to (Nearly) Swing, 1873–1938

—JEFFREY GREEN

In December 1938 at Carnegie Hall, New York City, various artists presented the black musical styles of gospel, blues, and jazz. This *From Spirituals to Swing* concert charted a route from Christian songs of uplift and protest, through folk music, to the sophistication of instrumental dance music.[1] The music of black Americans has tended to be seen in that progression ever since.

In Britain, where access to black American music was dominated by recordings into the 1950s, enthusiasts copied records of those genres they so admired, and produced skiffle, trad jazz, and—notably in the case of the Beatles and the Rolling Stones—a British rock 'n' roll. Before this impact from recordings there were other influences, and this survey will suggest that the history of the influences of African American music in Europe may need to be reconsidered. These influences were sustained and substantial, but seldom preserved on disc.

First, before the late 1920s, when discs of black American music started to appear in British and continental record catalogues, there had been several black Americans whose performances reached countless thousands. Secondly, performances by black Americans in Britain were not—as at Carnegie Hall in 1938—a break in the racial barriers or color-line that impinged on the daily lives of all Americans of African descent, but a normal part of social life. Thirdly, the music of at least one black Briton crossed the Atlantic and had some considerable influence on Americans.

One hundred years ago the majority of Americans of African descent lived in the southern states; all of them knew of slavery times or had relatives who had been slaves. In Britain considerable sympathy and support had been given to abolitionists and those who had experienced slavery. For example, Virginia-born Thomas Lewis Johnson's autobiography, *Twenty-eight Years a Slave*, went into eight editions, the first published in London in 1882 and the last in 1909 in Bournemouth, where he had settled and where he died in 1921.[2] After slavery, a group of black students drawing on northern white sympathies, ventured out in 1873 to sing in aid of their college, a former Civil War barracks in Nashville, Tennessee, that was now Fisk University. Their presentation of Spirituals was especially well received. The choir, named the Fisk Jubilee Singers, set off across the Atlantic in a sustained presentation of the music of black Americans in Europe.

Their spiritual music, in the Nonconformist Christian tradition, would have been immediately recognized by Mitchell's Christian Singers who were to appear at Carnegie Hall in 1938. But in the 1870s the music was a revelation in Britain (and in Germany, Italy, Denmark, the Netherlands, and Switzerland). Their first concert (May 6, 1873) led the London *Times* to comment: "Though the music is the offspring of wholly untutored minds, and, therefore, may grate upon the disciplined ear, it possesses a peculiar charm."[3]

A few days later they sang for Queen Victoria who said, "Tell them we are delighted with their songs, and that we wish them to sing 'John Brown.'" The Prime Minister of Britain, William Ewart Gladstone, attended a recital and remarked "Isn't it wonderful? I never heard anything like it." Music had won them influential friends including philanthropist Lord Shaftesbury who commented on the choir: "coming here in such a spirit, I don't want them to become white, but I have a strong disposition myself to become black."[4] The Queen, the Prime Minister, and the venerable aristocrat were just three Britons who were committed to the black cause as evidenced by the Fisk choir. This may often have been patronizing, but patronage was welcome and, despite republican sympathies, many Americans were impressed when the ancient families of Europe invited black Americans to grace their social gatherings.

At this time racial stereotypes were ill-formed. It could be argued that the Fisk Singers created a stereotype by presenting a music that looked back into the slavery decades. According to one doughty imperialist (and superb linguist and artist), Harry Johnston, who was in the South thirty years later, the Spirituals tradition was backward-looking. He "was enormously impressed with the beauty of the voices in the singing of Negro men and women at Tuskegee, Hampton, and other centers [*sic*] of education; but I soon got weary of the verbal rubbish of the hymns, and still more the plantation songs, to which their talent was directed." Admitting that grand opera, which these black students could have sung (and played: for he praised their violin, piano, and organ playing), had words and themes "nearly as idiotic as the worst hymns," he recommended Gilbert and Sullivan operettas to them.[5] His *The Negro in the New World* (1910) carries further details, for Johnston was never short of words.

The Fisk Jubilee Singers numbered ten in 1876, eleven in 1884, and eight later. All but one had been house-slaves, and thus alert to the manners and expectations of the ruling elite: not "untutored." Edmund Watkins, however, had picked cotton and had been whipped in Texas.[6] When another Fisk choir set off for Europe in 1875, it was led by freeborn Frederick Jeremiah Loudin. Loudin, ably assisted by his wife and business manager Harriet Loudin, took the music around the world. He was to tell audiences of the black experience of slavery, and explain how his people had been sustained by the music during those evil times. As well as public appearances the group sang for private gatherings, and sold many copies of *The Story of the Jubilee Singers, with their Songs*. A London edition dated 1876 is the sixth edition "completing forty-fourth thousand." Fresh editions appeared almost yearly, each with photographic portraits of the choir members. It contained 112 songs, with their words. Pianists and singers all over the country played Spirituals as a consequence. Members of the Fisks took advantage of opportunities that came to them in Britain. Two women studied music when the 1875 tour ended in 1878, and Isaac Dickerson went to Edinburgh University and settled in London where he became a Christian minister in Plumstead. He died there in 1900, and his funeral was accompanied by Spirituals.[7] His colleague Thomas

Rutling taught music in England, living in Harrogate (Yorkshire) where he died in 1915. His *Tom: An Autobiography, with Revised Negro Melodies*, was published in England around 1910.[8] He had been presenting black American music in Britain for over forty years.

With Loudin's choir, the book, and the activities of ex-members, the music reached many Britons. Three examples from *The Story of the Jubilee Singers* would have been known to the performers at Carnegie Hall in 1938. "Go Down Moses" and "Swing Low, Sweet Chariot" remain in the gospel/ spiritual repertory to this day. The 1920s recordings by Blind Willie Johnson, a mix of blues and spirituals in sound but the latter in intent, included "Keep Your Lamps Trimmed and Burning." The words are very similar to those in the 1876 Fisk book (the melody is different), hinting at a shared folk base, probably Biblical in origin. The Fisk book also has "Trouble in Mind." This has words and melody quite distinct from the jazz/blues tune recorded in the 1920s that became a stalwart of New Orleans revival bands across Europe. However, its three-word theme is an essential definition of the inspiration for blues music. Many devotees have not been aware of the legacy of the Fisks of the 1870s in the blues and other black American music that led to so much European enthusiasm.

The Fisks were not at the margins of musical performance, for they were briefly reviewed in the London *Musical News*, which noted their appearance at the Albert Hall in Sheffield in February 1899 and at London's new concert hall, the Queen's Hall, on November 17, 1899.[9] The success of the choir and the acceptance of spirituals as a black American art form led to bootleg editions of the book, and—as with skiffle and New Orleans jazz in the 1950s— white copiers. The East London Jubilee Singers of Hackney numbered up to forty, according to a late nineteenth-century flier that has somehow survived.[10]

By 1877 Loudin's choir was independent of Fisk University. They were back in Britain in 1884 and two years later sailed to Australia. They were there and in New Zealand for over three years, and returned via India and Japan after an absence of six years.[11] There are two massive scrapbooks of cuttings from this tour in the Detroit Public Library.

Other black Americans realized that Loudin's Fisk Jubilee Choir was making considerable amounts of money. The Wilmington Jubilee Singers pretended to be collecting for a school in North Carolina, and dogged the footsteps of the Fisks, even following them to the Netherlands in 1877. There were also two groups each called the Original Nashville Students.[12] There may have been other African American choirs touring Europe; certainly it was known that profitable opportunities were available across the Atlantic.

Eugene and Orpheus McAdoo from North Carolina were in a group of singers who went to South Africa, and then Australia, in the 1890s. An African referred to them as "McAdoo's Vaudevilles" in 1899, for this group had become more of a minstrel show by the time they were entertaining in diamond-mining Kimberley in 1898.[13] And all this stimulated a white South African to take an African choir to Britain in 1891 and then on to the United States.[14]

Black choral groups were far from rare in Britain from the final years of Victoria's reign. Eugene McAdoo and two female colleagues (billed as the "Fisk Jubilee Trio") appeared in Plumstead, London, in June and in Brighton in August 1908. It was declared that they "have sung before our King and Queen, and practically every living Monarch and Ruler."[15] The Kingston Choral Union, renamed the Native Choir from Jamaica, toured Britain in 1906 and in 1907–8.[16] The local press reviewed their performances.

Frederick Loudin, like the later- and better-known Paul Robeson, had a deep interest in the black experience. During the Spanish-American war of 1898, he expressed his wish that Spanish battleships would bombard the "hell holes" of Charleston, New Orleans, and Savannah, ports of Southern states where blacks were still in servitude.[17] He was aware that white attitudes to blacks did not have to be that experienced by his kinfolk in the United States. He informed a black contact that "I have been under the British flag in nearly all quarters of the globe [and] have never with the single exception of Canada—which draws its inspiration more from America than England—been denied any right a white man enjoys."[18] Two months later, at the end of July 1900, Frederick and Harriet Johnson attended the Pan-African Conference in London. This gathering of more than thirty men and women from the Caribbean, Africa, Canada, the United States, and Britain, led to a declaration that observed that the problem of the twentieth century would result from "denying to over half the world the right of sharing to their utmost ability the opportunities and privileges of modern mankind."[19]

The conference led to the London-based Pan-African Association, to press for global black rights. There were six people on its committee including both Loudins. Loudin, who became unwell and spent months in a sanatorium in Peebles, Scotland, had his choir cease activity in October 1902. He returned to Ohio where he died in 1904.[20]

Attending the Pan-African Conference, and serving on the committee, was Samuel Coleridge-Taylor, the son of an African, born in London in 1875. His father, a medical student from Sierra Leone, had returned to Africa before his birth and Coleridge-Taylor was raised by his mother and her family in Croydon. He had violin lessons from his English grandfather, a shoeing smith or farrier who paid for further tuition and set the lad, who clearly showed his African descent, on a path that led to him starting at the Royal College of Music in 1890, aged fifteen. There he studied the violin and, after two years, composition. He was awarded a scholarship in 1893 and remained at the college for a total of seven years. The London and British musical press praised his student creations. He became a professional composer, writing pieces for voice, the piano, violin and piano, and other concert and recital music. In 1898 he had his first commission from a music festival (a very necessary form of recognition for composers at this time), and considerable success with *Four Characteristic Waltzes*. These were published in versions for solo piano and for the piano with other instruments: there was a full orchestral version too. His cantata (a work for tenor and orchestra) based on part of the very well-known poem *The Song of Hiawatha* by Longfellow, became the talk of musical England in 1898. After a rushed premiere performance at the Royal College of Music in November 1898, Coleridge-Taylor's *Hiawatha's Wedding Feast* entered the repertoire of almost every one of the many hundreds of amateur choirs in Britain.[21]

Samuel Coleridge-Taylor was widely known as a composer by the winter of 1898–99. He was also in contact with Loudin. The black Englishman brought Spirituals into his compositions, arranging them for the piano, and using one melody in the overture he wrote for the complete, three-part, *Song of Hiawatha* (1898–1900). The overture was premiered at a music festival in Norwich in 1899. The complete work was performed by the Royal Choral Society at the Royal Albert Hall in London in March 1900.

Oliver Ditson of Boston, Massachusetts, commissioned Coleridge-Taylor in 1903 to write piano arrangements of black music. The *Twenty-four Negro Melodies, arranged for the Piano* (opus 59) were published in 1905. Of those originating in America, Coleridge-Taylor regarded "Deep River" as "the most beautiful and touching melody of the whole series."[22] It was in the Fisk Jubilee Singers' book, of course.

Black American music had entered the concert and recital world. Not merely the Spirituals which choirs presented, as we have seen, at British concert venues, but in Britain, Europe, and the United States. Anton Dvorak, the Czech maestro, had incorporated a black theme into his *Symphony: From the New World* inspired when working in the United States in the 1890s. And now Ditson, a major American musical press had issued Coleridge-Taylor's *Twenty-four Negro Melodies*. As far as I am aware, no American had been able to convince a mainstream publisher to consider a volume of black music before 1905. The collection had a preface by race-spokesman, Booker T. Washington.

Coleridge-Taylor's contacts with black Americans had been in England, but he crossed the Atlantic in 1904 as a guest of enthusiastic supporters in Washington, D.C., who had planned a series of concerts of his music. He visited Harriet Loudin in Ohio.[23] He returned to America in 1906 and in 1910, invited by white Americans who admired his music. He had both black and white Americans sharing his platform at some concerts, again breaking the color line that so restricted others of African descent. His music had removed these barriers. Coleridge-Taylor was, after all, used to directing white musicians and presenting his music to white audiences in Britain, and he was a total professional, unwilling to compromise. Washington, D.C., lacked a black orchestra so he refused to make his initial visit until a suitable ensemble was assembled—he was not prepared to conduct a choir without orchestral support. It took three years before his American friends obtained the services of the U.S. Marine Band (Coleridge-Taylor was disappointed by the band).

His warm personality and his musicianship made many friends among Americans. Concert violinist Maud Powell, who had been the first to record solo violin works on disc (for Victor, the leading artistic label), took up his version of "Deep River" and kept it in her repertory. The composer's violin concerto was written for her, an artistic exchange that was normal in the European art world but which was all but prohibited by the color line of the United States.

Coleridge-Taylor's achievement was to expose Americans (and others in the English-speaking world) to the music of one black musician working in the field of art or recital music. His success encouraged other black men and women to persevere both with their musical ambitions and with their determination to achieve despite the odds. He had taken black American music back across the Atlantic. His reputation and the quality of his music led to it being performed by both whites and blacks—and not just in the United States.[24] The *Twenty-four Negro Melodies* included one Nigerian theme (collected from London's black community), some from southern Africa and others from the Caribbean. And it was in Jamaica in 1911 that George Goode took over the Kingston Choral Union, members of which had toured Britain in 1906–8. He directed this choir until 1934. Nearly sixty people were members over those years. Their repertoire included items by Gounod, Elgar, and Sullivan, but Coleridge-Taylor's pieces outnumbered works by others. Included was Loudin's "I'm Troubled in Mind" and "My Lord Delivered Daniel," as well as all of *The Song of Hiawatha* and a dozen other works by Coleridge-Taylor.[25] George Goode named his son, born in 1914, Coleridge Goode. He studied engineering in Scotland in the 1930s and played the bass with many groups, making recordings, working with Django Reinhardt and other jazz musicians.[26]

Samuel Coleridge-Taylor, the black Londoner who died aged thirty-seven in 1912, had written music that reached around the English-speaking world: to blacks and whites in America, in the Caribbean, and in Africa. In 2004 the Johannesburg Symphony Orchestra recorded his Violin Concerto of 1912.

One of the American musicians inspired by Samuel Coleridge-Taylor was Edmund Thornton Jenkins of Charleston, South Carolina. Born in 1894, son of the Rev. Daniel Jenkins, who had founded the Jenkins' Orphanage in Charleston in 1891, he was well aware of the reception of African American musicians in Britain. Three of his brothers had been in a band from the orphanage, which had visited England in 1895.[27] Music tuition was part of the orphan home's vocational education program: other skills included shoe repairing, tailoring, farming, and printing. And it is in a copy of the orphanage weekly *Charleston Messenger* (May 7, 1898) that we see another and unexpected connection, for the orphanage was the sole agent for the musical instruments made by Abraham Collins of London.[28]

Edmund Jenkins studied music at Morehouse College in Atlanta, under Kemper Harreld, who trained orchestras and musicians to perform Coleridge-Taylor's works—and visited the composer's widow when in England in 1914.[29] By that time Edmund Jenkins was in London, studying at the Royal Academy of Music. He had arrived in England as a member of an orphanage band that played the Anglo-American Exposition from May 1914 until the outbreak of war closed the exhibition in September. Others in that group included future Jelly Roll Morton bassist William Benford, jazz trumpeter Gus Aiken, and Bessie Smith's trombonist Jacob Frasier.[30]

At the Academy, Jenkins studied composition with Frederick Corder, an enthusiast for Wagner. He was awarded medals, prizes, a scholarship, and other honors. He taught the clarinet at the Academy, leaving in 1921 after seven years. He had made a brief visit back home in the summer of 1920, but otherwise his awareness of developments in African American music was through contacts made in Britain, including Will Marion Cook whose Southern Syncopated Orchestra toured Britain from 1919 to 1921. Its clarinetist was Sidney Bechet of New Orleans. The white New Orleanian clarinetist Larry Shields was also working in London, in the Original Dixieland Jazz Band, at this time.

Like Shields and the O.D.J.B., and in the tradition of music students who often played in theater and music hall bands, Edmund Jenkins worked in a dance hall. The band recorded in 1921. The recordings of the "Queens" Dance Orchestra, renamed Jack Hylton's Jazz Band for issue on a less expensive label, document the skilled playing of Jenkins on both clarinet and alto-saxophone in an otherwise unexceptional band.

More important to Jenkins were his orchestral creations, notably his folk rhapsody later named *Charlestonia.* This used Charleston fishermen's song and two Spirituals as its themes. It was presented, under its creator's baton, at the Wigmore Hall in London in December 1919 in a concert otherwise devoted to the works of Coleridge-Taylor. It was performed again in Belgium in 1925. By this time Jenkins had relocated to Paris, and it was there he died in 1926, aged thirty-two.[31]

Using his extensive knowledge of African American culture, focused through his close associations with students from Africa and the Caribbean, Edmund Jenkins attempted to merge black musical ideas into the European concert music traditions. There was an audience for this, just as there were audiences for the music of Coleridge-Taylor and for the Spirituals that Loudin had spread widely. In America the mainstream concert stage (in the Northern states of course) had started to be available to black performers only in 1922.[32] As we have seen, Britain's concert stages had been available far longer.

Georgia-born tenor Roland Hayes worked the British concert platform from 1920 into 1923, appearing before royalty and forming friendships with British artists, as did Philadelphia-born contralto Marian Anderson in 1928.[33] These performances were much on the lines formed by Loudin and colleagues fifty years earlier and in the European artistic tradition.

The black colleges (where the concert platform had always been available, of course) and urban music tutors of America utilized Spirituals and Coleridge-Taylor's works in their lessons. Music-making African Americans emerged from these lessons, from schools for the blind, the Charleston orphanage of Daniel Jenkins, Morehouse College, and other institutions. Many had this background, even when these performers' concerts and recordings were in other fields.

Just as Jenkins composed in the European concert tradition and played jazz on his clarinet, Francis Mores who (as Rainer Lotz observes elsewhere in this collection) was a singer with showman Lewis Douglass, gave a recital of "African Folk Songs and American Negro Spirituals" at London's Wigmore Hall on May 31, 1924. He had earlier performed Coleridge-Taylor's works in Washington, D.C., and some were included in this London presentation. The leaflet also quotes the *Referee*: "His interpretations showed keen musical sense, refinement and dramatic perception," and the *Musical News*: "His voice is exceptionally rich and powerful."[34]

There were other performers in this tradition who followed Hayes and Mores, notably Paul Robeson and Jules Bledsoe. In 1931–32 Texas-born Jules Bledsoe (1897–1943) toured France, England, and the Netherlands, presenting on the platform "the emotional expression associated with black music" with "the sophisticated, urbane style associated with art music."[35] He recorded for Decca in England, and entertained at private parties. So widespread were performances by African Americans at high society events that the novelist Evelyn Waugh included a comment in his *Black Mischief* of 1932. In it the Oxford-educated African emperor Seth is described, by the wife of the British Ambassador, as "'Got up just as though he were going to sing Spirituals at a party.'"[36]

These presentations, despite their long history, have been virtually ignored because of the European concentration on recordings of African American music. By the 1930s there were other sources, including radio broadcasts and films, and pioneering television programs, but the shellac disc has dominated and twisted our understanding of the British and European inheritance of American music. Paul Robeson, for example, resident of Britain in the 1930s, made films, broadcasts, and recordings, and despite having the same pianist (Lawrence Brown) as Hayes, is usually perceived as a pioneer in the presentation of Spirituals and world music as art music. The British seldom pay attention to Hayes (who sang African songs in London in 1921).[37] Similarly, almost every summer from 1923 to 1939 a dramatized version of Coleridge-Taylor's *Song of Hiawatha* was presented by the Royal Choral Society at the Albert Hall, to such crowds that the finances of the Society were set firm and the hall made an annual profit, but this financial and cultural success has been ignored in studies of the black presence in Britain.[38]

Historians of early jazz in Britain relied on Jack Hylton's 1930s recollections and so it was "Al Jenkins" who appears in *A History of Jazz in Britain*; and using band leader Ted Heath's 1957's autobiography just "Jenkins" who appears in *Jazz Away from Home*.[39] The domination of discs led Jim Godbolt, who relied on the *Melody Maker* files and on recordings, to write "the black contribution to British jazz was slight."[40] Yet it was Hylton—whose orchestra toured with tenor sax star Coleman Hawkins in the 1930s—and Heath, whose swing orchestra toured the United States in the 1950s and 1960s—who entered the jazz world through contacts with Jenkins in London. Perhaps their gaining access to commercial jazz-style careers through Jenkins was not a black contribution?

The all-black swing band of Ken "Snake Hips" Johnson of 1937–1941 featured Barbados-born trumpeter Dave Wilkins who Johnson had recruited from Trinidad. Wilkins had first heard American jazz on the radio. His fiery attacking solo style later led him to broadcast (and record) with the Radio Rhythm Club in the 1940s and then earned him a place in the Ted Heath orchestra of 1947–49 and in many informal sessions.[41]

Godbolt states that only eight of the Johnson band recordings were "jazz orientated." He overlooked the fact that in the 1920s, 1930s, and 1940s when a British audience saw and heard (on the radio—and the Johnson band was a prolific broadcaster) a group of black instrumentalists playing American popular tunes, their perception was that they were hearing jazz. And the thousands who attended the city theaters where Johnson's band was one of

several performers, along with those who heard their broadcasts, vastly outnumbered those who purchased records. Wilkins, at the request of Leonard
Feather, traveled from Glasgow where he had been appearing with Johnson,
to London to make records with Thomas "Fats" Waller in 1938. It was a few
minutes' work in a hectic schedule of public performances.[42]

If historians of jazz in Britain misunderstand the contribution of Edmund
Jenkins and—despite his discs—pay little or no attention to Dave Wilkins, what
chance do they have of getting to grips with the music of black Americans?
George Chisholm, the trombonist with Wilkins on the Waller recordings, is
widely recognized as a British star and jazz pioneer. His wife had first been
married to Wilkins. These 1930s jazz players were closely knit inside and outside music.

Wilkins's colleagues in the Johnson band were of African descent, but
born in Jamaica, Guyana, Trinidad, Barbados, South Africa, England, and
Wales. In Britain in the 1930s they met visiting African Americans (who
gravitated to the after-hours spots where the Johnson band members were
also to be found), and in this and other ways these black musicians were
influenced by Americans. You did not have to be European to experience the
music of black Americans in Europe. On the other hand, jazz, by the 1930s,
was seen as having African American origins, and so it was often assumed
that others of African descent could play it. A racial stereotype of musical
abilities had been innocently created by decades of skilled and widespread
performances of black visitors to Britain.

Those enthused by jazz, from Wilkins in the relative isolation of Barbados
and Trinidad, the Guyana-born and England-educated Ken Johnson, who ventured to America to take dance lessons in Harlem, and countless instrumentalists who learned their "licks" from discs, worked in dance halls and clubs
in the 1930s. Their audiences thought they were hearing jazz and hot dance
music. The era ended with war—Johnson was killed (and Wilkins injured)
by a bomb that hit the Café de Paris in 1941, others changed their style as
fashion demanded.[43]

When dancers had enjoyed themselves at the small hall at the Queen's
Hall, London, in 1921 (a surviving fragment of contemporary newsreel has
revealed Jenkins playing) they were dancing to American tunes played in an
American way by a group led by an African American. They were not dancing the steps approved by their parents. This new music was the beginning

of the Jazz Age. When recital rooms and elitist social gatherings hushed as a dinner-jacketed male prepared himself to sing Spirituals, audiences were about to hear an authentic rendition of African American music. When they heard the compositions of Samuel Coleridge-Taylor they felt they were hearing music by an individual whose African descent had provided a unique creative talent. These aspects of the European reception of black music from America have been largely overlooked.

There was a Fisk Jubilee Singers group at the Royal Festival Hall, London, in September 1952, on a tour that had taken them to Bristol, Manchester, and Cardiff. The program included Spirituals, and Arthur Sullivan's *The Lost Chord*, items by Purcell, Strauss, and Verdi. The males wore white tie and black jackets, and could be transposed to those sepia photographs of Loudin's choirs of the late nineteenth century. In the mix of their music they presented a program that Roland Hayes, Coleridge-Taylor, and Edmund Jenkins would have been comfortable with.

The music associated with all these artists over the decades, in Britain and on the continent, has been part of the complex story of the presentation and reception of African American music by Europeans. Unlike many performers of blues and folk music, these men and women were well educated. They could read music. They were at ease on the concert platform, in the salons of high society, and as unofficial representatives of black America. These black performers had presented diverse aspects of music to European audiences for decades. They should not be underestimated any longer.

NOTES

1. John Hammond, *John Hammond on Record: An Autobiography* (London: Penguin, 1981), 200–6.

2. Jeffrey Green, "Thomas Lewis Johnson (1836–1921): The Bournemouth Evangelist," in Rainer Lotz and Ian Pegg, eds., *Under the Imperial Carpet: Essays in Black History 1780–1950* (Crawley: Rabbit Press, 1986), 55–68.

3. Andrew Ward, *Dark Midnight When I Rise: The Story of the Jubilee Singers Who Introduced the World to the Music of Black America* (New York: Farrar, Straus and Giroux, 2000), 210 quoting the *Times* (London), May 7, 1873, 5.

4. Ward, *Dark Midnight*, 214, 224, 288–89.

5. Sir Harry H. Johnston, *The Story of My Life* (Garden City, NY: Garden City Publishing, 1923), 395.

6. Ward, *Dark Midnight*, 191.

7. Ward, *Dark Midnight*, 373–74, 376, ill. 22; Susan Okokon, *Black Londoners* (Stroud: Sutton, 1998), 88 misidentified Loudin as Dickerson.

8. Fryer, *Staying Power*, 440; Ward, *Dark Midnight*, 374–75.

9. *Musical News* (London), February 25, 1899, 205; ibid. December 2, 189, 493.

10. Ward, *Dark Midnight*, 291; Jeffrey Green collection.

11. Ward, *Dark Midnight*, 389.

12. Ward, *Dark Midnight*, 198, 331.

13. Brian Willan, ed., Sol Plaatje, *Mafeking Diary. A Black Man's View of a White Man's War* (Meridor Books, 1990), 47; Doug Seroff, "The Zulu Choirs," *Keskidee* (London), vol. 1 (1986): 20–26.

14. Veit Erlmann, *African Stars: Studies in Black South African Performance* (Chicago University Press, 1991); Jeffrey Green, *Black Edwardians: Black People in Britain 1901–1914* (London: Cass, 1998), 103–4.

15. Green, *Black Edwardians*, 96–97.

16. Green, *Black Edwardians*, 89–96.

17. Willard B. Gatewood, *Black Americans and the White Man's Burden, 1898–1903* (Urbana: University of Illinois Press, 1975), 45.

18. Adelaide C. Hill and Martin Kilson, eds., *Apropos of Africa. Sentiments of American Negro Leaders on Africa from the 1800s to the 1950s* (London: Cass, 1969), 124.

19. Imanuel Geiss, *The Pan-African Movement* (London: Methuen, 1974), 190.

20. Lynn Abbott and Doug Seroff, *Out of Sight: The Rise of African American Popular Music, 1889–1895* (Jackson: University Press of Mississippi, 2002), 458–59.

21. W. C. B. Sayers, *S. Coleridge-Taylor, Musician. His Life and Letters* (London: Cassell, 1915), has several flaws. See vol. 21, no. 2 of *Black Music Research Journal* (Chicago), for recent Coleridge-Taylor research, edited by Jeffrey Green.

22. S. Coleridge-Taylor, *Six Negro Melodies* (London: Winthrop Rogers, 1905 [?]), 12.

23. Abbott and Seroff, *Out of Sight*, 459; see the *Cleveland Gazette*, December 24, 1904.

24. Doris Evans McGinty, "'That You Came So Far to See Us'—Coleridge-Taylor in America," *Black Music Research Journal* (Chicago), vol. 21, no. 2 (Fall 2001): 197–233.

25. Ethel Marson, *George Davis Goode: The Man and His Work* (privately printed, Kingston, Jamaica: 1964), 26.

26. Coleridge Goode and Roger Cotterrell, *Bass Lines: A Life in Jazz* (London: Northway, 2002).

27. George Brown Tindall, *South Carolina Negroes, 1877–1900* (Baton Rouge: Louisiana State University Press, 1966 [1952]), 279; Howard Rye, "Visiting Fireboys: The Jenkins' Orphanage Bands in Britain," *Storyville* (London), vol. 130 (June 1, 1987): 137.

28. Jeffrey Green, *Edmund Thornton Jenkins: The Life and Times of an American Black Composer, 1894–1926* (Westport, CT: Greenwood Press, 1982), 20.

29. Jeffrey Green, "Conversation with Josephine Harreld Love," *Black Perspective in Music* (New York), vol. 18, nos. 1 and 2 (1990): 193.

30. Rye, "Visiting Fireboys," 138.

31. Green, *Jenkins*, 106–10, 151, 158–59.

32. Lynette G. Geary, "Jules Bledsoe: The Original 'Ol' Man River,'" *Black Perspective in Music* (New York), vol. 17, nos. 1 and 2 (1989): 28.

33. Valerie Langfield, *Roger Quilter, His Life and Music* (Woodbridge: Boydell Press, 2002), 70–72.

34. Jeffrey Green collection.

35. Geary, "Bledsoe," 35.

36. Evelyn Waugh, *Black Mischief* (London: Penguin, 1971 [1932]), 108; Jeffrey Green, "High Society and Black Entertainers in the 1920s and 1930s," *New Community* (London), vol. 13, no. 3 (Spring 1987): 431–34; Green, *Black Edwardians*, 188–89.

37. Jeffrey Green, "Roland Hayes in London, 1921," *Black Perspective in Music* (New York), vol. 10, no. 1 (Spring 1982): 29–42.

38. Ronald W. Clark, *The Royal Albert Hall* (London: Hamish Hamilton, 1958), 179–81; Jeffrey Green, "Requiem: *Hiawatha* in the 1920s and 1930s," *Black Music Research Journal* (Chicago), vol. 21, no. 2 (Fall 2001): 283–88. See Peter Fryer, *Staying Power*, 261.

39. Jim Godbolt, *A History of Jazz in Britain, 1919–50* (London: Paladin, 1986 [1984]), 58; Chris Goddard, *Jazz Away from Home* (London: Paddington, 1979), 60.

40. Godbolt, *History*, 185.

41. Val Wilmer, "David Livingstone Wilkins," *Oxford Dictionary of National Biography* (London: Oxford University Press, 2004), article 74817.

42. Jeffrey Green, "'Bix in Barbados'—Dave Wilkins, Trumpet," *Storyville* (London), 118 (April–May 1985): 136–48.

43. Kneller Hall medal winner, military bandsman Leslie Thompson of Jamaica, played Latin American music with Edmundo Ros in the 1940s, for example; Cardiff-born Afro-Welsh Joe Deniz, guitarist with Ken Johnson and with the Radio Rhythm Club, worked in the "African musical" *Ipi Tombi* in London in the late 1970s. See Jeffrey Green, "Joe Deniz: A Guitarist from Cardiff," *Keskidee* (London), vol. 1 (1986): 13–18.

5

Black Music Prior to the First World War

AMERICAN ORIGINS AND GERMAN PERSPECTIVES[1]

—RAINER E. LOTZ

The presence of African American entertainers in Europe and the impact of African American music in Europe around the end of the nineteenth century, as well as aspects of cross-fertilization, remain largely unresearched. Most of the early authors of scholarly books and discographies on blues and jazz were Europeans, who had little or no first-hand impressions of Sedalia, or New Orleans, or Clarksdale, or Chicago. Their only contact with the music was through recordings available to them in Europe from the 1920s up to the 1960s. And they did not have access to recording ledgers, black papers, and other such research materials, that have only recently been discovered, or re-discovered.

Today we take it for granted that for all practical purposes just about any jazz or blues recording is readily available on CD.[2] During the 1920s up to the 1940s, however, very little authentic jazz and even less blues was made available by British record companies, and hardly any in the rest of Europe. Prior to 1942 some seven thousand double-sided blues and gospel records were released in the United States by commercial companies, involving some twelve hundred artists,[3] and an estimated total of twenty-two thousand titles when including archival recordings for the Library of Congress. Of this total only about fifty were available to record buyers in Europe, almost all of them released in Britain.[4]

Lizzie Miles's "You're Always Messin' Round with My Man" (1923) from Victor 19083 was probably the first blues issue in Europe on HMV B1703 (coupling Sissle and Blake for the reverse side). Her Brunswick 2462 (also 1923) was likewise issued in Britain. Other 1920s issues were Clara Smith's Columbia 14183-D (1926) on English Columbia 8938, as were the various issues in the Guardsman *Negro Race Dance Record* series of 1926 (Lena Wilson, Viola McCoy, Edna Hicks), as well as the various issues in the English Oriole *Race Series* of 1927 (Viola McCoy, Edmonia Henderson, Rosa Henderson), and The Memphis Jug Band coupling on Regal-Zonophone MR2331.[5] Several items by the Louisville jug groups were issued in Britain, though most of the foreign 78s listed in *Blues and Gospel Records 1890–1943*, are postwar reissues. HMV B5398 by Dixieland Jug Blowers is contemporary, so is Brunswick 01265 by Philips' Louisville Jug Band.

Among the few continental European contemporary issues are the Fisk University Jubilee Singers issues in the French Columbia 14000 series—these are only listed in the amendment service, but two of the couplings involved were also on English Regal. Douglas Williams's "Thrill Me" was issued in both Spain and Italy with a reverse by the Washboard Rhythm Kings. There are a lot of Eva Taylor's on English labels. Mamie Smith's "Jenny's Ball" was issued by Parlophone in Britain and Italy and on Odeon in Germany. Reverses are by Lonnie Johnson, whose records with Ed Lang were also widely issued across Europe.[6] A remarkable freak issue is a coupling of "Long Gone"/"I'm Looking for a Woman" by Papa Charlie Jackson on a German flexible Biberphon B.536, and labeled Manhattan Roof Orchestra ("Farewell Blues"/"Memphis Blues"). Apparently the wrong stampers were shipped from the United States by the Paramount company, and the error was only realized after a couple of test pressings.[7] The situation is not quite as striking with regard to jazz releases in Europe. In Germany, American "jazz" was represented almost exclusively by performers such as Ed Kirkeby, Vincent Lopez, Mike Markel, Harry Reser, Ben Selvin, and Paul Whiteman. Authentic hot performances by black bands are as rare as hens' teeth and could not have had a wide distribution. A German Beka featuring Thomas Morris only surfaced in the Czech Republic some seventy-five years after its original "publication" and to-date is not listed in any discography.[8]

After the world war, technologies such as the phonograph cylinders, player pianos, or musical boxes were at best vaguely remembered by a past generation in Europe. The pre-history of jazz and blues has tended to disappear. Record collectors are guilty of neglecting of areas of musical tradition which are under-represented or unrepresented on record.[9]

But is it really true that no early tangible, factual evidence exists to discuss the prehistory, protohistory, origins, and development of Afro-American musical phenomena on the American continent? Could the cakewalk and ragtime, blues and jazz, could the Cuban son, the choro and matchiche of Brazil, the beguine of Martinique and Guadeloupe, the cumbias in Colombia, the marimba bands in Mexico and Guatemala all have suddenly surfaced at about the same time, and without interlinkage? Do we really have to rely on hearsay, speculation, and the blurred recollections of octogenarians? And is it really true that Europeans first heard of African American music and performance styles with the advent of imported gramophone records of the jazz era?

In the absence of recorded sound documents we need to examine other sources to determine early repertoires and performance styles. Potential sources of information could be photos and etchings, notations, printed music, manuscripts. Unfortunately folk traditions are rarely documented, oral traditions do not often find their way into printed music; songsters, minstrels, vaudevillians do not normally make use of printed material, and only rarely do we find tangible artifacts. But they do exist if we look for them. For more than a hundred years historians, musicologists, and performers have speculated about the musical and etymological origins of "rag" and ragtime until Karl Gert zur Heide, yet another European researcher, suggested a plausible solution of the riddle (which he published in 2005).[10] There is still controversy about what the first published ragtime song may have been: Irving Jones's "Possumala Dance" (1894), "La Pas Ma La" by Ernest Hogan (1895), or Max Hoffmann's arrangement of Hogan's "All Coons Look Alike to Me" (1896).[11] The first printed composition with a twelve-bar-blues structure was published in St. Louis in 1904: "One o'them things," a ragtime/two-step by James Chapman and Leroy Smith.[12] The sheet music "was there" all the time, but it was not until one hundred years after its original publication that its historical significance was recognized.

Similarly, what do we know about tub, jug, and washboard bands? When did spasm bands appear on the scene, and what sounds did they produce? As recently as 2001 an entry in the *New Grove Dictionary of Jazz* provides the following definition: "Spasm Band—An ensemble consisting largely of homemade instruments. . . . They generally included a chord-playing instrument, such as a ukulele or guitar, a kazoo or comb-and-paper, and various percussion instruments—for example washboard or tambourine . . . also the boom-bam, a broom handle on which metal bottle-tops are nailed. . . . Spasm bands were active in New Orleans during the first three decades of the twentieth century, and performed a repertory of blues, ragtime, and the popular songs of the day."[13]

Now let us examine a postcard that occasionally turns up on eBay (figure 1). Obviously it is not a snap-shot but a staged or posed scene of the "water melon and alligator" variety. But the card clearly shows a spasm band.

FIGURE 1: "The Coon Creek Rehearsal in Florida." Source: Postcard no. 12813 "Florida Souvenir," copyrighted 1893 by O. P. Havens. During the 1920s the same photographic image was used for a "C. T. Art-Colortone" postcard in the series *C. T. Pickaninny Scenes* no. S.425, now captioned "The Blackville Serenade—Greetings from Lexington, N.C." From the Rainer E. Lotz collection, Bonn, Germany.

The location is Florida, not New Orleans. And the date is not the 1930s, not the 1920s, not the 1910s: the card is copyrighted and postmarked 1893; a German traveler sent it back home. The fact that such cards had been on sale during the early 1890s is a strong indication that this was a familiar, or typical sight, and must have been so for quite a while, perhaps for decades.[14] In other words, there is both photographic and printed evidence of pre-recorded black American music, and there is a case for continued efforts to look for it.

My starting point was: we need to examine other sources because there are no sound documents of Afro-American music styles. But is this hypothesis really valid? And is it really true that the Europeans were first exposed to such musical forms during the 1920s? It is a little-known fact that German

FIGURE 2: Kapelle Backes from Jettenbach/Palatinate, playing for prison inmates, around 1900. Source: Original photo captioned "Schwarz und Weiss in Eintracht vereint! Emil Backes (2.v.l.) und seine Musikanten aus Jettenbach inmitten einer schwarz-weissen Zuhörerschaft um die Jahrhundertwende in Amerika." From the Rainer E. Lotz collection, Bonn, Germany, courtesy Museum Zehntscheune, Burg Lichtenberg.

musicians played to entertain American audiences up to the First World War and were in turn, therefore, exposed to a variety of American music. Vast parts of Germany were extremely poor. Poverty and overpopulation in the marginal agricultural hinterlands left people with three choices: to emigrate, to become either a home worker (or out-worker), or else to survive in some itinerant activities. Many became itinerant musicians, earning their living in England and the United States. Stretches of Germany became known as the "musicians' belt." There is plenty evidence that rags and cakewalks—by both white and black composers—had been played by itinerant professional German musicians in the United States, and to both white and black audiences, during the 1890s.

Other musicians, who did not leave their villages, earned their living as home workers. In the Black Forest and other poor neighborhoods they spent the winter manufacturing mechanical music instruments for export. It is fascinating that those people, who had not even heard of St. Louis or Sedalia, arranged and manufactured authentic cakewalks and ragtime for piano rolls and metal disc symphonions.

FIGURE 3: Symphonion 33.5 cm-diameter metal disc no. 12362 "Schorschl ach kauf mir doch ein Automobil. K_Kb BOKb (Cake-Walk). Thurban." This composition was originally titled "The Perman's Brooklyn Cakewalk." Source: Manufactured around 1908 by the Symphonion Musikwerke. Leipzig, Germany. From the Rainer E. Lotz collection, Bonn, Germany.

On German-made metal discs you can hear a cakewalk composed in 1895 by the Afro-Caribbean comedian Bert Williams, and dedicated to the greatest of all cakewalk dancers, Dora Dean, who toured Europe for decades.[15] This "Dora Dean Cakewalk" was never recorded—not on piano rolls, not on cylinders, not on flat disc shellacs, not on LPs, since the time it was composed, and that was before the end of the nineteenth century. To say that this tune was never recorded is not entirely correct, though. In 1896—one year after Williams saw his original composition in print—one Charley Sydney O'Brien published "Ma Angeline," which is a note-for note, word-for-word theft, except that the reference to "Dora Dean" was replaced by "Ma Angeline" (it still rhymes), and the music was recorded under this name by an unnamed orchestra in that same year 1896.[16]

FIGURE 4: Flyer for "Carroll Johnson's Electric Hit—Greatest Coon Songs of the Age—'Ma Angeline' by Charles Sydney O'Brien" (18 × 11 cm). Source: Copyrighted 1896 by The Zeno Mauvais Music Co., S.F.; printed by Lyon & Healey, Chicago, Illinois. From the Rainer E. Lotz collection, Bonn, Germany.

Scott Joplin composed his masterpiece, "The Entertainer," in 1902. Again, it was never recorded on either cylinder or shellac disc, but a contemporary music box metal disc did exist—in the slow tempo that Joplin prescribed. I have documented an astonishing number of cakewalks and coon songs on German-made metal discs,[17] but in contrast to disc recordings very few are currently available on re-issue CDs for further analysis. "Dora Dean" and "The Entertainer" are played slowly, but there are certainly also fast cakewalks, and the highly syncopated "Whistling Rufus" (written by a white composer) even combines a slow and an up-tempo arrangement on the same disc, with bells added.[18]

We can thus draw the conclusion that Europeans had been exposed to black music, and even knew how to perform and arrange it for mechanical music before the end of the nineteenth century. By the time the early writers got interested in blues and jazz, the memory had faded, many important tunes were not even recorded although they were widely distributed in middle-class households both as sheet music and on mechanical media.

We have mentioned photographic evidence, and also musical evidence based on mechanical music. And I now pose another question: Is it really true that African Americans left no trace on early sound documents—not mechanical but analogue recordings (phonograph cylinders and flat discs records)?

Contrary to widespread belief, black artists not only recorded, they were actually among the pioneers of recorded music. Banjoist Louis "Bebe" Vasnier Jr. was a New Orleans housepainter who also ran his own Johnson and Vasnier's Colored Minstrel Company. By January 1891 the Louisiana Phonograph Company made and marketed musical cylinders by Vasnier. The company was undoubtedly the very first to record New Orleans musicians and music. And Louis Vasnier, born a free Creole of color in 1859, possibly became the first black recording artist in the world.[19]

His "Brudder Rasmus Sermons" and minstrel songs were actively promoted. A July 1892 "Price List of Musical Records Etc," which appeared in the *Phonogram*, a short-lived journal of the affiliated Edison phonograph companies, shows for sale five "Negro Sermons" by "Brudder Rasmus" at one dollar each. And the small print reads: "All of these are very popular and good for the blues: Try them!"[20] According to one *Phonogram* advertisement, "These sermons, while very humorous, are characteristic Negro delineations

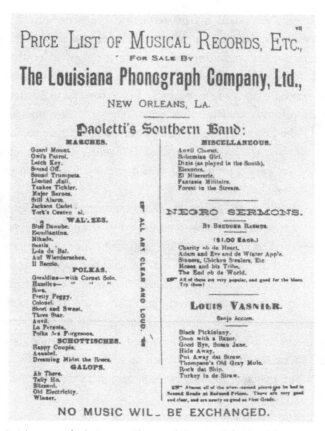

FIGURE 5: Advertisement for the Louisiana Phonograph Company, Ltd., New Orleans, Louisiana, 1891. Source: *The Phonogram* (July 1892); previously reprinted in *The Jazz Archivist*, vol. 4, no. 2 (December 1989), courtesy the National Park Service, Edison National Historic Site. Repro from the Rainer E. Lotz collection, Bonn, Germany.

and are faithful reproductions of a dusky style of pulpit oratory that is rapidly passing away. . . ." Also available by Vasnier were banjo versions of eight "plantation negro songs," presumably in the minstrel tradition, including "Black Pickaninny," "Coon with a Razor," "Good Bye, Susan Jane," "Hide Away," "Put Away dat Straw," "Thompson's Old Grey Mule," "Rock dat Ship," and "Turkey in de Straw." The advertisement concluded with the comment "The sermons are very popular among both whites and blacks and have proved among the most profitable of exhibition records."[21]

At least one of the Vasnier cylinders has survived, but is in extremely poor shape.[22] Other notable recordings took place in New York: the Unique

Quartette in 1890; the Standard Quartette in 1891, the Dinwiddie Quartet in 1902. The recordings show distinctive Afro-American characteristics, although the sound quality leaves much to be desired. Of much better sound is a duet recording made by Cousins and DeMoss taken in 1897 for a single-sided Emil Berliner disc. Two singers alternate verses in the black gospel tradition to fervent banjo accompaniment; the speed is accelerating throughout this exciting record "Poor Mourner."[23] Blues singer Frank Stokes was born shortly after Cousins and DeMoss recorded "Poor Mourner"; three decades later, in 1927, Stokes selected this tune as his first choice for a recording session for the Paramount label! By 1909 the recording technology had advanced to a degree that cylinders can provide listening pleasure even to "spoiled" modern ears. A splendid example would be "Watermelon Party" by "Polk Miller and the Old South Quartette" which demonstrates call-and-response patterns (the white impresario, Polk Miller, plays the guitar and sings) on this upbeat number.[24]

There are also unsung early female soloists. Tim Brooks in his groundbreaking study on black recording pioneers published in 2004 identified concert singer Daisy Tapley as the first African American woman to make a commercial recording, on the basis of a single duet recording of 1910 in which she did not take a solo line. It is the sacred hymn "I Surrender All," released by Columbia in 1911.[25] Sadly even Brooks missed out on May C. Hyers, who recorded some fifty cylinders for the Kansas City Talking Machine Company in 1898. Her repertoire ranged from opera and patriotic songs to minstrelsy items and coon songs such as "Hot Coon from Memphis."[26] May C. Hyers was less well-known than her sisters Anna Madah and Emma Louise, but through her recordings may well prove to be more important in historical perspective—if they could be found. There were more black female singers pre-dating Tapley whom we shall mention later.

We can thus draw the conclusion that African American vocalists and musicians were among the pioneers of recorded music. As was to be expected, all those recordings I just mentioned were made in the United States. For some one hundred years those cylinders and discs indeed contained "lost sounds"; only over the past few years have they been rediscovered and some are now accessible to researchers.

Afro-American performers had been part of Europe's entertainment scene from the eighteenth century, in particular with regard to the popular "negro impersonations" in the British Isles. Their share was maintained into the nineteenth century and, during that time, increasingly spread to the continent. The Ku Klux Klan was founded only two years after abolition, and discrimination in the United States reached an unprecedented intensity by the 1890s. Given the extent of violence and discrimination experienced by African Americans, it is not surprising that an astounding and ever-increasing number pursued their livelihood overseas—including instrumentalists and bands, musical clowns and dancers, singers and theatrical performers, minstrels and eccentric acts. *Der Artist*, a German weekly for traveling artists, has references to more than one hundred black performers in Germany in 1896 alone.[27] Considering the vast number of African Americans touring Europe, wouldn't it be surprising if they did not cut cylinders and discs over here? And once again, the answer is: Yes, they did record.

The first were probably the African Canadian banjoists brothers Bohee—James Douglass Bohee (born 1844, Indiantown, Saint John, New Brunswick, Canada; died on tour 1897, Ebbw Vale, Wales) and George Bohee (born 1856, Indiantown; died after 1929). St. John's black population had its origins in the Caribbean and the United States, and the Bohee family moved to Boston by 1859. Boston was the center of banjo manufacturing and the brothers took up that instrument. Around 1876 the Bohee brothers started their own, racially mixed Bohee Minstrels which also included James Bland, the composer of "Carry Me Back to Old Virginny," Virginia's state song 1940–97. They toured the United States in 1876, later in 1876 with Callender's Georgia Minstrels, from 1878 in Jack Haverly's Genuine Colored Minstrels. By May 1880 they had reached Canada, where James Bohee was reported as the drum major in the troupe's street parades. They opened at Her Majesty's Theatre, London, in July of that year. There were over sixty performers in the troupe, which toured Britain and returned to America in 1882.

James Bohee remained in Britain, owning a minstrel show (once again James Bland was hired) that toured theaters and halls. James, described as the "Paganini of the Banjo" established "The Great American Banjo Academy" in London and advertised himself as "the only Banjoist in London who has the honour of appearing by special command at Marlboro house before Their Royal Highnesses the Prince and Princess of Wales."[28] By 1890 the brothers had become London institutions, and members of royalty were among their pupils.

FIGURE 6: Afro-Canadian banjoists James and George Bohee, seated on stage, in formal dress, no date. Source: Originally published in Harry Reynolds, *Minstrel Memories*, 1928, opp. p. 196, previously reprinted in Rainer E. Lotz, *Black People*, 1997, p. 36. Repro from the Rainer E. Lotz collection, Bonn, Germany.

After James died of pneumonia, brother George first tried to continue the Bohee Operatic Minstrels but, by late 1898, was forced to disband. He consequently worked as a solo performer and toured the Empire Theatre circuit. His death has been variously dated from 1915 (in the United States) to the 1930s (in Britain). As well as singing, tenor George Bohee danced to his brother's banjo and played banjo duets with him (he also played piano). James provided banjo solos.

They kept in contact with America, introducing songs and providing employment opportunities. Catering for a white European audience, "Home Sweet Home" and "A Boy's Best Friend Is His Mother" are examples of the sentimental compositions that made them famous, but the Bohee brothers' repertoire also included anti-slavery protest material, cakewalks, and minstrel songs. Sometime between 1890 and 1892 in London, the Bohee brothers recorded banjo duets on Edison wax cylinders—they may thus be the first

FIGURE 7: Pete Hampton, harmonica, and his common-law wife, Laura Bowman, banjo, ca. 1906. Source: Photo previously published in Rainer E. Lotz, *Black People*, 1997, p. 99. Repro from the Rainer E. Lotz collection, Bonn, Germany.

Afro-Americans to do so. These recordings are known only from a report of their being played in Australia, and it is impossible to assess their musical character. George Bohee made at least another eleven banjo solos for the Edison Bell Supply Co. in Liverpool in 1898, but the titles (including "Darky's Dream" and "Darky's Awakening") are at present only known from catalogs.[29]

However, the most recorded American visitor to Europe, black or white, in the period under review, was an African American, Pete George Hampton (b. 1871, Bowling Green, Kentucky; d. 1916, New York City).[30] As a teenage member of a banjo-playing vocal quartet, Pete Hampton appeared in Medicine Shows in Ohio. During the 1890s he toured with prominent minstrel troupes; first Al G. Fields's Darkest Africa-Company, then Mahara's Minstrels, P. T. Wright's Nashville Students, and John W. Isham's Octoroons (1898). He then became associated with Bert Williams and George Walker.

By 1900 he was in the roster of the Sons of Ham Company, and a couple of years later in *In Dahomey* (1902). A company totaling eighty-one took this revue to England in 1903.[31] Hampton fell in love with Laura Bowman, also with *In Dahomey*; they had a common-law marriage until Hampton died in 1916.

The company toured successfully in the United Kingdom, and apparently were socially accepted; Hampton became a member of the Free Masons Grand Lodge of Scotland. After the tour ended in 1904, Hampton and Bowman continued their career in Europe, until the outbreak of the world war in 1914 forced them to return to the United States.

Having grown up in the African American minstrel tradition, Hampton must have been an above-average comedian, actor, singer, instrumentalist (five-string banjo, harmonica), dancer, and composer (e.g., "Lindy, Lindy, Sweet As Sugar Cane," lyrics by Bowman, later sold to the famous husband-and-wife team of Charles Johnson and Dora Dean). His talents were recognized and within a few years he had made not only a movie but well over 150 cylinders and discs. Like many of his fellow song and dance artists and the Bohee Brothers before him, he heavily relied on "coon songs" written by white composers, but he performed them in a distinctively black style. What is more, he also performed his own compositions, such as "Dat Mouth Organ Coon." Dating from 1904, "Dat Mouth Organ Coon" has an interesting ragtime piano introduction, Hampton sings a few stanzas of a typical ragtime song, suddenly he doubles the tempo and the piano accompaniment gets into a frenzy. Right in the middle of the performance Hampton abruptly takes out the tempo. He switches to harmonica, hence the title "Dat Mouth Organ Coon," and he quotes "The Last Rose of Summer." Hampton's specialty was playing the harmonica through his nose, but on this cylinder, after stating the melody, he performs at such a break-neck speed, that this is difficult to believe. He bends the melody, he adds blue notes, he produces all sorts of queer sounds that must make Thomas Moore rotate in his Irish grave, and he adds shouts and vocal interjections just like recorded blues singers would do decades later. Some recordings by Hampton are clearly in the minstrel tradition, while others are inspired by gospel and camp-meetings, such as "When You Die You Are a Long Time Dead," a jumpy and truly swinging tune, performed to piano accompaniment.[32]

Among the black female singers pre-dating Tapley were Belle Davis (1902), Laura Bowman (1906), Arabella Fields (1907), and Lavina Wilson

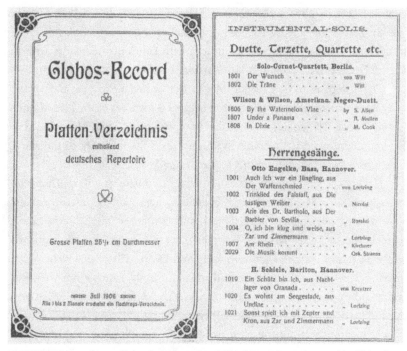

FIGURE 8: Excerpts from a Globos Records catalog, 1906. Source: Originally printed by Globophon-Fabrik, Hannover, Germany. Repro from the Rainer E. Lotz collection, Bonn, Germany.

(1906). Theodore Walton Wilson (b. 1879) was from Philadelphia and his wife Lavina (b. 1878) from New Orleans. In 1906 the Wilsons recorded at least three duets, and Mrs. Wilson at least another five solo titles, by some of the most prominent contemporary black composers: Tim Brymn, Will Marion Cook, Alex Rogers, and James Vaughn. They recorded for Globos, an obscure record company in Hanover, Germany.

Among the titles recorded were numbers from *In Dahomey:* "Why Adam Sinned" was the specialty of Aida Overton Walker; while "When the Moon Shines" was a featured duet by Williams and Walker. No copies of any of the Wilson discs have been found as yet, but when they surface, we would have the only recorded examples of the tunes, since Aida Overton Walker never recorded herself, and Williams and Walker never recorded that particular tune. We know very little about Wilson and Wilson, although they spent half a decade in Europe, touring widely, from Liverpool to Zwickau, Saxony. They very well represent the hundreds of other pioneers in their respective

FIGURE 9: Poster for the African American Character Concert Company—Foote's Minstrels; directed by William Foote for a performance at "Zur alten Harmonie," Frankfurt, August 26, 1891. Source: Original lithograph by Great Western Company, New York, printed in Germany by Enz & Rudolph, Frankfurt am Main, 1891. The Historisches Museum Frankfurt holds a set of different posters. Repro from the Rainer E. Lotz collection, Bonn, Germany.

fields of entertainment who remain unrecognized. They returned to New York from Boulogne, France, in 1909.[33]

We can thus draw the conclusion that African American musicians were among the pioneers of recorded music not only in the United States, but also in Europe. A serious effort should be made to locate those elusive artifacts. Judging from those that have turned up, and considering the titles of those that still need to be located, we may have to rewrite the chapters on early black music.

The motion picture technology was developed at about the same time as the sound recording technology. And indeed, black artists were also among the pioneers in the fledgling movie industry. A surprising number of films had been shot in Europe prior to the First World War, demonstrating what was then known as "nigger song and dance." I have in my personal collection three examples of such film material: first a French music hall act,

Frenchs Original-Neger-Ensemble

Gesang, Tanz, Bagno- und Gitarre-Spiel
Duette, Quartette

Spez.: **Cake-Walke**

Direktion: **French**

Monat Mai:

Zittau, Sonnensäle

Solo-Agentur: **Konzertdirektion Oscar Scherff, G. m. b. H., Leipzig,** *Hainstraße 19 I.*

FIGURE 10: Advertisement for Arthur French's Neger Ensemble, for a performance at the Apollo, Posen, 1910. Source: *Der Künstler*, vol. 2, no. 37 (June 15, 1910), p. 33. Repro from the Rainer E. Lotz collection, Bonn, Germany.

with blacks and whites performing on stage at the same time; next a British film showing a dancer performing "black steps" to banjo accompaniment; and lastly a series of three equally short "takes" featuring Belle Davis. and her "pickaninnies" presumably in Germany.[34] I also have the sound for what was clearly a similar piece of film material entitled "Coontown Ragtime Dance" on a 30cm-diameter disc dating from 1907, for which we still lack the film. The sound quality of the copy available to me is unfortunately poor, but the recording engineers nevertheless did a remarkable job. Remember, at that time they had to record through an open horn. It was already quite difficult to capture the sound of an individual singer or instrumental soloist, but in this case they had to capture a rousing performance by a troupe known as The Georgia Pickaninnies.[35] The engineers (of the Gramophone Company, working on commission for the Messter-Film Company) had to cope not only with an entire orchestra, but in addition with a troupe of several lead singers, and a responding chorus, and step dancers, and all of them used to wildly gyrate on stage.

FIGURE 11: Label for Messter Biophon disc no. 879 "Coontown Ragtime Dance." Source: Recorded and pressed by the Deutsche Grammophon AG for Messters Projection G.m.b.H., 1908. Repro from the Rainer E. Lotz collection, Bonn, Germany, courtesy Tom Hawthorn.

An impressive number of black vaudeville acts were featured on European sound films. In Germany alone between ten to twenty interest us as they feature black dancers, entertainers, minstrel troupes, and musicians. Only very recently it was brought to my attention that the black minstrel veteran Will Garland and his "Negro Operetta Troupe"[36] recorded a couple of sound films in Berlin in 1910, and there are two films by Arabella Fields (1907). There are also several films by Josephine Morcashani (1908) who may thus claim to have been the first black drag artist to make a sound movie. The artist's real name was Joseph Morcashani—a female impersonator who wore gorgeous dresses.

Continental European audiences were not free from prejudices and stereotypes, and people of African descent were certainly often disregarded and despised as a racial minority in the Old World. Nevertheless, racially mixed stage acts—often performed by husband-and-wife teams—were common, and socially acceptable. True, Polk Miller toured the Untied States with the

FIGURE 12: John Friedmann's The Georgia Piccaninnies Troupe. Source: Program for the Scala, The Hague, 1907. Repro from the Rainer E. Lotz collection, Bonn, Germany, courtesy Albert L. Kramer.

Old South Quartette, but the overall situation in Europe was markedly different. Black performers—singers, dancers, and musicians—made their living as rural songsters and urban minstrels and vaudevillians. The latter in particular had to provide what the mainly urban, white lower- and middle-class audiences expected. All blacks traveling overseas had to bear in mind that they performed for exclusively white audiences. Their niche in vaudeville entertainment was twofold: by exotic appearance and by eccentric performances. *Black People* quotes contemporary German reviews and comments at length. Exotic they were on account of their dark skin and facial features, and eccentricity was achieved by posing as knockabout clowns and by introducing African American elements in dancing, singing, and playing instruments—even though many, if not most, may not have had any affinity for African American musical traditions. They had to provide a carefully balanced selection of popular tunes and Tin-Pan-Alley "coon songs," spiced with both European elements—recognizable by their audiences—and black elements.

Just how continental European audiences reacted to black performance styles we shall probably never know. Although, in contrast to Britain, the

FIGURE 13: Poster for "The Georgia Piccaninnies of America. Grown up. Manager John E. Friedmann." Source: Poster No. 4677 printed by Adolf Friedländer, Hamburg-Altona, 1909. Repro from the Rainer E. Lotz collection, Bonn, Germany, courtesy Jaap Best.

language barrier seems to have been something of a problem in countries such as Germany, there had nevertheless been an ever-increasing demand for what was then often advertised as "nigger song and dance" until the war dramatically changed the situation. Many of these performances left a legacy of recordings and moving pictures, as well as postcards, publicity shots, and illustrated publicity items. Thanks to their rediscovery we now have a much better understanding of this subject than only a few years ago. As a result, we shall have to amend the blues, gospel, country, music hall, and ragtime discographies, and rewrite chapters of the research on early black music.

NOTES

1. This is the slightly revised and expanded version of a paper delivered as a "multi-media chat" at the University of Gloucestershire, Saturday, July 24, 2004, "'Overseas Blues'": European Perspectives on African American Music" Conference. Besides the illustrations (transparencies), the original presentation also included sounds and moving images, now where possible, referred to in the text.

2. Document Records, now based in Britain, attempts to maintain a complete catalog of all historical blues and gospel recordings by black performers <http://www.document-records. com>. It should be noted that the situation with regard to white blues and vaudeville is dramatically different.

3. Robert M. W. Dixon, John Godrich, *Recording the Blues* (London: Studio Vista, 1970), 104–5.

4. Robert M. W. Dixon, John Godrich, and Howard W. Rye, *Blues and Gospel Records 1890–1943* (Oxford: Oxford University Press, 4th ed., 1997).

5. The Junkshop Three, "A glimpse of the past #13: Guardsman," in *Storyville* 23 (1969): 192–94; Laurie Wright, "A glimpse of the past #6: The Oriole 1000 Series," in *Storyville* 6 (1966): 26–27.

6. Howard Rye to Lotz, and conversation with Alan Balfour, Andy Cohen, Howard Rye, Elijah Wald, February 7, 2005.

7. Pete Whelan, ed., "The Rarest Country Blues," in *78 Quarterly* 6: 37. The disc is not listed in H. H. Lange, *Die deutsche '78er' Discographie der Hot-Dance und Jazz-Musik 1903–1958* (Berlin: Panther Verlag, 3rd ed., 1992).

8. Brian A. L. Rust, *Jazz and Ragtime Records 1897–1942* (Denver: Mainspring Press, 4th ed., 2002); Horst H. Lange, *Die deutsche '78er' Discographie der Hot-Dance und Jazz-Musik 1903–1958* (Berlin: Panther Verlag, 3rd ed., 1992). It should be mentioned though, that dedicated collectors—such as Antoine Cyriax, Charles Delaunay, Albert McCarthy, Hugues Panassié, Hilton Schleman, to name just a few—have always been able to import original pressings from the United States, or to buy them from specialized importers such as Levy's, and discs pressed in Europe were thus not the only source material. "After the war, the British were prevented from importing but the French and Swiss were not and a comparison between Jazz Directory and the works of Kurt Mohr or the contents of a magazine such as Jazz Statistics quickly reveals the consequences for scholarship" (Rye to Lotz, February 8, 2005). In contrast to jazz and black blues there is still neither a comprehensive discography of white blues, nor a book-length analysis.

9. Among more recent book-length studies are: R. E. Lotz, *German Ragtime and Pre-History of Jazz* (London: Storyville, 1985); R. E. Lotz, *Black People—Entertainers of African Descent in Europe and Germany* (Bonn: Birgit Lotz Verlag, 1997); Edward S. Walker, *English Ragtime* (Stamford: Walker 2000, 2nd ed., 2000); Chris Ware, *The Ragtime Ephemeralist* (Chicago: ACME Novelty Library, 1998, three volumes published); Lynn Abbott and Doug Seroff, *Out of Sight: The Rise of American Popular Music, 1889–1895* (Jackson: University Press of Mississippi, 2002); Allan Sutton, *Cakewalks, Rags and Novelties, 1894–1930* (Denver: Mainspring Press, 2003); David Wondrich, *Stomp and Swerve: American Music Gets Hot, 1843–1924* (Chicago: A Cappella, 2003); Tim Brooks, *Lost Sounds—Blacks and the Birth of the Recording Industry, 1890–1919* (Chicago: Chicago University Press, 2004).

10. Following a 1898 statement by rag pioneer Will Marion Cook, zur Heide presents additional evidence for an "oriental" origin of rag the rhythm, rag the dance, and rag the word, which he traces to the Arabic word for dance, viz. raqs. Karl Gert zur Heide, "Chicago, 1893, Part 2," in *Doctor Jazz* (Hilversum), 188 (2005): 6–16.

11. Chris Ware, *The Ragtime Ephemeralist* 1 (1998): 45; David A. Jasen and Gene Jones, *That American Rag* (New York: Schirmer, 2000), 32, 45–46.

12. Trebor Jay Tichenor, *Ragtime Rarities* (New York: Dover, 1975), vii; Karl Gert zur Heide, "Saint Louis, 1904, Part 1," in *Doctor Jazz* 185 (2004).

13. Barry Kernfield, ed., *The New Grove Dictionary of Jazz*, Vols. 1–3 (London: Macmillan Press, 2001), quote from original Vol. 2, 1986, 483.

14. Perhaps the Grove editor considered that only in New Orleans are spasm bands ancestral to jazz, those elsewhere being ancestral to blues. Published evidence for their existence in Louisville and entries on Louisville musicians show awareness of this (Rye to Lotz, February 8, 2005).

15. "Dora Dean Cake Walk"—Bert Williams (1895) 0:50, from "Black People" CD: Track 2. This CD is attached to the book, R. E. Lotz, *Black People—Entertainers of African Descent in Europe and Germany* (Bonn: Birgit Lotz Verlag, 1997); it has no order number and cannot be ordered separately.

16. Chris Ware, *The Ragtime Ephemeralist*, online edition http://home.earthlink.net/~ephemeralist/cakewalkdoradean.html.

17. Lotz, *German Ragtime*, op. cit.

18. "The Entertainer"—Scott Joplin (1902) 0:55, from "Black People" CD: Track 4; "Whistling Rufus"—Kerry Mills, Part 1 = 0:56, Part 2 = 0:57–2:03, from "Black People" CD: Track 1.

19. Vasnier's rivals for this claim are George W. Johnson and the Unique Quartet, both of whom started recording in 1890, but the exact dates are not known for any of the three. Vasnier's recordings were first *advertised* in January 1891 and must have been made in 1890.

20. Quoted by Dan Weisman, "The Louisiana Phonograph Company," in *The Jazz Archivist—Newsletter of the William Ransom Hogan Jazz Archive*, Tulane, vol. 4, no. 2 (1989).

21. Facsimile reproductions in the *The Jazz Archivist*, as they originally appeared in an April–May 1892 issue of *The Phonogram*, the national trade paper of the phonograph industry.

22. It has been reissued on Document DOCD-5321.

23. Cousins and DeMoss (1897) 2:00, from Document DOCD-5216 "Too Late, Too Late, Volume 2": Track 1.

24. "Watermelon Party"—Polk Miller and Old South Quartet (1909) 3:40, from Archeophone CD ARCH-1003 "Stomp and Swerve": Track 16.

25. T. Brooks, *Lost Sounds*, op. cit., 254.

26. The facsimile of a catalogue listing is in my possession. A different catalogue was provided by researcher Quentin Riggs, letter to Lotz, August 29, 2004.

27. *Der Artist—Central-Organ der Circus, Variété-Bühnen, reisenden Kapellen und Ensembles*, Düsseldorf, Vol. 1 (1893) to date. The chief editor in 1896 was Hermann Waldemar Otto ("Signor Saltarino").

28. British Library, Evanion Catalogue, www.bl.uk. The Bohee Brothers regularly advertised in the *Times*: see August 3, 1881; December 28, 1883; December 31, 1883, through to January 10, 1888.

29. Lotz, *Black People*, 35–50; Lotz, "The Bohee Brothers: Were the Afro-Canadians the Best Banjoists Ever?" in *78 Quarterly*, vol. 1, no. 7 (1992): 97–111.

30. The white banjoist Vess Ossman (b. 1868 at Hudson, NY) recorded more titles in total, but in Europe far less than Hampton.

31. Jeffrey P. Green, "*In Dahomey* in London in 1903," in *The Black Perspective in Music*, vol. 11, no. 1 (1983): 39–40.

32. Lotz, "Pete Hampton, Laura Bowman & The Darktown Aristocrats in Europe, 1904–1912: A preliminary Bio-Discography," in *International Discographer*, vol. 1, no. 1 (1992): 1–13; Lotz, *Black People*, 89–124; "Dat Mouth Organ Coon"/"It's the Last Rose of Summer" (1904)—Pete Hampton—2:11; "Black People" CD: Track 6; "I'm Going to Live Anyhow Till I Die" (1904)— Pete Hampton—2:34, from "Black People" CD: Track 7.

33. Documentation consulted includes passport application by Theodore Wilton Wilson at the Consulate of the United States at Hanover, March 9, 1906; the files of the Hanover municipal registration office for 1906; a Globos record catalogue dated 1906; and the Ellis Island Foundation passenger records for 1905 and 1909 <http://www.ellisislandrecords.org/>.

34. Stage performances at the Nouveau Cirque, Paris (1903)—Banjo and stepdance (date unknown)—Belle Davis and Piccs (1906), from DVD, not commercially available.

35. The Hungarian-born theatrical manager Johann "John" Eugen Friedmann emigrated to the United States in 1888, where he was naturalized in 1893. Around 1903 he joined forces with an as-yet-unidentified black lady impresario and brought a troupe of some ten "pickaninnies" to Europe. There were frequent changes in personnel until Friedman had to return to the United States upon the outbreak of the First World War. Until the original footage turns up, it will not be possible to establish beyond doubt which films were taken by Will Garland's troupe, and which by John Friedman's troupe. "Coontown Ragtime Dance"—Georgia Piccaninnies (1907) 3:10, from CD, not commercially available.

36. This fact is therefore not mentioned in my earlier publications: "The Negro Operetta Company and the Foreign Office," in *New Community—Journal of the Commission for Racial Equality* (London), vol. 13, no. 2 (1986): 204–7; "Will Garland's Negro Operetta Company," in Lotz and Ian Pegg, ed., *Under The Imperial Carpet—Essays in Black History* (Crawley: Rabbit Press, 1986), 130–44; "In Retrospect: Will Garland and the Negro Operetta Company," in *The Black Perspective in Music*, vol. 14, no. 3 (1986): 291–302; and *Black People*, 1997, 199–224.

6

Fascination and Fear

RESPONSES TO EARLY JAZZ IN BRITAIN

—CATHERINE PARSONAGE

The "Jazz Age" of the 1920s has become romanticized in retrospect, and indicative of the supposedly universal appeal of jazz on both sides of the Atlantic. Although jazz, both as a specific musical style and an abstract idea, was omnipresent in British society at this time, its obvious popularity was balanced by the correspondingly strong outrage and antipathy that it provoked among some quarters in Britain. Indeed, R. W. S. Mendl thought it necessary to include a chapter on the dislike of jazz in *The Appeal of Jazz*, the first British book on the subject (1927).[1] While jazz represented a welcome escape from the complexities of modern life, it could also present a significant threat to the foundations of tradition. However, those who were opposed to jazz had often never experienced the music for themselves; Canon Drummond, as cited in Neil Wynn's introduction, admitted that he "had no personal experience of the art of Jazz dancing."[2] Therefore, to understand the variety of responses to early jazz in Britain, it is necessary to look beyond the musical material to consider the image of jazz. As I have argued elsewhere, this had been firmly established in Britain before the well-documented arrival of the Original Dixieland Jazz Band in 1919 and was extremely influential on the reception of jazz in Britain.[3]

Jazz was certainly not viewed as an isolated development when it appeared in Britain, as it was initially presented in revue shows as the latest in a series of American dance music styles to cross the Atlantic. Jazz was incorporated into revues as a modern and fashionable replacement for ragtime, a style that had been popular since around 1912 but was considered to be outdated after the War. Jazz was also linked with previous forms of African American music that had been presented in Britain through the inclusion of the banjo in almost all jazz bands well into the 1920s. The banjo was the instrument most closely associated with black music due to the minstrel show, and had developed a clear musical and symbolic identity by the end of the nineteenth century. The continued use of the banjo also enabled black-face stereotypes, which had been established in the nineteenth century as truisms for a public that had limited acquaintance with black people, to continue to influence the reception of jazz in the twentieth century. Therefore the importance of previous experiences of African American culture in influencing the reception of jazz in Britain cannot be underestimated.

When discussing the response of white South Americans to black culture, Christopher Small writes that "white people have always viewed black culture with a mixture of fascination, fear and even envy."[4] Two specific and important factors emerge in the British reception of minstrelsy that can also be observed in reactions to jazz, and exemplify Small's premise. Firstly, the idea of the Negro as "primitive" influenced the positive reception of black entertainers in Britain as representative of a culture that was fascinatingly "other" in its simplicity. Specifically, an innate musicality was considered to be one of the characteristics of the otherwise "primitive" Negro, an idea that was confirmed through the centrality of music in the minstrel show. At the same time, the "primitivism" of the Negro could engender an attitude that black culture was fundamentally inferior in an extension of "scientific racism." This imagery was also used in support of colonialism, particularly in British exhibitions in the late nineteenth and early twentieth centuries.[5]

Secondly, although the popularity of minstrel shows from the 1840s onwards[6] demonstrates that "there was need in white culture for what black culture had to offer,"[7] black entertainment that was understood to be founded on realism was less popular than versions presented by whites in blackface. The apparently threatening nature of the "realistic" portrayals of black culture to the British public is shown by problems encountered by Sam Hague, who brought an all-black troupe to Britain in 1866. In the end, Hague had to replace most of the troupe with white, blacked-up performers "as the public seemed to prefer the imitation nigger."[8] The competition between black and blackface minstrel shows would have increased the pressure for black minstrels to conform to white stereotypes for their survival. The threat of "genuine" black minstrel performers was clearly being felt in Britain as late as 1912, as one writer commented: "When the nigger-minstrel can wash his race off after office hours he is harmless; but the true negro singer is often a dangerous fellow to be let loose in a hall—we dare not be so familiar with him."[9]

In this essay, I will consider the different responses to jazz in Britain in the 1920s, which demonstrate the manifestation of the emotions of fascination, fear, and envy. I will conclude with close analysis of the reactions to Louis Armstrong's first appearances in Britain in 1932.

When jazz came to prominence in Britain during the 1920s, the understanding of its links with black culture were the source of some extreme responses of fascination and fear. The appeal of jazz as a black music in the 1920s was inherently linked with the contemporary interest in the primitive. Jazz had appeal as an exotic music, which like minstrelsy, whose protagonists opposed "the dominant moral and institutional order" of the Victorians, offered escapism to British audiences by providing an "inverted image of society."[10] Stanley Nelson described the postwar embrace of "primitive" culture through the adoption of jazz as dance music: "The War shattered many of our illusions and brought us nearer to earthy things. That is why the artificiality of the Victorians in their dance music was superseded by a dance music [jazz] which was unashamedly proud of showing its crude emotional stress."[11]

In the 1920s, the perceived simplicity and freedom of black culture could be something desirable for whites to emulate, rather than just observe or imitate, and jazz "seemed to promise cultural as well as musical freedom" for young people.[12] Although this was tinged with misunderstanding based on the long-held assumption that black art was the unsophisticated "low other" of Western culture, this attitude seems to demonstrate genuine interest and appreciation of the perceived "authentic" qualities of black culture. For the

"Bright Young Things" caught up in the aftermath of a war that prompted the basis of Western civilization to be questioned, the values of "primitive" black culture could act as a constructive replacement for the ruined past, offering a less complicated alternative to modern life, and were also a way in which they could subvert tradition: "Whites gravitated toward black music and black culture in general because they felt it expressed the abandon and hedonism toward which they liked to think they were moving."[13]

Paradoxically, primitivism can also be read as the rejection of the whole idea of the modern age, with the Negro as a cultural primitive who "maintained a kind of escapist innocence in the face of technology—a myth perpetuated by blacks who were gaining respectability in white society."[14] But yet, the prominence of black culture in so many art forms in the 1920s, particularly through the art and literature of the Harlem Renaissance, established the "primitive" Negro, ironically, as a primarily modern idea. Jazz was unique in presenting this "primitive" culture in a way in which it could be assimilated, reproduced and experienced directly by whites, and thus "became a cultural shorthand for that which was both supremely modern and, through its African roots, connected with the exotic origins of things. It was the music of the urban jungle."[15] The paradoxical expression "urban jungle" is particularly apt when describing the simultaneous expression of "supreme modernity" and "the exotic origins of things" in London in the 1920s. Jazz encapsulates musically the metaphor of the "urban jungle," as its modernity was expressed through its perceived "primitive" rhythmic qualities.

Jazz provoked a "primitivist" response through dancing that was increasingly improvisational. Dancing was now a response to the basic rhythm of the music, rather than a formal series of steps, and required participants to become absorbed in the music. Jazz dancing as a social activity encouraged the division between young and old, freedom of expression, and the liberation and sexual freedom of women. Significantly, dancing was a more overtly sexual experience than previously as partners could dance pressed closely together for balance, and women's dresses were more revealing. The "primitive" and exotic associations of the music were enhanced by the environment of the new dance clubs, which were decorated in unusual, otherworldly color schemes, and the prevalence of drink and drugs within these venues, which pointed to the function of jazz as a source of escape from the modern world.

The "primitive" associations of jazz also provoked fearful responses from sections of British society. The popularity of jazz as a subversive alternative to convention meant that it presented a threat to those that felt responsible for upholding tradition and moral values. In particular, the overt sexuality of the jazz dance provoked strong opposition to jazz at this time. Canon Drummond referred to jazz as "a dance so low, so demoralizing and of such a low origin—the dance of the low niggers in America" and Sir Dyce Duckworth described "wild dance—amid noises only fit for West African savages—held in London drawing rooms."[16] Adverse comparisons between jazz and classical music were used as a fundamental source for those that wished to denigrate jazz. Essentially, comparing jazz to classical music could show that jazz was simple and underdeveloped particularly with respect to its harmonic basis, and its supposed dependence on rhythmic aspects clearly identified it as "lowbrow." This was a source of misguided criticism, particularly, as Mendl points out, from "some of the most notable men in the musical world" whose views were often published in the national press and thus perpetuated the misunderstanding of jazz.[17] Such comments contributed to an image of jazz that clearly rendered it unsuitable as entertainment in civilized British life.

This opposition to jazz was clearly symptomatic of the racial prejudice in British society at this time. Racially motivated violence was prevalent in Britain in the postwar period, due to fierce competition for jobs between black workers and demobilized white soldiers. The violence was often also sexually motivated, as black men were perceived to have "taken" white women while white men were at war.[18] Objections to black workers extended to the entertainment profession, where African American performers appearing on the stage were perceived to be putting British actors out of work. Negative aspects of blackface stereotypes, such as the supposed propensity of black men to steal and to have extreme sexual urges, were used in support of this discrimination. African American performers were often restricted to performing racially specific entertainment on the British stage in order to be granted work permits, as it could be shown that this could not be provided by the local population, but this often had the effect of perpetuating stereotypes still further. Numerous all-black shows were staged in London, including the "plantation revues" *The Rainbow* and *Dover Street to Dixie* in 1923. These productions had imported African American casts and caused significant controversy in the national and theatrical press.[19]

Black people and jazz found refuge from prejudice within mainstream society in the nightclubs of the underworld of London. Many nightclubs had sprung up even within the relatively small area of Soho in London's West End in the postwar period, an area that Robert Fabian, a policeman in the 1920s, called "The Square Mile of Vice ... where you can buy anything and see everything."[20] There were in fact many different sorts of club in London at this time, embodying varying degrees of "vice," and Seabrook, in his guide to London nightlife in *Brightest Spots in Brighter London*, wrote that "London night clubs are not at all to be avoided as seats of Satan."[21] Nevertheless, in the 1920s "the very words 'night-club' immediately suggest to some people the picture of something degraded and disreputable,"[22] due to the fact that for most of the general public, knowledge of nightclubs was restricted to stories of scandalous activities that were published in newspaper reports. Although the image of nightclubs described in newspapers tended to be exaggerated, sensationalist, and presented in such a way that it was seen as representative of all establishments, there were elements of truth contained within it. Criminal activity, ranging from holding dances without a license to armed robbery and drug dealing, was rife in nightclubs of all types. The fact that jazz flourished as the main form of entertainment in this environment, which had close associations with alcohol, drugs, and prostitution, and also was increasingly understood as a black music at a time of growing racial intolerance, served to cement a negative image of jazz for the general public.

While black people were suffering increasing racism in mainstream British society, there is strong evidence that they were probably much more welcome in the alternative communities of underworld London which represented "the negative image of daytime society."[23] Seabrook noted the racial mix in nightclubs: "The types of frequenters are as diverse as are their races, colors and creeds."[24] Fabian describes the existence of "colored clubs," such as the "Big Apple," and gives a fascinating insight into the music that could be heard in such places: "I learnt all about jazz, boogie-woogie and calypso from my colored friends years before they became known outside the murky little 'colored clubs.' When we were all in the mood—which was often—I would persuade them to give me a 'jam session' that would have opened new doors to any white musician, who had cared to spare the time to listen, in those days."[25]

It was probably only in nightclubs that jazz performers, and particularly black musicians, were able to express themselves fully through their art. However, the increasing presence of black people in this underworld environment in the 1920s meant that they could be held publicly responsible for its associated social problems; for example, dark-skinned foreigners were held responsible for supplying drugs to vulnerable young white girls, often with fatal consequences.[26] Although few published songs of 1919 depicted black performers of jazz, those that do are derogatory or patronizing in nature, for example, "You ought to hear those crazy tunes/Played by all those crazy coons" in the 1918 song *Jazz!* by Grey and Ayer. Similarly, the black origins of jazz were generally only mentioned in contemporary articles by those who wished to criticize jazz. Mendl suggests in the chapter entitled "The Dislike of Jazz Music" that people in Britain were averse to jazz in the twenties because of their "antipathy towards everything connected with the nigger" and that jazz was regularly denounced in the 1920s as "vulgar, coarse and crude and ugly; it is described as a debased product and its popularity is said to be the sign of a decadent age."[27]

These attitudes are epitomized in J. B. Souter's painting *The Breakdown*, in which the corrupting influence of jazz as a black music is clearly implied.[28] The picture was included in the 1926 Royal Academy Summer Exhibition and was commended as "a work of great promise executed with a considerable degree of excellence" by the President of the Royal Academy, Frank Dicksee.[29] However, after only five days the picture was removed from the exhibition under instruction from the Colonial Office, as the subject "was considered to be obnoxious to British subjects living abroad in daily contact with a colored population," showing continued governmental concern for imperial integrity.[30] The painting depicts a black man in evening dress playing the saxophone. In the 1920s, as we have seen, jazz was increasingly identified as a black music, and the saxophone was adopted as a distinctive new musical timbre and a clear visual symbol of modern dance music; hence this figure represents "jazz." A naked white woman, a shingled, androgynous figure, dances to the music of the saxophonist, representing 1920s youth. The saxophone player is seated on a shattered Greek statue, possibly Minerva, a goddess associated with virginity, wisdom, and the arts, traditional values with which the figures in the painting are apparently in disregard. Similarly, it is clear that due to the increasing representation of jazz as black music, and the concurrent move of black musicians into the nightclubs, by the end of the decade jazz was firmly positioned, metaphorically and literally, as the musical accompaniment to the other perceived evils of the underworld of London.

This had a direct effect on the musical evolution of jazz in Britain in the 1920s. Jazz, as primitive, low, black culture, was perceived to be in need of an injection of "civilized" white culture to elevate and improve it, thereby rendering it suitable as mainstream entertainment. This strategy is particularly clear in the BBC's approach to popular music in the 1920s. Jazz rarely appeared in BBC program schedules; instead, the BBC presented "dance music," which consisted of standardized arrangements of popular songs broadcast from venues such as the Savoy Hotel or performed by the BBC's house bands. In the mid-1920s symphonized syncopation was adopted in Britain as a main form of popular music, strongly influenced by Paul Whiteman. "Symphonizing" meant, in effect, the white "civilizing" of "primitive" black music through the addition of symphonic harmony and orchestration. Even Mendl, who was generally a perceptive analyst of early jazz, says that it is unfair to criticize jazz just because it is a black music, as white musicians had since civilized and improved it. He then credits "Whiteman, Hylton and others" for improving the jazz band, bringing it "to so much higher a level that the modern syncopated dance band can hardly be put on the same footing or appropriately designated even by the same name, as the primitive organisms from which it took its origin."[31] The consistent presentation of symphonized syncopation on the radio, the main way in which popular music was disseminated prior to electrical recording, had the effect of standardizing London's dance music, to the extent that jazz was pushed further away from the mainstream.

Ironically, for a time, even those that supported jazz promoted the strategy of symphonizing in an attempt to elevate jazz from its perceived low status. Most of the early British writing on jazz shares the common feature of the use of "classical" music to provide the criteria against which jazz is evaluated. Therefore supporters of jazz attempted to validate the music by pointing out similarities with classical music, attempting to position jazz within the canon and the evolution of music in a bid to make the music seem less radical and to emphasize its artistic qualities. This reliance on classical criteria when assessing jazz meant that it was often difficult for the traditional hierarchy of composer, performer, and arranger to be reconsidered, which was necessary for the importance of improvisation in jazz performance to be recognized. Writers including Mendl and conductor and composer Constant Lambert appealed for a better standard of composition to secure the future of jazz by providing more possibilities for improvisation, and furthermore, pointed to the future of jazz within the work of high art composers rather than as a musical form in its own right. Lambert wrote: "The next move in the development of jazz will come, almost inevitably, from the sophisticated or highbrow composers."[32]

Symphonic syncopation was at its peak of popularity for a few years in the mid-1920s, but even Gershwin's *Rhapsody in Blue* (1924), which had been upheld as an example of excellence in symphonic syncopation, began to be criticized in the late 1920s to early 1930s. Mendl had described the piece as "technically an extremely efficient composition . . . skilful in form . . . the work is a kind of instrumental fantasia written for jazz band," but in 1934 Lambert criticized the piece as being "neither good jazz nor good Liszt."[33] There was a sense that the compromise offered by "symphonic syncopation" was no longer sufficient for everyone as the music was not successful as either jazz or art music. The increasing availability of American jazz on record and the high-profile visits of Louis Armstrong and Duke Ellington to Britain in the early 1930s were vital to this realization and the subsequent re-evaluation of jazz.

Records allowed more people to become acquainted with the sound of jazz and other popular music, as they were no longer reliant on BBC radio. It was possible for Britons to begin to understand spontaneous expression in performance as an artistic quality, particularly in relation to African American musicians. This prompted a deeper understanding of the artistic and cultural validity of jazz that allowed it to be appreciated in its own right without persistent reference to classical music. At the same time, the growing awareness and criticism of the commercial motivation of the pervasive dance music "industry" contrasted with the relative scarcity of American jazz records. In the early 1930s, the continuation of the "primitivist" mode of reception of black culture meant that black musicians were now regarded as innocent of commercial motives. Although this was an essentialist notion that perpetuated stereotypical beliefs about black musicians, African American jazz was profoundly different in sound to the overtly commercial, large, uniform, and controlled presentations by dance orchestras that could be heard on the BBC and seen in established venues in the capital. The music critic Stanley Nelson, writing in 1934, described the changing perceptions of African American jazz in Britain:

> In the early days of jazz the Negro exponents were usually condemned by the experts as too crude. . . . [T]heir jazz had a blatancy which was far from pleasing to white ears. . . . [I]n our opinion, their jazz was a poor thing beside the refined product of the best white bands. . . . It is my belief that most of the future development of Jazz will come from the colored race themselves, and not from us. . . . We lack the spontaneity of the colored people and their innate feel for the jazz idiom. . . . Their playing is characterized by its extreme fervor; instead of playing in the detached manner of white bands, these colored artists subordinate every feeling to the job in hand.[34]

The discourse of primitivism remains inherent in Nelson's description of the "spontaneity," "feel," and "fervor" of black musicians, whereas their white counterparts have been responsible for "standardization" and a "detached" style of playing. However, it can be seen that black music held similar escapist appeal as a cultural alternative to the complexities and failings of Western civilization as in the immediate postwar period. Constant Lambert wrote in *Music Ho!*: ". . . the only jazz music of technical importance is that small section of it that is genuine Negroid. The 'hot' Negro records still have a genuine and not merely galvanic energy, while the blues have a certain austerity that places them far above the sweet nothings of George Gershwin."[35] Black music was now being appreciated in its own right for its complexity and quality, and "civilizing" impulses were beginning to be recognized by many people as being unnecessary, superficial, and even racist.

Despite this intellectual re-evaluation of jazz, African American jazz performers were generally underrepresented on records and in live performance in Britain in the early 1930s. Black musicians generally came to Britain to accompany music theater productions, and unlike their white compatriots, their participation in British dance bands was very limited. Recordings by black musicians were often not as readily available as those by white Americans, and British critics could treat their work disparagingly. Although Louis Armstrong's records could be obtained by determined enthusiasts and musicians, it is likely that Nat Gonella's imitations of them might have been more familiar to British audiences prior to Armstrong's

1932 visit. British audiences, even those who had encountered Armstrong's recorded performances, were generally unprepared for the impact of his live performances, and fascination, fear, and the discourse of primitivism are very much in evidence in the audiences' responses.

Armstrong's performances at the London Palladium, a leading variety theater, in July 1932 certainly provoked extreme reactions.[36] While several audience members left the theater in disgust, others hailed him as a virtuoso genius. In comparison, Duke Ellington performing at the same theater in the following year (commencing in June 1933) was more consistently well received. Ellington's publicity machine had been in action to enhance his profile in Britain since the previous November. This was aided considerably by reports of his performances in the Cotton Club in *Melody Maker* by the British musician, critic, and Ellington fan Spike Hughes. Ellington's performances were appropriate for the Palladium, as the polished and controlled presentation related to the familiar aesthetics of dance bands in variety. Ellington also selected balanced programs of his own compositions and popular songs, for which he was roundly criticized by Hughes, but which appealed to the variety audience.[37]

The reactions to Armstrong were partially due to his musical performance, which was extreme in comparison to the dance band music normally presented at variety shows. Reviewers who attempted to validate Armstrong's performances as art often emphasized quantifiable or technical aspects in an attempt to highlight his virtuosity in line with the qualities valued in the performance of Western art music:

> [Armstrong said] "This tiger runs very fast, so I expect I'll have to play five choruses to catch him up!" He played *eight*—all different! . . . Top F's bubble about all over the place, and never once does he miss one. He is enormously fond of the lip-trill, which he accomplished by shaking the instrument wildly with his right hand.[38]

> His phrasing is unique by reason of his quaint manner of breaking up four bars, for example, by singing the first bar, remaining tacet for the next two, and suddenly singing all the words in the last bar! It is ludicrous, yet astoundingly rhythmic.[39]

Armstrong's performance style and stage presence particularly prompted a continuation of the primitivist mode of reception. This was at the root of both positive and negative reactions depending on the weighting of "fascination and fear and even envy" in the psychology of audience members when faced with this latest example of black culture. A combination of these emotions is exemplified in the "fascination" that led to so many people going to see Armstrong, but the "fear" that prompted them to leave during his performances. Here these fluctuating emotions are described:

> The business for Armstrong's first visit to the Palladium was said to be a record for the theatre at that time. So that every performance would be full at Louis' opening, but by the time he had to finish the theatre was half empty.[40]

> Armstrong . . . was heartily applauded . . . although the reception at the conclusion of the act was somewhat mixed, some booing being noticeable.[41]

As Jones and Chilton have suggested, the fact that Armstrong was "an extremely fervent exponent as well as an unbridled presence on stage" was the main reason for the exodus of the Palladium audiences.[42] However, Armstrong's performances could be found to be variously attractive and mystifying as well as threatening. Many critics simply noted that Armstrong "puts a tremendous amount of energy into his work"[43]: "All the time he is singing he carries a handkerchief in his hand and mops his face—perspiration positively drips off him. He puts enough energy in his half-hour's performance to last the average man several years."[44]

Robert Goffin, the Belgian poet and music critic who dedicated his book *Aux Frontières du Jazz* to Armstrong, came to London to hear Armstrong play in 1933 and provided a particularly vivid description: "In action Armstrong is like a boxer, the bell goes and he attacks at once. His face drips like a heavy-weight's, steam rises from his lips . . . the whole right side of his neck swells as though it must burst; then, summoning up all the air in his body for another effect, he inflates his throat till it looks like a goitre."[45]

Descriptions such as Goffin's, although intended to be affirmative, nevertheless suggest that Armstrong would have had the ability to shock and threaten British sensibilities. Reviewers such as the famous journalist Hannen Swaffer reacted viciously to Armstrong's performances:

> Armstrong is the ugliest man I have ever seen on the music hall stage. He looks, and behaves, like an untrained gorilla. He might have come straight from some

African jungle and then, after being taken to a slop tailor's for a ready-made
dress-suit, been put on the stage and told to "sing."

Armstrong's head, while he plays, is a unique as his music. Gradually, it
is covered by a thousand beads of perspiration. . . . He tries in vain to keep dry
with a handkerchief. He is a living shower-bath.

And his neck swells out like a gorged python.[46]

Louis Armstrong's reception in Britain was often dependent upon the
way in which the aspects of his performance that were understood as "primitive" were received: with fascination or fear. It is interesting to note some
similarity in the description, but not in meaning or intent, of Armstrong
in Swaffer's and Goffin's accounts. Indeed, the primitivist evaluations
of Armstrong were not confined to his critics, because for writers such as
Goffin, one of Armstrong's most devoted supporters, a performance style
that suggested unmediated emotional expression had the effect of confirming Armstrong's artistic originality and creativity, qualities which were
perceived to be inherently linked with his race: "Armstrong is primarily a
trumpeter, a stylist and a creator. No white man could have evolved such a
style. It is as colorful as he is colored."[47]

Rhythm magazine noted that Swaffer's review of Armstrong "adequately
describes the whole show as it must have appeared to anybody who did not
understand how perfectly amazing is Armstrong's trumpet work."[48] It is
interesting to note that in general those that wished to acclaim Armstrong
tended to focus on his trumpet playing, regarded as a more "artistic" feature of his performances, while those that sought to criticize it neglected
this aspect in favor of consideration of his singing, which could more easily
be regarded as "primitive," as when the criteria of value of Western classical
music were applied: "To the listener oriented to 'classical' singing, Louis's voice,
with its rasp and totally unorthodox technique, usually comes as a complete
shock."[49] An article in the *Daily Express*, in summarizing the questions being
asked by Londoners about Armstrong's performances, contrasted these two
modes of performance: "Louis Armstrong! For or against? Can he play the
trumpet or is he a crazy, enraged negro blurting noises at a long suffering
public?"[50] Gabbard has noted the difference between Armstrong's performance
style when singing and playing with reference to films of the early 1930s, in
that "when he puts his trumpet to his lips, he becomes a different man."[51]

Even Armstrong's singing could be perceived diversely, as noise or art. Whereas Swaffer wrote "His singing is dreadful, babyish, uncouth. . . . [H]e makes animal noises into the microphone . . ."[52], another critic evaluated Armstrong's singing in a more positive light, still resorting to the jungle metaphor, but emphasizing the artistic nature of primitivism: "Singing, indeed, is hardly an adequate description of those incoherent, ecstatic, rhythmical jungle noises which none of Armstrong's imitators have yet succeeded in rivalling. . . . This savage growling is as far removed from English as we speak or sing it—and as modern—as James Joyce."[53]

Armstrong did begin to receive more overt praise by his second week at the Palladium, albeit still vague in detail, suggesting that after the initial shock audiences and critics had indeed taken him to their hearts, or that those that attended the later performances had a better idea of what to expect:

> . . . [T]he reception accorded Louis Armstrong is now considerably warmer than it was on the first night. . . .
>
> [Armstrong] was a great hit with his admirers, the applause completely holding up the interval.
>
> Louis Armstrong is retained, and the King of the Trumpet too had an enormous reception. There is no doubting the cleverness of Louis' playing, I have never heard anything quite as good.[54]

According to *Variety News*, Armstrong "worked a little more piano than last week and was, consequently, more acceptable to English audiences," suggesting the possibility that Armstrong might have responded to the initial criticism of the extreme nature of his performances.[55]

There is evidence to suggest that by the mid-1930s, the availability of recordings and the high-profile visits of Louis Armstrong, Duke Ellington and others led to some dominance of fascination over fear in the reception of black jazz musicians in London. Nelson recalled a change in attitude, whereas in the past famous Negro bands "were all very well in their way, in our opinion, but their jazz was a poor thing beside the refined product of the best white bands. . . . To-day Ellington, Armstrong and the other colored bands have practically assumed the position of arbitrators of modern rhythmic style."[56] Indeed, it can be seen that by the time of the 1935 restrictions on American musicians in Britain, there was a demand for black musicians to provide performances of jazz that were appreciated as "authentic" by the British public. This need was met by musicians from the resident black population in Britain, including many from the ethnically diverse Tiger Bay area of Cardiff in Wales, and immigrants from the West Indies. The presence of so many talented black musicians in London allowed the trumpeter Leslie Thompson, who had been resident in Britain since 1929, to realize his dream of forming an all-black dance band which was later taken over by Ken "Snakehips" Johnson. The Johnson/Thompson band was to contribute to the re-definition of the artistic status of jazz in Britain as entertaining and exhilarating dance music. Although Britain was by no means free from racial discrimination, the performances and reception of black musicians could now transcend the stereotypes that were the legacy of blackface entertainment and their music could be appreciated seriously.

NOTES

1. Robert W. S. Mendl, *The Appeal of Jazz* (Glasgow: Robert Maclehose, 1927).

2. *Times*, March 15, 1919, 7.

3. Catherine J. Parsonage, *The Evolution of Jazz in Britain, 1880–1935* (Aldershot: Ashgate, 2005).

4. Christopher Small, *Music of the Common Tongue: Survival and Celebration in Afro-American Music* (London: Calder, 1994), 141.

5. Marika Sherwood, "White Myths, Black Omissions: the Historical Origins of Racism in Britain," in *International Journal of Historical Learning, Teaching and Research*, vol. 3, no. 1 (2003) (http://www.ex.ac.uk/education/historyresource/journal5/journalstart.htm).

6. See Michael Pickering, "White Skin, Black Masks: 'Nigger' minstrelsy in Victorian Britain," in Jacqueline S. Bratton, ed., *Music Hall: Performance and Style* (Milton Keynes: Open University Press, 1986); Michael Pickering, "John Bull in Blackface," in *Popular Music*, vol. 16, no. 2 (1997); Harry Reynolds, *Minstrel Memories: The Story of Burnt Cork Minstrels in Great Britain 1836–1927* (London: Alston Rivers, 1928).

7. Ben Sidran, *Black Talk* (New York: Da Capo, 1981), 32.

8. Reynolds, *Minstrel Memories*, 165.

9. William R. Titterton, *From Theatre to Music Hall* (London: Stephen Swift, 1912), 213.

10. Pickering, "White Skin, Black Masks," 88–89.

11. Stanley R. Nelson, *All About Jazz* (London: Heath Cranton Ltd, 1934), 170.

12. Simon Frith, *Performing Rites: Evaluating Popular Music* (Oxford: Oxford University Press, 1996), 128.

13. Sidran, *Black Talk*, 54.

14. Sidran, *Black Talk*, 54.

15. Adam Lively, *Masks: Blackness, Race and the Imagination* (London: Chatto and Windus, 1998), 99.

16. *Times*, March 15, 1919, 7; *Times*, March 18, 1919, 7.

17. Mendl, *The Appeal of Jazz*, 60.

18. See Jacqueline Jenkinson, "The 1919 Race Riots in Britain: A Survey," in Lotz/Pegg, eds., *Under the Imperial Carpet: Essays in Black History 1780–1950* (Crawley, Sussex: Rabbit Press, 1986).

19. See Parsonage, *The Evolution of Jazz in Britain,* Chapter 7.

20. Robert Fabian, *London After Dark* (London: Naldrett Press, 1954), 10.

21. Sydney A. Moseley, ed., *Brightest Spots in Brighter London: A Comprehensive Guide to London Amusements, Shopping Centres and Features of Interest to the Visitor* (London: Stanley Paul Moseley, 1924), 137.

22. Kate Meyrick, *Secrets of the 43* (London: John Long, 1933), 88.

23. Marek Kohn, *Dope Girls: the Birth of the British Drug Underground* (London: Lawrence and Wishart, 1992), 125.

24. Moseley, *Brightest Spots*, 138.

25. Fabian, *London After Dark*, 15.

26. For example, the case of the nightclub hostess Freda Kempton, who was supplied with cocaine by the notorious Brilliant Chang. Kempton's death from an overdose in 1922 received extensive coverage in the national press. See Kohn, Chapter 8.

27. Mendl, *The Appeal of Jazz*, 71, 25.

28. The painting can be seen on the cover of Parsonage, *The Evolution of Jazz in Britain.*

29. Joan M. Matthew, *J. B. Souter, 1890–1971*, an exhibition catalogue (Perth: Perth Museum and Art Gallery, 1990).

30. Royal Academy Annual Report 1926, 13.

31. Mendl, *The Appeal of Jazz*, 72, 49.

32. Constant Lambert, *Music Ho!* (London: Faber, 1934, rpt. 1966), 198.

33. Mendl, *The Appeal of Jazz*, 177–78; Lambert, *Music Ho!*, 195.

34. Nelson, *All About Jazz*, 162–63.

35. Lambert, *Music Ho!*, 186.

36. Armstrong remained in Britain until October 1932, and returned in July 1933 for a visit that lasted a year. See Howard Rye, "Visiting Firemen 2: Louis Armstrong," in *Storyville*, vol. 89, 184–87.

37. Extensive comparative analysis of Armstrong and Ellington at the Palladium can be found in Chapter 9 in Parsonage, *The Evolution of Jazz in Britain.*

38. *Melody Maker*, August 1932, 617.

39. *Rhythm*, September 1932, 11.

40. Gonella, quoted in Max Jones and John Chilton, *Louis: The Louis Armstrong Story 1900–1971* (St. Albans: Mayflower, 1975), 161.

41. *Performer*, July 20, 1932, 10.

42. Jones and Chilton, *Louis*, 162.

43. *Stage*, July 21, 1932, 3.

44. *Melody Maker*, August 1932, 617.

45. Goffin, trans. Beckett in Nancy Cunard, *Negro: Anthology Made by Nancy Cunard 1931–1933* (London: Nancy Cunard at Wishart and Co., 1934), 292.

46. *Daily Herald*, July 25, 1932.

47. *Rhythm*, September 1932, 11.

48. *Rhythm*, September 1932, 9.

49. Gunther Schuller, *Early Jazz: Its Roots and Musical Development* (New York: Oxford University Press, 1968), 100.

50. *Daily Express*, July 28, 1932, 9.

51. Krin Gabbard, ed., *Jazz Among the Discourses* (Durham: Duke University Press, 1996), 210.

52. *Daily Herald*, July 25, 1932.

53. *Daily Express*, July 20, 1932, 15.

54. *Stage*, July 28, 1932, 3; *Performer*, July 27, 1932, 10; *Era*, July 27, 1932, 19.

55. *Variety Music, Stage and Film News*, July 27, 1932, 4.

56. Nelson, *All That Jazz*, 162.

7

"Un Saxophone en Mouvement"?

JOSEPHINE BAKER AND THE PRIMITIVIST RECEPTION
OF JAZZ IN PARIS IN THE 1920S

—IRIS SCHMEISSER

The metropolis of Paris was particularly receptive to the influence of African American jazz in the arts and popular culture in the 1920s for two reasons that are integral to its history as a center of transatlantic modernism: French consumer culture was, on the one hand, increasingly shaped by American entertainment culture, a result of increasing commercial exchange in the postwar period, and on the other hand, by cultural forms to which one attributed African origins, a result of colonialism. "Jazz" was associated with cultural modernity, such as an urban lifestyle, technological progress, mobility, etc., and, at the same time, cultural primitivism—as it was considered a black musical tradition with past African origins. However, jazz as it was played and represented to a French audience at first and predominantly by African American performers, drew different responses from different groups. There was, according to historian Jeffrey H. Jackson, great liberty among French recipients of African American performers and the dance styles they imported to Paris as to what was defined and interpreted as "true" jazz. As

Jackson argues: "what people meant when they used the term jazz depended on who was using it—just as in the United States, where the term was also being used to describe a wide variety of dance music."[1] In other words, if certain cultural and aesthetic properties indicative of jazz could be partially identified, those parts were quickly projected upon the whole, thus making the label "jazz" a broadly and loosely interpreted category. As a result, the focus of this essay will not be on the types and variations of jazz in Paris in the 1920s, but rather on its aesthetic representation and cultural imagination in French visual culture.

Inspired by a number of recent contributions contextualizing the reception of African American jazz and its dance styles in general, and of singer/ dancer Josephine Baker in particular within a diasporic framework, this essay seeks to accomplish two things. First, to read Josephine Baker's performance in the all-black musical revues *La Revue nègre* (1925) and *La Folie du jour* (1926) and subsequent representations of Baker in French art and popular culture as a case study regarding the primitivist reception of jazz in Parisian visual culture in the 1920s, a culture shaped by the consequences of colonialism. And second, to problematize an either/or perspective in critical approaches to Baker that a) either represent her as a figure of cultural power and influence who resisted a racist power structure or b) that identify her as a perpetrator and even victim of white primitivist stereotypization. The very complexity of her figure, to use a jazz metaphor applied to Baker by the French critic Pierre de Regnier in his review of *La Revue nègre*, might be comparable to "un saxophone en mouvement" and as such incredibly fascinating yet impossible to pin down into one single frame.[2] This doubly moving complexity of Josephine Baker's (self-)representation was, as I will argue, the main ingredient of her lasting originality.

Seeking to answer the difficult question why "American black music had so much greater a capacity to conquer the Western world than any other," Eric Hobsbawm proposes two answers that well illuminate the major cultural coordinates that constituted the historical context of Baker's primitivist reception: first, the fact that African American jazz was perceived not only as primitive, but also as modern, and second, because "[j]azz made its way and triumphed, not as a music for intellectuals, but as a music for dancing." Significantly, Hobsbawm uses the term "dance revolution" to account for its broad social and cultural consequences, namely its impact upon class and gender structures: Baker's popularization of the Charleston, for instance, and its eager adaptation not only by the French middle-class but also the French haute-bourgeoisie, well illustrate Hobsbawm's argument concerning the dissolution of class and gender conventions as a result of this "dance revolution."[3] Whether this "dance revolution" triggered by the import of African American jazz also resulted in a loosening of race-based structures will be problematized in light of Baker's primitivist reception. If, as Jack Sullivan optimistically concludes that "[j]azz is where real integration occurs, mixing races, cultures, and sensibilities in a unified design," the example of Baker's primitivist reception shows that this integration—the dissolution and transgression of social borders—also resulted in their very re-inscription.[4]

Like Hobsbawm, Jeffrey H. Jackson attributes the popularity of jazz and the "dance craze" it unsettled in Paris to broader cultural tendencies having to do with the Americanization of French entertainment culture in the postwar period. As Jackson argues: "Americans and other tourists from around the world along with nouveaux riches French poured money into Parisian show business, helping to make jazz profitable in nightclubs and music halls."[5] However, Josephine Baker's premier in *La Revue nègre* (1925) and her performance one year later in *La Folie du jour* (1926) were events that simultaneously hit *two* major commercial trends regarding the modernization of French popular culture through transatlantic import: they featured a star and cultural material imported from America, but they also—regarding the exoticist themes both revues played with—betrayed the modernization of French visual culture through import from Africa. Thus, Baker was perceived as a cross-over of these two trends, an advantage she commercially exploited for her own ends and with great success. Obviously, Baker herself made a career as a French chansonnière rather than a jazz singer, yet her performance was typically read—especially by visual artists who saw her perform in Paris at the time—as the "embodiment" of jazz based on her debut in *La Revue nègre* and the Parisian night club scene, no matter how much she actually danced to musical pieces that deserve to be placed under the category of jazz. It was also significantly in France and not the United States, that Josephine Baker's primitivist modernist performance based on a jazz aesthetic was appreciated as a form of art that inspired other works of art.

In the early twentieth century, African objects had achieved a new significance among modernist primitivist artists such as Pablo Picasso and

Guillaume Apollinaire and French art connoisseurs such as Paul Guillaume. African objects were now valued as art as opposed to merely ethnographic curiosities. In the fall of 1912, Guillaume Apollinaire's programmatic essay "Exotisme et Ethnographie" appeared in the French magazine *Paris-Journal.* In this essay, Apollinaire demonstrated the stylistic impact of "art nègre"—traditional African sculpture—upon European modernists and the simultaneous valorization of African objects as art that went with it. Another contemporaneous voice and prime instigator of what would transform into a craze for African objects, a craze referred to as "vogue nègre" was the French art dealer Paul Guillaume. Guillaume promoted the cultivation of a taste for these African objects and would become one of the most renowned collectors of "art nègre" in the interwar years. In February 1914, Guillaume had opened his own gallery in Paris where he exhibited works by contemporary European modernist painters next to African art objects. The catalogue of the exhibition praised the artistic value of the African objects by inverting the traditionally negatively charged meaning of the categories "savage" and "primitive" while transposing and thus ameliorating them into positively connoted aesthetic classifications to designate and celebrate black cultural difference. The hype for "art nègre" and Africanism—exoticist art and popular culture based on African motives—played a crucial role regarding the reception of Josephine Baker in Paris.[6] She drew upon the aesthetic codes of black exoticism in her performances, yet also, in turn influenced the vogue of black exoticism herself.

However, the craze for traditional African objects did not represent the only manifestation of the black exoticist vogue that characterized Parisian culture at the time. The other primary ingredient that fueled Parisian "vogue nègre" was the impact and influence of African American jazz, mainly introduced to the French by African American soldiers in France. Approximately 370,000 African Americans had served in the American Expeditionary Force in France—needless to say in segregated units—during the First World War. The majority of French civilians received these African American soldiers who fought in the war with benevolence and gratitude, a circumstance that led to an often uncritical version of francophilia among black Americans who spread a myth of French racial liberalism that was blind towards the abuses of French colonial rule, as Michel Fabre has shown. Josephine Baker had also believed in and perpetuated that myth of French racial tolerance—which also contained at least a grain of truth: "Mrs. Baker, why did you leave the United States?" the young Henry Louis Gates had asked in an interview he conducted with black American expatriates in Paris in 1973, among them Josephine Baker. The answer was:

> I left in 1924, but the roots extend long before that. One of the first things
> I remember was the East St. Louis Race Riots. . . . That was the beginning of my
> feeling. . . . The French adopted me immediately. They all went to the beaches to
> get dark like Josephine Baker. . . . I felt liberated in Paris. . . . Once, I dined in a
> certain restaurant with friends. An American lady looked at our table and called
> the waiter. "Tell her to get out," the lady said. "In my country, she is belonging
> only in the kitchen." The French management asked the American lady to leave.[7]

As Brent Hayes Edwards has pointed out, if one looks at the presence of Africans and peoples of African descent in Paris in the mid-1920s, the time when Josephine Baker arrived there, one realizes that the exoticist craze for black culture known as "vogue nègre," white primitivist fantasies about Africa and peoples of African descent, co-existed with the real and tangible presence of hundreds of black soldiers, visitors, students, and expatriates in the metropole. It was thanks to military bands like James Reese Europe and Noble Sissle's 369th Infantry Regiment "Hellfighters" Band and black American performers—men and women—like Palmer Jones and his International Five, Louis Mitchell, Arthur Briggs, Will Marion Cook's Southern Syncopated Orchestra, Bricktop, and Florence Embry Jones that "vogue nègre" not only implied the craze for traditional African art but also the appreciation of African American jazz. As jazz historian William A. Shack has put it, "before the end of the decade, [James Reese] Europe had created his own revolution in France."[8] It was *those* former black American soldiers who decided to stay in France after the Armistice that formed the *core* of the African American expatriate community in Paris. This was made possible by an arrangement between the French and American governments to permit American ex-soldiers to study at a French university which hence made it possible for them to remain in an environment which many black Americans perceived to be less oppressive than the United States.

Regimental bands of black American soldiers had toured the country in 1918, thus spreading the taste for the "modern tunes" of jazz At "Zelli's," one of the first jazz clubs in Paris, two non-European dance bands, in fact, alternated: black American jazz musicians and an Argentine tango band; the place was so popular that young women were hired by Joe Zelli, the owner of the place, to dance with unaccompanied male guests. Before Josephine Baker took Paris with a sweep, two African American women performers, Florence Embry Jones and Ada Smith, nicknamed Bricktop because of her red hair, were famous among the Montmartre cabaret scene. Bricktop, next to Josephine Baker, triggered the hype for the Charleston and it was her jazz club "Bricktop's" which introduced the latest tunes from New York to its international clientele.[9] The visibility and success of African American jazz performers in Paris in the interwar years fueled the commodification of black cultures that black exoticism signified and subjected African Americans to the mixed blessing of French primitivist "negrophilia" that on the one hand celebrated yet on the other hand also stereotypically fixed a white exoticist concept of black cultural difference.

The primitivist avant-garde in Paris celebrated the "African roots" of jazz; this was particularly the case with so-called "negrophile" surrealists. But the white cultural practice of projecting a "primitive mentality" upon blacks because of the racial difference they were perceived to embody had its own popular and controversial tradition in the United States: the theatrical history of blackface minstrelsy which, as a form of urban mass entertainment, was revitalized in the interwar years and also exported to Paris. Fixed constructions of black otherness thus constituted the aesthetic repertoire of blackface minstrelsy. This mechanism of white racialized ascription, underwritten by a strange mix of desire and aversion resurfaced in the "jazz age" and the transgressive allure associated with black American performance in the 1920s.[10] There is, however, another dimension to the uneasy theatrical tradition and racist heritage of minstrelsy in black American popular culture as Berndt Ostendorf has pointed out: it not only paved the way for the entry of black music and dance into the mainstream of American entertainment culture, but also for African American performers' *subversive* emergence on stage which they entered—in disguise and thus double-conscious—behind the white minstrel mask. In white primitivist scenarios, black otherness was ambivalently connoted as attractive and desirable, but also repulsive and threatening. The white primitivist perception of African American expressive culture essentialized its aesthetic difference by celebrating it as an expression of "primitive mentality" and idolizing its "African descent." Significantly, African American artists and writers could ironically reappropriate and parody those primitivist codes which informed either the popular vogue for "art nègre" or the representations of white modernist primitivists.[11]

Already at the turn of the century, a group of black singers called the "Four Black Troubadours" had performed comic burlesque in *European* concert halls and had, in fact, popularized the cake-walk in Parisian entertainment culture, an equivalent to the American minstrel show. A song-and-dance team called Nègres Joyeux presented minstrel acts, clowning, buffoonery, and blackface in front of a Parisian audience at the Nouveau Cirque. Exotic black minstrel groups such as the Four Black Spades, the Four Black Diamonds, and Bonnie Goodwin's Picaninnies all played and entertained a white European audience eager to indulge in the racist amusement of "cooning," as it was called, at the Folies-Bergère in 1904. Will Marion Cook's all-black musical *In Dahomey* featuring the vaudeville comedians Bert Williams and George Walker was not only the first African American musical show to play on Broadway—it opened at the New York Theatre in 1903—but also went on tour in London and Paris where it made the cake-walk famous.[12]

During the 1880s, minstrel shows had become a popular form of entertainment in Paris.[13] The cake-walk is said to have originated in the slave culture of Southern plantation life, supposedly a form of theatrical entertainment African Americans practiced around Christmas time or other holidays when their owners "allowed" them to pose as or rather mimic high society whites in order to win a prize—a cake. The cake-walk spectacle of the 1890s did not share much with the cake-walk of antebellum plantation culture, rather, cake-walk became a popular form of entertainment as it crossed over into vaudeville performance, and cake-walk contests were staged throughout the United States topped, according to Nathan Huggins, by the annual national cake-walk championship held in Madison Square Garden.[14] Around the turn of the century, Parisians were introduced to the "cake-walk" at the Nouveau Cirque and the Folies-Bergère—the debut of African American entertainers in Paris—well before the arrival of jazz bands in 1918.[15] Both the syncopated tunes of ragtime and the cake-walk were perceived as "exotic images of antebellum plantation life" and through the primitivist lens applied to so-called "indigenous" Africans.

The white artistic avant-garde—a typical motive of the jazz age—compared the "arrival" of jazz in Paris and its cultural and aesthetic influence to the "discovery" of African art and its impact. Thus jazz, despite its undeniably transcultural origins, was perceived as authentically "black." This meant that the "African roots" of jazz were considered exclusively significant and hence stood for the black identity of jazz, the obvious hybridity of its cultural and aesthetic origins notwithstanding. Instead, the primitivist reception of jazz music and dance typically zoomed in on its African "nature." The "blackness" of African American jazz performers was read as a visible embodiment of their cultural difference. It thus adopted the quality of a metaphor for the "primitive" *as well as* the "modern." "Vogue nègre" in Paris meant that jazz was, like traditional African sculpture, appreciated for its cultural difference and its African origins. The idea of "art nègre" that circulated among the artists and writers in Paris in the interwar years thus conceptually fused the aesthetic quality of traditional African sculpture with that of African American jazz. Surrealist intellectuals—such as the group that gathered around the jazz amateur Georges-Henri Rivière, a museologist and curator at the Musée du Trocadéro in Paris and fervent admirer of Josephine Baker's—typically looked at the so-called "indigenous" Africans whose expressive culture they studied through a prefabricated primitivist lens.

The other way around, descriptions of contemporary African American jazz orchestras of the time were also frequently perceived through an ethnographic lens. To contemporary observers, at the high tide of "vogue nègre," African American jazz and the dance styles supposedly expressing it, i.e., the Charleston, shimmy, black bottom, lindy hop, etc., were approached through the aesthetic filter of black exoticism that resembled that of ethnographic studies of African "natives" and their ritual dances. This phenomenon can be illustrated with a passage from John Banting's essay "The Dancing of Harlem." Banting, an artist from England who had been to Harlem, wrote that

In many travel films the ritualistic dances performed by natives have the identical rhythms and steps of the "Charleston," "Shimmy," "Black-Bottom" and "Lindy-Hop," done to-day on Harlem stages and dance floors and in the more enthusiastic evangelical churches . . . Six years ago, the New York revue producer George White introduced the "Charleston" to Broadway, the chorus being taught by children from Harlem. He claims the honour of being its inventor. The dance is named from the town in South Carolina and its fast rhythm and flashing steps are the same as those performed in many parts of Africa.[16]

La Revue nègre, announced as "a show of authentic Negro vaudeville" consisting of more than twenty black musicians, singers, and dancers (including Sidney Bechet and Josephine Baker), and staged by Rolf de Maré at the prestigious Théâtre de Champs-Élysées, newly renovated into a music hall, came to Paris at the postwar climax of the music hall and jazz craze—in 1925.[17] This show, in which Josephine Baker had the main role, would launch her international fame. Her career as a performance artist started in the early 1920s when she joined the Dixie Steppers, a Southern vaudeville group that toured small towns playing before an all-black audience. Later, she managed to find a job in the chorus line in Noble Sissle and Eubie Blake's black musical comedy *Shuffle Along* in 1921. The show was a big hit and ran for more than five hundred performances.[18] Significantly, Baker was cast in a role in which she parodied the popular conventions of vaudeville and the minstrel show as she played the comic chorus girl at the end of the line.[19] In the summer of 1925, Baker performed as "Topsy Anna"—in blackface—in another musical comedy by the successful team Sissle and Blake, *The Chocolate Dandies.* "Topsy Anna" was a minstrel figure especially created for Baker; she appeared on stage as a ragamuffin in blackface with oversized clown shoes doing a Charleston parody.[20]

Caroline Dudley Reagan (the well-off wife of an attaché to the American embassy in Paris and patron of the arts) had seen and admired Baker's dancing in these performances and subsequently decided to cast her in a black musical show she was planning to stage for a Parisian audience. Among the people she had begun to recruit for such a project were the composer Spencer Williams, the bandleader and pianist Claude Hopkins, the dancer and choreographer Louis Douglas, as well as the set designer and caricaturist for *Vanity Fair* Miguel Covarrubias. The musicians who would make up the band for *La Revue nègre* were Joe Hayman (saxophone), Daniel Day (trombone), Bass Hill (tuba), Percy Johnson (drums), Sidney Bechet (clarinet), and finally, Josephine Baker as lead dancer and singer.[21]

La Revue nègre opened on the night of October 2, 1925, at the Théâtre de Champs-Élysées. The performance, originally modeled after a vaudeville show designed for white urban America's nostalgic yearning for the idyll of Southern plantation 'life, featured tap dancing and spirituals, and thus directly fed on the tradition of minstrelsy. Yet it was also to be transformed to suit the *Parisian* vogue of black exoticism. As a result, American-derived codes of minstrelsy were blended with French-derived codes of primitivist Africanity and concocted into a spectacle which mixed elements taken from African American entertainment culture with those taken from French manifestations of "vogue nègre." The French craze for Baker's black body in motion in *La Revue nègre* dwelt on the exotic, and also erotic dimension of the "primitive" African Other enacted through a mise-en-scène of the colonial gaze. Wendy Martin hence conceives of Baker's modernist performance as an act of appropriation as well as exploitation as she deliberately bought into the commodification of African art and cultures which characterized "vogue nègre."[22]

Baker played on and acted out representational conventions of the black "primitive" historically derived from minstrelsy, but also borrowed from contemporary white fetishizations of the African body as mediated in ethnographic missions, avant-garde art, "art colonial," and colonial exhibitions. The "danse sauvage," for instance, was a fabricated composite dance without any "authentic" origins; it would become Baker's signature style. It consisted of an African American and a Martinican performer, Joé Alex, masquerading as African "savages," their semi-nude and oiled black bodies decorated with an assortment of supposedly "African" or "tribal" props. The opening night of *La Revue nègre* staged a series of familiar (yet) exotic settings interrupted by short tap dance numbers and musical solos culminating in the great finale, Baker and Alex's "danse sauvage" in a Harlem nightclub and "Charleston Cabaret" in which Baker appeared entirely nude with just a set of pink feathers draped around her waist and ankles. These highlights of the show were supported by a troupe of nine "Charleston Steppers," backed by a seven-piece "Charleston Jazz Band."[23]

Though largely invented, Baker's "danse sauvage" can be nevertheless traced back to the popularity of two "real" cultural origins which stirred the French "vogue nègre" at the time: first, the publication of the Martinican author René Maran's novel *Batouala,* and second, the ethnographic expedition sponsored by the car manufacturer André Citroën, commonly referred to as *La Croisière noire.* Both the literary evocation of African tradition in

Maran's *Batouala* and the visual inventory (painting, film, as well as photography) produced of "non-assimilated" Africans and their cultural customs during *La Croisière noire* were most famous for their depiction of the so-called Gan'zaa dancers, the annual danced performance of an initiation ritual among the Gan'zaa.[24] In *Batouala*, the literary depiction of the Gan'zaa dancers was famous for a scene entitled "danse de l'amour," in which Yassigui'ndja, Batouala's wife, dances with a wooden phallus around her waist. Maran's novel represented this ritual in an exoticist, erotically charged manner, a projection of sexual transgression that found its popular primitivist correlative in jazz and its corresponding dance moves, the Charleston which, according to the American journalist and Paris correspondent, Joel Rogers who drew this connection, "calls for activity of the whole body."[25]

There was yet another transatlantic link to this scene; it had inspired Countee Cullen's poem "The dance of love," a poetic tribute to the erotic quality of an African woman's body and dancing.[26] The Gan'zaa received their popularity from the erotic and exotic appeal this initiation ritual entailed for a white metropolitan audience. Baker and Alex's bodies were adorned with a cross breed of Caribbean-style jewelry and Oceanic style "tribal" feathers reminiscent of the Gan'zaa dancers as well as of contemporary Afro-Déco jewelry by Parisian designers such as Paul Poiret or Jean Dunand.[27] A similar connection between West African dance and African American jazz and dance was drawn by Joel Rogers in his essay "Jazz at Home" which was filled with primitivist allusions to Parisian "vogue nègre." It addressed the popular metaphor for the jazz craze/"nègromanie" of the time by referring to its sweeping success as an "epidemic contagiousness." And more so, in Rogers's phrasing, jazz became the ultimate emblem of modernity; it represents an Afro-modernist spectacle:

> The direct predecessor of jazz is ragtime. That both are atavistically African
> there is little doubt, but to what extent it is difficult to determine. In its barbaric
> rhythm and exuberance there is something of the bamboula, a wild, abandoned
> dance of the West African and the Haytian Negro, so stirringly described by
> the anonymous author of *Untrodden Fields of Anthropology*, or of the *ganza*
> ceremony so brilliantly depicted in Maran's *Batouala*. But jazz time is faster
> and more complex than African music. With its cowbells, auto horns, calliopes,
> rattles, dinner gongs, kitchen utensils, cymbals, screams, crashes, clankings

and monotonous rhythm it bears all the marks of a nerve-strung, strident, mechanized civilization. It is a thing of the jungles—modern man-made jungles.[28]

In April 1926, Baker starred in a new, this time French musical show at the Folies-Bergère, *La Folie du jour* produced by Paul Derval. In this show, Baker was at once coded as American and as African in a theatricalization of the jazz craze. Preceding Baker's appearance on stage was a series of eight tableaux featuring Parisian shop-windows and eight young white American women who in the process left the stage dressed in the elegant Parisian fashion they selected from the store. Not so Baker in her role as "la sauvage" Fatou. To underline *her* (rather than Fatou's) African origins, she was accordingly submitted to a different setting, that of the African "jungle" featuring a white male ethnologist (identifiable by his tropical helmet) asleep, yet another allusion to the (all-male) ethnographic mission *La Croisière noire*.[29] Dressed in a phallic mock-traditional, mock-African banana skirt, bare-breasted, Baker was most definitely transgressing the social and moral conventions regarding female sexuality at the time. While her quite scandalous appearance made international headlines and, according to Wendy Martin, the American film clip of this dance was touched up so that the scene would meet the censor's requirement that Baker wear a brassiere, Baker's parody frivolously mocked the "Africanization" of metropolitan taste and hence consumption, yet also articulated the African Americanization of French entertainment culture, the "jazz craze" apparently induced by her arrival in Paris.

Around the same time that *La Revue nègre* starred at the Théâtre de Champs-Élysées, Baker and the French illustrator Paul Colin collaborated on a different project: a portfolio of illustrations entitled *Le Tumulte noir*. During the production of *La Revue nègre*, Colin, a poster artist for the music hall of the Théâtre des Champs Élysées, had studied the movements of Baker's body during her performance.[30] In collaboration with Baker, Colin, inspired by what he saw during the rehearsals and performances of *La Revue nègre*, produced a portfolio entitled *Le Tumulte noir* comprising forty-five hand-colored lithographs published in January 1927. It sold out immediately. The narrative and illustrations of *Le Tumulte noir* related the story of the "Charleston epidemic" and captured the modernizing influence of jazz and its aesthetic codes on other artistic media. Baker's performance of the

Charleston was the prime influence on the popularization of these dance moves as a form of public entertainment among Parisians. Montmartre was the center of this Charleston fever, where these new moves that swept across the Atlantic were danced, taught, and passed on in clubs modeled after Harlem's jazz bars and speakeasies. The fascination for the Charleston among the white high society (ridiculed in Colin's *Le Tumulte noir*) had to do with the fact that it represented, as an expression of black culture, an exotic tease. The fact that the Charleston was perceived as an "authentic" form of black American cultural entertainment with "African roots" was significant concerning the primitivist reception of jazz (and its moves) of which *Le Tumulte noir* is a controversial document. The primitivist connotation that characterized the Parisian reception of the Charleston in the 1920s had to do with the fact that the Charleston, danced to a syncopated jazz rhythm, differed from "classic" European dance conventions. Its cultural difference was signaled by the hyperbolic and pelvic-based body movements attributed to its "African roots," a theme that Colin caricatured.

The story that *Le Tumulte noir* told was that of Baker's (i.e., the Charleston's) "minstrelizing" impact upon all kinds of Parisians: from the artistic avant-garde to the French haute bourgeoisie. Colin illustrated this obsession with the Charleston Baker personified by a number of identifiable celebrities of the time satirically depicted in blackface. The preface by Rip, a well-known French critic at the time, mocked common colonial conventions regarding the ethnographic perception and categorization of cultural difference at the time. What was observed and studied in this case was, however, the French cultural phenomenon of "vogue nègre." Rip's text was printed in typescript, Baker's—an ironically inflected authentication strategy—was rendered hand-written, and more or less corresponded to oral speech. Rip's text cast Colin (after all, *Le Tumulte noir* was about a black theatrical genre) in the role of "portraitiste attiré de l'impératrice Joséphine Baker," which purposely resonated with the French national symbol of Napoleon's wife Joséphine, yet most certainly also signified the carnivalistic habit of black artists and political figures of the time to appropriate royal titles. What then followed, according to Rip's rendition, was a musically and performatively induced "black colonization" of French culture, symbolized by the artistic and cultural influence of African American jazz. This racist trope of "black assimilation" represented the satirical inversion of the ideology of the French "mission civilisatrice," namely, a "primitivizing mission" launched by African American jazz musicians and dancers. Baker's Charleston moves—the appearance of her "derrière frénétique"—demarcated the apex of this "black tumult" (Rip's satirical humor not only fed on racist, but also sexist stereotypes). Several of Colin's illustrations even depict Baker having regressed into a monkey under the primitive spell of her dancing.

Though meant as a parodic representation of her performance, such allusions at the time had a deeper and uncanny resonance betraying cultural anxieties linked to the question of race that were on the rise emanating from the more conservative wings of French society: fear of miscegenation. Such nativist tendencies stressed, as Jeffrey H. Jackson has pointed out, a "clearly biological conception of racial categories" particularly raised by the eugenics movement.[31] Jody Blake similarly relates such racial fears unleashed by the growing influence of jazz to conservative nationalist strands in French society that even proclaimed the end of Western civilization and the degeneracy of the white race.[32] It is difficult to determine whether Colin's visual representation of the Charleston craze as equivalent to the inversion of French civilization was meant as a parodic critique of such tendencies or not. He was a true admirer of Baker, yet driven by the most reprehensible racial and sexist fantasies about her. It is telling, though, that the French critic André Levinson is indirectly quoted in Le Tumulte noir: as Jody Blake's scholarship has brought to light, Levinson had published an article in Le Temps in September 1927 in response to the Charleston craze entitled "La danse et l'exotisme" in which he precisely announced the racial inversion of Western civilization.[33] Levinson had attributed "la fureur du Charleston" to Baker's arrival in Paris, and, directly referring to Baker and Joé Alex's performance of "la danse sauvage" in La Revue nègre, not only conceived of their movements as beast-like and primitive ("ce bref pas de deux des 'sauvages' dans le finale, avec Joé Alex, atteint à une grandeur farouche et une superbe bestialité"), but, as Sieglinde Lemke has shown, also compared Baker's "poses"— yet another primitivist stereotype as cultivated by the art connoisseur and dealer Paul Guillaume—to the African sculptor's apparently innate "sens plastique."[34]

In Paul Colin's Le Tumulte noir, the story that is told and the black primitivist stereotypes that were displayed, in several instances of the crudest kind, were both meant satirically. Rip's preface, which equally satirized white primitivist responses to jazz *and* ridiculed the artistry of black performers, packaged its parody of "vogue nègre" in a narrative that symbolically inverts the cultural and racist hegemony of colonialism. "Armed" with the weapon of jazz, African American jazz artists "invade" Paris to "enslave" its citizens who cannot resist this incredibly powerful temptation. Historically, the theatrical practice of blackface minstrelsy, performed by white actors in front of a white (primarily) urban audience, originated during times of slavery in the early nineteenth century, a form of cultural borrowing, as Eric Lott argues, "that ultimately depended on the material relations of slavery."[35] If Rip, and by extension Colin, "minstrelize" the white reception of Baker's performance (i.e., the Charleston) and symbolically render it as a phenomenon of "black assimilation" and even "enslavement," one may wonder about the ethical limits of such a highly questionable type of "humor" that suggests "black power" in terms of cultural influence and (white) entertainment when colonial domination and racist oppression was the reality. Baker's parody of primitivist codes was ambivalent, how she commodified and hyperbolized her "Africanity" was an equally controversial endeavor. Who was deceived, after all, in the satirical scenario that *Le Tumulte noir* unfolded?

Despite this ambivalence Josephine Baker's success in Paris, specifically for her primitivist performance and parody in the black musical shows *La Revue nègre* and *La Folie du jour* illustrates the reception and representation of jazz—jazz as a black musical tradition with African roots—through a primitivist lens among many artists, writers, and intellectuals who resided in Paris at the time. What united them was a—though admittedly often uncritical, often racist—fascination with black cultural difference epitomized by jazz and its performance. The white patrons who sponsored and supported the black artists and the white audience which consumed the art they produced had a very clear and very limited idea of what constituted black culture and a black aesthetic. This idea was often the result of white fantasies about the black Other, the identification with cultures considered non-Western and therefore primitive. The basic assumption behind primitivist modernism was the conflation of cultural and racial essentialism—African descent was considered to be exclusively significant, and turned into a (modernist) abstraction. As a result, this primitivist construction concealed that it was not race, but racism that produced essentialist notions of race and that it was racism, the cultural consequences of slavery, which had produced the uniqueness of African American expressive culture of which Josephine Baker's internationally acclaimed artistic performance was a case in point. Her performance in *La Revue nègre* and *La Folie du jour* drew an international mass audience, and many artists and writers residing in Paris at the time who went to see her, found in her performance more than just mere entertainment, but a modernist style and black aesthetic influenced by and based on the primary organizing principles of jazz—syncopation and improvisation. Josephine Baker transformed her body—Régnier's "un saxophone en mouvement"—into an artistic medium of self-expression. Rather than conforming to the aesthetic dictates of a white audience, she was freely improvising upon them, creating her own distinguished and inimitable style.

NOTES

1. Jeffrey H. Jackson, *Making Jazz French. Music and Modern Life in Interwar Paris* (Durham and London: Duke University Press, 2003), 10.

2. Quoted in Marcel Sauvage, *Les Mémoires de Joséphine Baker*, Recueillis et adaptés par Marcel Sauvage, avec 30 dessins inédits de Paul Colin (Paris, 1927), 20.

3. Eric Hobsbawm, "Jazz Comes to Europe," *Uncommon People. Resistance, Rebellion and Jazz* (New York: The New Press, 1998 [1994]), 266–67.

4. Jack Sullivan, *New World Symphonies* (New Haven and London: Yale University Press, 1999), 235.

5. Jackson, *Making Jazz French*, 2.

6. Jody Blake, *Le Tumulte Noir: Modernist Art and Popular Entertainment in Jazz Age Paris, 1900–1930* (University Park: Pennsylvania State University Press, 2003), 5.

7. Henry Louis Gates, Jr., "James Baldwin and Josephine Baker: an Interview," *Southern Review*, Summer 1985, 597.

8. William A. Shack, *Harlem in Montmartre: A Jazz Story Between the Great Wars* (Berkeley: University of California Press, 2001), 5, 37.

9. Shack, *Harlem in Montmarte*, 37, 44.

10. Eric Lott, *Love and Theft: Blackface Minstrelsy and the American Working Class* (New York: Oxford UP, 1995), 6.

11. Berndt Ostendorf, "Minstrelsy and Early Jazz," *The Massachusetts Review*, vol. 20, no. 3 (1979): 576, 597.

12. Shack, *Harlem in Montmartre*, 9, 28.

13. Petrine Archer-Straw, *Negrophilia. Avant-Garde Paris and Black Culture in the 1920s* (London: Thames and Hudson, 2000), 42.

14. Petrine Archer-Straw, *Negrophilia. Avant-Garde Paris and Black Culture in the 1920s*, 43–44, and Nathan Irvin Huggins, *Harlem Renaissance* (New York: Oxford University Press, 1971), 273.

15. Jody Blake, *Le Tumulte Noir*, 15.

16. John Banting, "The Dancing of Harlem," [1934] in Nancy Cunard, ed., *Negro. An Anthology.* Edited and abridged with an introduction by Hugh Ford (New York: Continuum, 1996), 203.

17. Shack, *Harlem in* Montmartre, 34–35.

18. Tyler Stovall, *Paris noir* (Boston: Houghton Mifflin, 1996), 51.

19. Wendy Martin, "'Remembering the Jungle': Josephine Baker and Modernist Parody," in Elazar Barkan and Ronald Bush, eds., *Prehistories of the Future: The Primitivist Project and the Culture of Modernism* (Stanford: Stanford UP, 1995), 310–11.

20. Henry Louis Gates, Jr., and Karen C. C. Dalton, *Josephine Baker and La Revue nègre: Paul Colin's Lithographs of Le Tumulte noir in Paris, 1927* (New York: H. N. Abrams, 1998), 6. All factual information on *La Revue nègre* (1925) and *La Folie du jour* (1926) has been taken from this source.

21. Ibid.

22. Wendy Martin, "'Remembering the Jungle': Josephine Baker and Modernist Parody," 311.

23. Blake, *Le Tumulte Noir* (1999), 254.

24. The connection between Baker's danse "sauvage" and ethnographic representations of Africans dancing is also analyzed in Blake *Le Tumulte Noir*, 2003 ed., 124–26.

25. Rogers, "Jazz at Home," in Alain Locke, ed., *The New Negro* [1925] (New York: Touchstone Books, 1999), 219.

26. See Michel Fabre, *From Harlem to Paris: Black American Writers in France, 1849–1980* (Urbana: Univ. of Illinois Press, 1991), 150. Written in New York City, Countee Cullen's poem "The dance of love," subtitled "After reading René Maran's BATOUALA," was published below Alain Locke's essay "La jeune poésie africo-américaine" in *Les Continents* (September 1, 1924).

27. Dunand, in fact, depicted Baker in a semi-nude full body portrait wearing the jewelry he designed and posing with a small African object in front of an abstracted decorative jungle background on a panel that was lacquered in imitation of Baker's trendsetting Afro-modern streamlined hairstyle.

28. Rogers, "Jazz at Home," 216–18.

29. From October to December 1926, probably at a time when *La Folie du Jour* was still playing, the "Exposition de la Croisière Noire" took place at the Pavillon de Marsan of the Palais du Louvre.

30. Henry Louis Gates, Jr., and Karen C. C. Dalton, *Josephine Baker and La Revue nègre*, 9.

31. Jeffrey H. Jackson, *Making Jazz French*, 88.

32. Jody Blake, *Le Tumulte Noir*, 86.

33. Blake, 106.

34. André Levinson, "Extrait de la Danse d'aujourd'hui du 1/5/29," in Pepe Abatino, ed., *Josephine Baker vue par la presse française*, 37.

35. Eric Lott, *Love and Theft*, 3.

BIBLIOGRAPHY

Antheil, George. "The Negro on the Spiral." Nancy Cunard, ed., *Negro: An Anthology*. Edited and abridged with an introduction by Hugh Ford (New York: Continuum, 1996), 203–4.

Apollinaire, Guillaume. "Exotisme et Ethnographie." *Paris-Journal* (September 10, 1912).

Appel, Alfred, Jr. *Jazz Modernism. From Ellington and Armstrong to Matisse and Joyce.* New York: Knopf, 2002.

Archer-Straw, Petrine. *Negrophilia. Avant-Garde Paris and Black Culture in the 1920s.* London: Thames and Hudson, 2000.

Bhabha, Homi K. *The Location of Culture.* Routledge: London and New York, 1994.

Banting, John. "The Dancing of Harlem." Nancy Cunard, ed., *Negro. An Anthology,* 203–4.

Barkan, Elazar and Ronald Bush, eds. *Prehistories of the Future: The Primitivist Project and the Culture of Modernism.* Stanford: Stanford UP, 1995.

Barnes, Albert C. "La musique nègre Américaine." *Les Arts à Paris* 12 (1926): 3–7.

Barnes, Albert C. "Negro Art and America." Locke, *New Negro,* 19–29.

Barnwell, Andrea D. "Like the Gipsy's Daughter or Beyond the Potency of Josephine Baker's Eroticism." Powell et al., eds. *Rhapsodies in Black,* 82–90.

Blake, Jody. *Le Tumulte Noir: Modernist Art and Popular Entertainment in Jazz Age Paris, 1900–1930.* University Park: Pennsylvania State University Press, 1999 [hardcover].

Blake, Jody. *Le Tumulte Noir: Modernist Art and Popular Entertainment in Jazz Age Paris, 1900–1930.* University Park: Pennsylvania State University Press, 2003 [paperback].

Blanche, Jacques Emile. *A Propos de Peintre: De Gauguin à la Revue Nègre.* Paris: Emile-Paul Frères, 1928.

Clifford, James. *The Predicament of Culture: Twentieth Century Ethnography, Literature and Art.* Cambridge: Harvard University Press, 1988.

Colin, Paul. *Le Tumulte Noir.* Paris: Éditions d'Art Succès, 1929.

Cunard, Nancy, ed. *Negro. An Anthology.* Edited and abridged with an introduction by Hugh Ford. New York: Continuum, 1996 (1934).

Edwards, Brent Hayes. "The Ethnics of Surrealism." *Transition* 78 (1999): 84–135.

Ezra, Elizabeth. *The Colonial Unconscious: Race and Culture in Interwar France.* Ithaca: Cornell University Press, 2000.

Fabre, Michel. *From Harlem to Paris: Black American Writers in France, 1849–1980.* Urbana: University of Illinois Press, 1991.

Gates, Henry Louis, Jr., and Karen C. C. Dalton. *Josephine Baker and La Revue nègre: Paul Colin's Lithographs of Le Tumulte noir in Paris, 1927.* New York: H. N. Abrams, 1998.

Gates, Henry Louis, Jr. "James Baldwin and Josephine Baker: An Interview," *Southern Review* (Summer 1985).

Gendron, Bernard. *Between Montmartre and Mudd Club.* Chicago and London: University of Chicago Press, 2002.

Hobsbawm, Eric. "Jazz Comes to Europe." *Uncommon People. Resistance, Rebellion and Jazz.* New York: The New Press, 1998 (1994): 265–74.

Huggins, Nathan Irvin. *Harlem Renaissance.* New York: Oxford UP, 1971.

Jackson, Jeffrey H. *Making Jazz French. Music and Modern Life in Interwar Paris.* Durham and London: Duke University Press, 2003.

Lemke, Sieglinde. *Primitivist Modernism. Black Culture and the Origins of Transatlantic Modernism.* Oxford and New York: Oxford University Press, 1998.

Levine, Lawrence. "Jazz and American Culture." O'Meally, ed. *The Jazz Cadence of American Culture,* 431–48.

Levinson, André. "Extrait de la Danse d'aujourd'hui du 1/5/29." Pepe Abatino, ed. *Josephine Baker vue par la presse française:* 37.

Locke, Alain, ed. *The New Negro.* New York: Touchstone Books, 1999 (1925).

Lott, Eric. *Love and Theft: Blackface Minstrelsy and the American Working Class.* New York: Oxford UP, 1995.

Martin, Wendy. "'Remembering the Jungle'": Josephine Baker and Modernist Parody." Barkan and Bush, eds. *Prehistories of the Future*, 310–26.

Ogren, Kathy J. *The Jazz Revolution. Twenties American and the Meaning of Jazz.* New York and Oxford: Oxford University Press, 1989.

O'Meally, Robert G., ed. *The Jazz Cadence of American Culture.* New York: Columbia University Press, 1998.

Ostendorf, Berndt. "Minstrelsy and Early Jazz." *The Massachusetts Review* 20.3 (1979): 574–602.

Ostendorf, Berndt. "Double Consciousness Revisited: African American Expressive Culture and the Dilemma of Interpretation." *Sources* 11 (Autumn 2001): 57–84.

Powell, Richard J., et al., ed. *Rhapsodies in Black: Art of the Harlem Renaissance.* Berkeley: University of California Press, 1997.

Rogers, Joel A. "Jazz at Home." Locke, *New Negro* 216–25.

Sauvage, Marcel. *Les Mémoires de Joséphine Baker.* Recueillis et adaptés par Marcel Sauvage, avec 30 dessins inédits de Paul Colin. Paris, 1927.

Sauvage, Marcel. *Voyages et aventures de Joséphine Baker.* Paris: M. Seheur, 1932.

Shack, William A. *Harlem in Montmartre: A Jazz Story Between the Great Wars.* Berkeley: University of California Press, 2001.

Shaw, Arnold. *The Jazz Age. Popular Music in the 1920s.* New York and Oxford: Oxford University Press, 1987.

Stovall, Tyler. *Paris Noir: African Americans in the City of Light.* Boston: Houghton Mifflin, 1996.

Sullivan, Jack. *New World Symphonies.* New Haven and London: Yale University Press, 1999.

8

Paul Robeson's British Journey

— SEAN CREIGHTON

One of the great inspirational figures of the twentieth century, the African American actor, singer, and political activist Paul Robeson was a frequent visitor and resident in Britain, and in turn Britain was an important influence on Robeson's singing, acting, and politics. He linked politics and culture in support of 1930s political campaigns against fascism and colonialism which then set the ground back in the United States for his political campaigning for black rights and colonial freedom during and after the Second World War. In the period of the Cold War he was victimized for these and his peace and anti-nuclear activities by the American authorities, but he continued to have many friends and admirers in Britain and elsewhere in Europe even after his death in 1976.

This essay outlines key events in Robeson's visits to and residence in Britain, its significance on his personal development, and the effect he had on those who heard and saw him act and sing. It also examines Robeson in the context of what he called "Negro" music and of organized black and anti-racist activity in Britain. It concludes with a discussion on his continuing relevance.[1]

Robeson, "Negro" Music, and Racism

Robeson was deeply rooted in spirituals, gospel, hymns, ragtime ballad, and blues as well as mainstream white American and British popular songs.[2] In the early 1920s he specialized in singing Negro spirituals and popular songs. He had reservations about U.S. black audience demands for the inclusion in his programs of German, French, and Continental classics. He feared "the eventual obliteration of their own folk-music."[3] But as he studied Negro and other music from around the world he saw links between African American and other folk musics. In 1939 he explained that while he had thought of himself as a concert artist, he was now "best as a singer of folksongs."[4] Robeson's own personal list of significant black composers, musicians and singers included Marian Anderson, Roland Hayes, William Handy, Samuel Coleridge-Taylor, Henry Burleigh, Nathaniel Dett, William Dawson, William Grant Still, Duke Ellington, Billie Holiday, Ethel Waters, Florence Mills, Bert Williams, Bessie Smith, Bill Robinson, Eddie Rector, Teddy Wilson, Turner Layton, Johnny Dunn, Hall Johnson, Will Marion Cook, Count Basie, Mahalia Jackson, Josephine Baker, Wayland Rudland, and Louis Armstrong.[5]

When he first came to Britain in 1922 there was a lively following for black musicians, singers, and dancers. Robeson stayed in the flat of John Payne, a black American who had originally come over in 1919 with the Southern Syncopated Orchestra led by Will Marion Cook. Here he met the black American pianist and arranger Lawrence Brown. Meeting again in New York in 1925 a life-long association as singer and accompanist began. For Brown, Robeson's was "the voice of the Negro people," "true with all the half-tones, the indefinable rhythm, the colors," "that ranged from a velvety black bass up to the tonal scale to light, clear, translucent overtones."[6]

Other contributors to this volume have shown that Afro-American performers in Europe were caught in a dilemma about how to present their music—in its original and raw form or to soften it by "Europeanizing" it. This was also Robeson's predicament. The rawer performance forms like cakewalk and early jazz, seem to have had three main sets of reactions among different groups of their white European audiences: enjoyment, moralistic horror, and "racism." Enjoyment could come in two forms: comic appreciation, and a sense of racial superiority. For those who simply enjoyed the comic aspects could this have been the same kind of enjoyment as of the cruder antics and songs of some white musical hall performers? These enabled music hall audiences to join in—singing along and laughing. There is some evidence emerging that there was a spectrum in British audience responses to blackface minstrelsy from the racist to the sympathetic and empathetic.[7] The songs that particularly seem to reveal sympathy and empathy are those of Stephen Foster, a white American songwriter on black themes. Robeson was just one of many black artists to perform these songs.

Perhaps the key to positive identification lies in what Robeson wrote in 1958: "The *power of spirit* that our people have is intangible. . . . A spirit of steadfast determination, exaltation in the face of trials—it is the very soul of our people that has been formed through all the long and weary years of our march toward freedom. That spirit lies in our people's songs—in the sublime grandeur of 'Deep River,' in the driving power of 'Jacob's Ladder,' in the militancy of 'Joshua Fit the Battle of Jericho,' and in the poignant beauty of all our spirituals."[8]

The tradition of adopting a more European classical concert approach was started by the Fisk Jubilee Singers from the 1870s. They found that by being dressed in formal clothing and singing a refined form of spirituals they generated considerable enjoyment and respect from their European white audiences, something they were not used to in the United States. They set the approach for many who were to follow, like Roland Hayes. This style meant that audiences listened rather than joined in, as if at a classical music or operatic performance.

Robeson adopted the concert and recital approach, his audiences listening in awe and reverence. This approach, however, seems to be in contradiction to his views about the difference between Negro music as a folk music rooted in feeling and the European classical approach rooted in thinking. Whether he was aware of this is not clear. He knew the limitations of his own voice. The concert style fitted him best. He knew that he could not adequately sing most opera, and when he recorded the bluesy "King Joe" backed by the Count Basie Orchestra, Basie commented that Robeson could not sing the blues.[9]

The ecstatic reception that many American black performers including Robeson received over the decades has raised the question of whether people could separate these performers' "blackness" from their singing or playing, allowing listeners still to be racist in their reactions to black people living in Britain. When Robeson himself experienced racism at the Savoy Hotel in 1929 there was shock in certain quarters. The press was full of the case and the matter was taken up with Prime Minister Ramsay MacDonald. West African and West Indian students were particularly active at a protest meeting. Paul became a patron of the West African Students Union. The incident prompted the *Daily Herald* to publish an article assessing the "present position and the future prospects of the negro in New York and the United States."[10] Examples of racial discrimination of course continued. A year later an editor walked out of Robeson's performance of *Othello*. He had clearly gone there to watch a black man perform, but walked out because he did not like sitting near "coloured people," of whom there were many in the audience.[11]

There were many people whose political, liberal, humanitarian, and religious beliefs led them to oppose racial prejudice. When owners and managers banned Africans and Asians from certain dance halls in the 1920s there were those in the white population who opposed their actions as being racially discriminating.[12] There has been a long history of solidarity and anti-racism in Britain running alongside and countering racism. There were probably even more people who while not actively opposing, were non-racist in their attitudes and behavior.

This polarity of views towards black people includes on the one hand the welcome reception in Wales of the Fisk Jubilee Singers and the groups that spun off from it before the First World War and the long love affair between Robeson and Wales, and on the other the race riots in Cardiff (and elsewhere) in 1919 and the ghettoization of the black community in Bute Town. Later similar issues were raised by the rise of popular interest in jazz and blues at the same time as the outbreak of race violence as in Notting Hill in London in 1958. Robeson recognized the polarity of views when he commented on those riots.[13]

Robeson in Britain

Robeson first came to Britain in 1922 to appear in *Voodoo*, a play in which he had already appeared in New York. Because of his singing his personal reception was greater than that for the play itself. Appearing in the London production of Eugene O'Neill's *Emperor Jones* in 1925, the script called for him to whistle a tune. As he could not whistle he sang a Spiritual. On the first night he was called back a dozen times, and had to make a speech. Closing night was a prolonged personal ovation to him. In late 1925 his first American recordings were released in England. He and his wife Eslanda found England "warm and friendly and unprejudiced" compared to the States, and they could dine at any public place. They were accepted into London's high society.

Six years later Robeson was back to play Joe in the London production of the Jerome Kern and Oscar Hammerstein musical *Show Boat* singing "Ol' Man River." Audiences were ecstatic about his performances. Robeson also undertook concert and private and public recital work.[14] *Show Boat* closed in early March 1929. After a tour of Europe, he sold out the Albert Hall, and then toured a number of British cities. During this visit he met some unemployed miners who had marched from Wales to publicize their plight. He spent several days in South Wales with them. He used his *Show Boat* earnings to give food and clothing for the children. These experiences led to his identification with the working class, an increasing desire to perform to working class audiences, and his politicization.

His early 1930 tour included performances at the Albert Hall in February, and Glasgow and Birmingham in March. While visiting Canterbury Robeson delighted his host Cathedral Dean Dick Sheppard with his rendition of "Were You There When They Crucified My Lord?"[15] After a trip to Europe, rehearsals began for *Othello*. The day after the opening on May 19, the *Daily Express* headlined "Paul Robeson's Triumph in Othello." "He triumphed as a negro Moor. . . . When his rage came it was magnificent. He threw himself on the floor in apoplexy, and it was a terrible fall. His jealousy was terrible to see." There were some complaints about a white actress and a black actor kissing. This was ironic given that Robeson's attraction to *Othello* was based on his belief that Shakespeare "was able to get to the root of the racial question."[16]

In the last months of 1930 he visited various cities and towns, including Manchester and Leeds, performing scenes from plays as well as singing.[17] After another trip to the States, he was back in 1931 for O'Neill's play *The Hairy Ape*, in which he was a ship's stoker. The play was cut short by his becoming ill. After starring in a revival of *Show Boat*, he was in England again in September 1932. These hectic two and a half years proved a severe strain on his marriage, especially as he was having affairs. It nearly ended in divorce, but he and Eslanda were able to rebuild their relationship. Early 1933 saw him in *All God's Chillun* directed by Andre van Gyseghem. Then back to the States for a film version of *Emperor Jones*. On his return Britain became more or less his permanent base until the outbreak of war. These were the years of his growing politicization and popularity, and his entry into British film-making.

Robeson's political development appears to have taken a significant leap forward in response to the Nazi attacks on Jews from 1933, reinforced by the racism he and Eslanda experienced traveling through Nazi Germany in December 1934 en route to the Soviet Union. The warm welcome they received there began his identification with the latter. A year later he attended the London meeting of the Congress of Peace and Friendship with the USSR which had a wide-ranging audience.[18] The anti-fascist environment of the British left nurtured his increasing involvement in politics. Lending his artistry to a range of political causes did not appear to damage his broad popular appeal.

A key attraction of Britain was clearly the reception he received and his effect on his British listeners. As early as 1930 the BBC's *Radio Times* magazine said that his broadcast recitals were "among the most popular of all programmes." This popularity is evidenced by the reception on his tours, and in the 1937 vote for him as the most popular radio singer. He undertook a number of nationwide tours and other performances outside London, and was frequently broadcast on BBC radio. His picture was front page of *The Radio Times* advertising a program of him singing on New Year's Eve 1933.[19] In January 1934 he was at Sheffield City Hall singing spirituals and traditional Russian, Hebrew, Slavonic, English, Scotch, and Welsh folk songs, and sea shanties. Three thousand people attended, five hundred having to sit on the stage behind him. He performed in seventeen towns and cities in February and March 1934, attracting huge crowds. The 1935 tour included thirteen concerts, the 1936 one lasted from January to April, and the 1939 tour took place in the summer.[20]

From 1934 Robeson began to act in British-made films, and these broadened his popularity. The first was *Sanders of the River*. Robeson was very happy with his role as an African chief, but when it was released in 1935, however, it had scenes that had been added without his knowledge glorifying the Empire and colonialism. He distanced himself from it and later disowned it. Many British filmgoers do not appear to have seen the film in this light.[21] After the experience with *Sanders* he tried to exercise more control over the films he starred in. 1936 saw *Song of Freedom*, in which he played a London-born dock worker, who goes to Africa. 1937 saw *Big Fella* (based on the novel *Banjo* by the Jamaican-born Claude McKay), *King Solomon's Mines*, and *Jericho*.[22]

The period from 1935 to 1939 saw increasing fascist aggression: the Italian and Japanese invasions of Abyssinia and China and the German and Italian support for the Franco rebellion in Spain. Robeson became an active supporter of campaigns against these aggressions, such as the League Against Aggressor Nations, the China Campaign Committee, and the Aid Spain movement.[23] The formation of Unity Theatre, a group with branches across Britain formed in 1936 to produce theater for and by working people, enabled him to act in front of politically left-wing working-class audiences. In 1938 he turned down West End roles to appear in its production of Ben Bengal's *Plant in the Sun* about a strike in a New York sweet factory. He went on supporting Unity in many ways, including tutoring at its night classes.[24]

Robeson clearly stirred his political audiences. Reporting the June 1938 Youth Rally my father, Campbell Creighton, wrote, "Paul Robeson caught the spirit best.... He sang 'How Long, O Lord?,' 'Old Man Ribber,' the Chinese national Anthem. The whole hall rose to its feet like one man. It was amazing. It made a little shiver run down your spine." This was followed by the "The Soviet Fatherland Song," and the "Himmo de Riego" (the Spanish National Anthem). "And again the audience rose.... And how it cheered when Robeson finished, and raising his great fist, cried 'Salud!'" To advertise the Rally his records were played from loudspeaker vans.[25]

Support for the cause of the Spanish Republic became a major focus of Robeson's political activity. 1937 saw an April concert in aid of homeless men and women in Spain, and in December two concerts and a broadcast to Spain. On December 19 he appeared at the Labour Party's Justice-for-Spain rally at the Albert Hall. At the Albert Hall Rally in aid of Basque children in June 1937 he stated: "The artist ... must elect to fight for freedom or slavery. I have made my choice. I had no alternative."[26] He made a record of *Sometimes I feel like a Motherless Child* for the Basque Children's Fund and visited Spain in early 1938. A rally was held in January 1939 at the Earls Court Empress Hall to welcome back the British International Brigaders from Spain, and commemorate those who had died. With nine thousand people inside and hundreds outside, "Paul Robeson's singing roused the gathering in wild enthusiasm."[27]

Robeson's last British feature film was *The Proud Valley* set in a Welsh mining community. It was not released until March 1940 by which time he was back in the United States because of the War. BBC radio broadcast a sixty-minute version of the soundtrack, the first time it had premiered a film. He continued to show his support for the British working classes and for left-wing causes during the war when he sent a message of support to the broad left People's Convention in January 1941.[28] He also continued to have a wide audience in Britain: in 1944 ten million listened to the BBC radio broadcast of him in *The Man Who Went to War*, a ballad opera by the black American Langston Hughes.

After the war, Robeson's political affiliations caused increasing difficulties for him in the United States as the Cold War intensified and the McCarthyite witch-hunting of actual and alleged Communists reached its heights. Following the cancellation of eighty-five concerts he returned to Britain in February 1949. It was something like a triumphal procession. His concerts were sell-outs. "The English public seemed as fond if not fonder of Paul than ever."[29] Robeson used his visit to highlight the case of the Trenton six, black Americans convicted and sentenced to death by an all-white jury for the murder of a white shop-keeper. He also visited the offices of the New International society where he sang to crowds gathered in the street.[30]

Robeson was active in a number of peace movements. He was a member of the International Liaison Committee that co-sponsored the Congress of the World Partisans for Peace in Paris in April 1949, for which Picasso painted his famous peace dove. Robeson sang and made some brief remarks and afterwards he supported the report-back meetings organized by the British Cultural Committee for Peace. Due to misreporting his remarks caused an uproar in the States. Racist mobs attacked two outdoor concerts he was performing at in Peekskill in New York State, while the police stood by. "I'm going to sing wherever the people want me to sing ... and I won't be frightened by crosses burning in Peekskill or anywhere else."[31] In 1950 he was back in Britain where he sang for the World Peace Council to twenty thousand people in Lincoln's Inn Fields.

His political activities and the anti-Communist hysteria in the States led in July 1950 to the U.S. government confiscating his passport. This was probably welcomed by the British Foreign Office. In a review of international student and youth groups which it regarded to be Soviet front organizations, it commented: "The latest collaborator is Paul Robeson." However, supporters in Britain took a leading part in the campaign to have his passport reinstated including the Scottish TUC, Equity, leading musicians, and the Workers' Sports Association. In Manchester in early 1956 one thousand attended a "Let Paul Robeson Sing" protest, to which he sent a message. He cabled the national Conference held in May. A national Committee was formed and a second national Conference held in Manchester in December.[32]

Enforced internment did not prevent ways being found to sing outside the borders of the United States. At the end of his transatlantic transmission of six songs to a day of celebration in London, the one-thousand-strong audience jumped out of their seats to shouts of approval. Robeson was "deeply moved" and towards the end of the concert "he was close to tears," thrilled at the prospect of "a new means for communication from the jailhouse." October 1957 saw a similar link up to the Welsh Miners' Eisteddfod.[33]

In June 1958 the Supreme Court ruled that the Secretary of State had no right to deny a passport to any citizen because of his political beliefs. With the return of his passport, the first country Robeson visited was Britain. As he left the States an anti-Robeson columnist wrote that he was "willing to bet" the British would meet him in the "spirit of heyday derision." He would have lost the bet. When his plane touched down in London on July 11 Robeson and Eslanda were met by two hundred friends and fans who shouted "Hip' hip' hooray," and sang "For he's a jolly good fellow." The *News Chronicle* reporter said that the press conference held later that day was the most remarkable he had ever attended.[34] Robeson was full of gaiety and excitement about his future.

His ten-year absence had not dulled Robeson's popularity. The coming weeks were a personal triumph. There are all kinds of touching snippets. A charwoman greeted him on an early morning walk; people on their way to work rushed up to shake his hand; a cab driver refused with indignation to accept payment. Robeson was euphoric at the reception he was getting. Tea and lunch with politicians, a signing party at Selfridges for his book *Here I Stand*, parties and events at embassies and private homes, a half hour "Paul Robeson Sings" on TV, and a sell-out concert at the Albert Hall were just some of the activities. He was at the Welsh Miners' Eisteddfod again in August. William Gallagher, the former Communist MP, wrote "Salute to Paul Robeson" for *Labour Monthly*, the journal edited by leading Communist Party theoretician Rajani Palme Dutt. In October he sang at St. Paul's Cathedral for the defense and aid fund established for those arraigned at the treason trials in South Africa; four thousand inside, five thousand outside. He was "mobbed" the moment he started leaving with people wanting to kiss him and shake his hand. "This is an heroic moment in my life. I am terribly moved by the tremendous demonstration for me. I came close to tears about it."[35]

A national tour covered the major British cities. At Blackburn children, teenagers, housewives, business and working men, and old people queued up for him to sign programs, autograph books, pieces of paper, and copies of his book. Enthusiastic fans "mobbed" him on his arrival in Sheffield. The capacity audience was "enthralled," "completely captivated." At Newcastle one of the audience wrote on their program "Thanks to God for sight and hearing. Grateful for return of so talented an artist."[36]

Then it was off to Moscow before the start of another British tour between September 21 and December 6. Another trip to Moscow and back to rehearse *Othello* at Stratford in February 1959, the month that also saw the first performance at the Albert Hall of *The World is His Song* by the Communist composer Alan Bush. Although *Othello* ran from April to November, Robeson found time in June to sing at an anti–H bomb rally in Trafalgar Square. The BBC recorded a radio series, and showed the *Paul Robeson Story* on TV. Fan mail flooded in. A second nationwide tour took place from February to May 1960 covering thirty-two cities. He also attended the funeral of the British Communist Party leader Harry Pollitt.[37]

Despite his successes, it was at this time that Robeson began to suffer bouts of depression. A tour of Australia and New Zealand from October proved difficult. The depression deepened as he journeyed back and forth between London and the Soviet Union, finally being admitted to the Priory, the private hospital in Roehampton, where his treatment involved ECT and drugs. His health spiraled up and down. It did not prevent him agreeing to be president of the Pete Seeger Committee, supporting the American left-wing folk singer who had been with him at Peekskill. Seeger was on bail pending his appeal against a ten-year sentence for contempt of Congress.[38] On good days Robeson was able to venture out, as in March 1962 when he saw Peggy Ashcroft and John Gielgud in *The Cherry Orchard*. A sympathetic visiting American doctor was appalled by the treatment at the Priory. With the help of British and East German friends, arrangements were made to send him to a clinic in the GDR. Because the *Sunday Telegraph* suggested he was going to be abducted, a clandestine operation had to be mounted to get Robeson away, with the press waiting outside the flat and the hospital.[39]

While in the GDR Paul decided to return to the States stopping off in London just before Christmas to collect things from his flat. Back in the States he never recovered his health and went into retirement. His seventieth birthday was celebrated at the Purcell Room on the South Bank in April 1968 in an evening of music, poetry, and drama. The Belfast Trades Council sent him a birthday present. His death on January 23, 1976, was widely reported in the British press.[40]

Robeson and Black and Anti-Colonial Politics and Culture in Britain

Interwar Britain had many black people living in cities like Cardiff, Liverpool, Manchester, and London. The 1919 race riots had boosted black organizational development, such as the African Progress Union. Union President John Archer had been a leading black Progressive and then Labour activist in Battersea since 1906, and Mayor in 1913/14.[41] He took part in the first postwar Pan African Conference organized by the black American activist W. E. B. Du Bois in London. 1922 saw the Indian Shapurji Saklatvala elected as Battersea's MP. William Miller was becoming a leading Labour figure in Plymouth.[42] There were black networks with which new arrivals from the United States, the Caribbean, and Africa could connect. Robeson made many connections and contributed to black political and cultural activity in Britain.

He and Eslanda became close friends of the British-based popular American black entertainers Turner Layton and Tandy Johnstone. He met Amanda Ira Aldridge, the British black composer and pianist and daughter of the great Victorian black actor Ira Aldridge. She gave him the earrings her father had worn playing Othello, and hoped that Paul would play the role. In 1928 Paul and Eslanda watched the West Indian Learie Constantine play cricket at the Oval, saw Layton and Johnstone at the Alhambra Music Hall, and heard Samuel Coleridge-Taylor's *Hiawatha* performed at the Royal Albert Hall. In 1930 Aldridge gave him diction and voice training for the part of *Othello*. In 1933 he enrolled at the School of Oriental Studies to study African linguistics. This led him to write further about African American culture.[43]

The 1930s were years of a new phase of black organization in Britain, including the League of Coloured Peoples led by the Peckham doctor Harold Moody, the International African Service Bureau, the Negro Welfare Association, and the International African Friends of Abyssinia, involving activists like C. L. R. James, Peter Blackman (the West Indian activist who was later to be organizer of Robeson's 1949 British tour), Robert Broadhurst, George Padmore, and Peter Milliard.[44] Robeson had links with these activists. On December 12, 1934, he addressed a League meeting on "The Negro in the Modern World." Although advertised to open the League's Bazaar in March 1935, he does not seem to have been able to as Sail Rodgers and John Payne provided the singing at it. At the 1938 Youth Rally at which Robeson sang, Peter Blackman "appealed for unity with the colonial people." In June 1938 Robeson took part in the India League meeting welcoming Nehru to London. Before singing he said: "The struggles that are going on in China, India, Abyssinia, and Spain are one. The struggle of the colonial people is a struggle for democracy and freedom for all."[45]

Robeson's films gave opportunities as actors and extras to black Americans, Africans, and West Indians living in London, including the American Elizabeth Welch and Jomo Kenyatta, who became the first President of Kenya.[46] Robeson was criticized for the way Africans were portrayed in *Sanders* by the black nationalist Marcus Garvey. Writing in the League's newsletter "G.M." thought Robeson was "completely wasted" in it. "In fact the whole cast—many of whom you will recognise—has been sacrificed to make room for some news-reel pictures of Africa, and some fine opportunities for real Negro acting have been withheld." But he concluded: "Still, if only to hear Paul Robeson sing, and to see some good Negro dancing, you should see this film." One of the film extras, Napoleon Florent, who had been out of work for six years, also pointed out that "*Sanders of the River* pays the rent and puts food on the table."[47]

In response to black criticism Robeson explained that he thought that the cinema was the most important medium for his work, and that he could best do this in England where he would not have to fight against the attempts of Hollywood to typecast him. His personal dissatisfaction with the roles he was offered led to his decision to stop appearing in films until he was given a part that did not degrade his people. However, in an assessment years later Sidney Poitier stressed the positive impact Robeson "had on the role of blacks in the (film) industry."[48]

Robeson told the *Observer* April 1935 that he "would like to found a negro [sic] theatre."[49] In the absence of one he worked with left-wingers in the theater, like Andre van Gysengham who directed him in *Stevedore*; Lawrence Brown and John Payne were also involved. More in tune with his aspirations was his role in January 1936 as Toussaint L'Ouverture, the leader of the Haitian revolt against French colonial rule. The play's author, the Trinidadian C. L. R. James, had come to Britain in 1932 and quickly got to know and become friends with Robeson. James was profoundly impressed by Robeson's views as published in *The Spectator* in 1934 which helped change James's perception of black identity. Their friendship was not disrupted by James's Trotskyism.[50]

Robeson's association with Unity Theatre helped lead to further opportunities for black actors. Because Robeson was in the States in July 1939 Unity cast Guyana-born Robert Adams in the main role in *Colony*, a play about a strike in Jamaica. Adams had starred in Robeson's films and was his understudy in *Proud Valley*. Unity continued to work with black actors through and after the War, helping the start of black theater in Britain. Robeson was able to connect with many postwar black actors and singers including Trinidadians Edric and Pearl Connor, and Nadia Cattouse from the British Honduras.[51]

In wartime and postwar United States Robeson was a leading member of the American Council on African Affairs, which supported the anti-colonial struggle. The British Foreign Office was not happy about his anti-colonialism. It linked Robeson's tour of Jamaica and Trinidad in 1948 to increased Communist activity in Trinidad. In 1949 the anti-colonial newspaper *New Africa* was referred to as "Paul Robeson's paper." This was the year that he wrote the foreword to Amanke Okafor's book *Nigeria—Why We Fight for Freedom*.[52] Not surprisingly, anti-colonialism was often associated with the Left and in the 1950s the British Communist Party called its branches among West Africans "Robeson" branches.[53] His continuing support for anti-colonialism included singing and speaking at the April 1959 African Freedom Day concert organized by the Movement for Colonial Freedom, of which he became a sponsor. At it he said : "Let nobody tell you that I'm just an artist in the void. I am fighting for the freedom of all Africans. . . . The struggle is not one of individual people. It is a collective struggle."[54]

Robeson saw the battle for his right to travel in the 1950s as linked to the wider cause of freedom: "From the days of chattel slavery until today, the concept of *travel* has been inseparably linked in the minds of our people with the concept of *freedom.* Hence, the symbol of a railroad train recurs frequently in our folklore. . . . And there are boats. . . . "[55]

His 1958 return to Britain included functions hosted by Indian journalists and the Nigerian Minister of Internal Affairs. During the tour around the United Kingdom he attended a mill children's party in Huddersfield. A photograph shows him party hat on his head with six-year-old Robert Barker and four-year-old Raashida Qureshi sitting on his lap. His previous support for the cause of Indian freedom saw the celebration of his birthday in 1958 in India. This prompted the American State Department to try to dissuade the Indian Government from letting Robeson visit India.[56]

In defense of freedom Robeson continued his association with people deemed persona non grata by the U.S. State Department. While in Moscow he let his American friend and political comrade W. E. B. Du Bois and his wife stay in his Maida Vale flat. His friendship in the States with the black Communist Claudia Jones was rekindled in Britain to where she had been deported. In 1959 he supported her activities centered around the *West Indian Gazette:* receptions for him in June and July 1959 at Lambeth and St. Pancras Town Halls, the *Gazette's* Anniversary Concert, and an evening with Robeson. At a *Gazette* Concert in 1960 Robeson advocated "art as a weapon for freedom, be it in Africa, the Caribbean Cuba or British Guiana." A recorded message from him and Eslanda was played at Jones's funeral in January 1965. He lent his name to her Memorial Committee, and sent a recorded message to her Memorial Meeting at St. Pancras Town Hall in February.[57]

The Development of His Repertoire

Robeson underwent his own musical, cultural, and political voyage of discovery. His time in Britain was central to this. His musical journey started with his family singing "Down by the Old Mill Stream," "Turkey in the Straw," "Silent Night," and "Annie Laurie". His progressed through church choir, school glee club, and university. His musicality was cemented in the Negro community of Princeton, with its "warmth of song. Songs of love and longing, songs of trials and triumphs, deep-flowing rivers and rollicking brooks, hymn-song and ragtime ballad, gospels and blues, and the healing comfort to be found in the illimitable sorrow of the spirituals."[58]

Lawrence Brown introduced him to a staggeringly broad range of European, African, Brazilian, and Caribbean music, to which Robeson added music from China and the Far East.[59] Robeson studied and thought carefully about the nature of Negro song and culture. He regarded Negro music as a form of folk-song with much in common with folk-song in other parts of the world. He spoke and wrote about this throughout his life.[60] His studies at the School of Oriental Studies deepened his understanding.

Robeson's personal manifesto *Here I Stand* was published in 1958. He reflected on his life, his approach to songs and his aspirations for the Negro race. As well as outlining his views on Negro culture and folk music, he argued for a non-violent crusade for freedom:

> Americans who wish for peace among nations—and I believe the vast majority of them do—can join with my people in singing our old-time song—
>
> I'm going to lay down my sword and shield
> Down by the riverside . . .
> I'm going to study war no more![61]

His belief in the unifying power of song is central to his broad appeal. In his singing he championed the cause of the common man. "In your search for freedom you experience a common bond between the suffering and oppressed folks of the worlds, that folk music is universal and that folks are alike everywhere."[62]

Through his mixed programs of songs from different parts of the world he introduced large numbers of people to the product of "world music" long before the concept was reinvented in recent times: "It may well be that today, after many fascinating and rewarding digressions, we are flowing back into the mainstream of world music—which includes the music of Asia, Africa, Europe and the Americas—with a future potential of immense musical wealth, all going to and taking from each other through this wonderful world bank of music."[63]

Robeson's Continuing Relevance

Today Britain's most deprived neighborhoods are not only home to 70 percent of the country's black and ethnic minority population, but also of deep-seated racism, ignorance, and intolerance among some of their white British residents. Action against deprivation and racism has to go hand in hand. This can partly be done through an increase in public work about the contribution of black and ethnic minorities in Britain's historic development. Robeson is an important part of that story. Using today's language Robeson not only stood for black culture and rights, anti-racism, social justice, multicultural-ism, and peace, but for something more. In *Here I Stand* he quoted Marx's statement: "Labor in a white skin can never be free while labor in a black skin is branded."[64] His life and work was devoted to the struggle for Negro rights and freedom, *and* the mutual benefit white people would gain from it. Song was a central tool through which he was able to reach people regardless of race or nationality. It is this that is one of the motivating reasons for the continued commemoration of Robeson in Britain since his death. Among the many celebrations were: 1978: James Earl Jones played Paul Robeson at the Haymarket; 1979: BBC 2 TV *Paul Robeson Story*; 1984: exhibitions by the Greater London Council and in Wales; 1985 & 1986: visits by Paul Robeson, Jr.; 1998: Birthday Commemorations; 2002: Cleo Lane unveiling of an English Heritage blue plaque on his 1929–30 Hampstead home, and the Manic Street Preachers' record *Let Robeson Sing*; 2003: Exhibition, National Library of Wales; 2004: Manchester cab driver Charles Ngandwe won ITV television's "Stars in Their Eyes" with a rousing rendition of "Ol' Man River"; 2005: the Stratford-upon-Avon Music Festival's "Paul Robeson Story: The Search for Ol' Man River." Similar celebrations have taken place across the world. Like the murdered trade union activist sung about in "Joe Hill," another of his hallmark songs, Robeson still lives comforting and inspiring people through his music.

NOTES

1. The two key biographical studies of Robeson are: Martin Bauml Duberman, *Paul Robeson: A Biography* (New York: The New Press, 1989), and Paul Robeson Jr., *The Undiscovered Paul Robeson: An Artist's Journey, 1898–1939* (New York: Wiley, 2001).

2. Paul Robeson, *Here I Stand* (London: Denis Dobson, 1958), 23.

3. "Paul Robeson and Negro Music," Interview. *The New York Times*, April 5, 1931, repro-duced in Philip S. Foner, ed., *Paul Robeson Speaks. Writings Speeches Interviews 1918–1974* (New York: Quartet Books, 1978), 81–82.

4. "A Great Negro Artist Puts His Genius to Work for His People," Interview by Eugene Gordon, *Sunday Worker* (USA), June 4, 1939, reproduced in Foner, 127–30.

5. *Songs of My People. Soviet Music,* no. 7, July 1949, and *The Negro Artist Looks Ahead,* Speech, November 5, 1951. *Masses & Mainstream,* January 1952, both in Foner, *Paul Robeson Speaks,* 217, 298–305, and *Here I Stand,* 79–80.

6. Rye and Green, "Black Musical Internationalism in England in the 1920s," *Black Music Research Journal,* vol. 15, no. 1 (1995): 93; See also, Stephen Bourne, *Black in the British Frame. Black People in British Film and Television. 1896–1996* (London: Cassell, 1998), 86–69, and Mary Seton, 1958 Concert Tour 1958 program.

7. Michael Pickering, "The Blackface Clown," in Gretchen Holbrook Gerzina, ed., *Black Victorians. Black Victoriana* (New Brunswick & London: Rutgers, 2003), 159–74.

8. *Here I Stand,* 108.

9. Robeson sang and recorded "St. Louis Blues" by W. C. Handy, the bluesy "King Joe" by Richard Wright and Count Basie. The Africana website contains a note "Did Paul Robeson Ever Sing the Blues?" "King Joe" was written by Richard Wright following black boxer Joe Louis's victory in 1941, with music composed by Basie. According to the note Basie whispered to the recording director John Hammond that Robeson did not have an ear for the blues. The *New York Times* said it was "mighty good jazz." (Quoted Hazel Rowley, *Richard Wright. The Life and Times* (New York: Henry Holt & Co. 2001). Stan Britt, author of *Frank Sinatra: A Celebration* (London: Hamlyn Books, 1995), states: "Richard Wright's dedicatory King Joe is sung with predictable Robeson commitment, supported with equally predictable potency by the Council Basie Orchestra." Notes to CD *The Inimitable Paul Robeson* (Parade, PAR 2065. 1996).

10. *Manchester Guardian,* October 23, 1929, *Daily Herald,* October 24, 1929; Hakim Adi, "West Africans and the CP in the 1950s," in Geoff Andrews, Nina Fishman, and Kevin Morgan, eds., *Opening the Books. Essays on the Social and Cultural History of the British Communist Party* (London: Pluto, 1995), f.21, 193.

11. *Daily Express,* May 20, 1930.

12. For example the Streatham Locarno, *Norwood News,* November 1 & 8, 1929.

13. John Williamson, *London Letter. The Worker* (U.S.), October 19, 1958. "I am glad that the majority of the British people and especially the Labour Movement, recognised the need is for unity of all peoples and was sure they would not allow continued attacks on West Indians and Africans, since it was against the interests of white citizens also."

14. *The Times,* September 6 & 26, 1928. For the importance of *Show Boat* in the development of American music see William G. Hyland, *The Song's Ended. Songwriters and American Music 1900–1950* (Oxford: Oxford University Press, 1995), Chapter 11.

15. See for example *Glasgow Evening Citizen,* March 4, and *Birmingham Post,* March 19, 1930; Carolyn Smith, *Dick Sheppard. A biography* (London: Hodder & Stoughton, 1977), 179.

16. *Daily Express,* May 20, and *Daily Herald,* May 21, 1930. For a detailed account of the production see Michael Billington, *Peggy Ashcroft* (London: John Murray, 1988), 37–42; Interview, *The Era,* May 21, 1930, which also contains a review of the play.

17. See for example *Manchester Guardian,* September 2, and *Leeds Mercury,* November 21, 1930.

18. William Gallagher, "Salute to Paul Robeson," *Labour Monthly,* September 1958; Marc Wadsworth, *Comrade Sak. Shapurji Saklatvala MP. A Political Biography* (Leeds: Peepal Tree Press, 1998), 118.

19. *Radio Times,* April 18, 1930, December 29, 1933.

20. *Yorkshire Telegraph & Star,* January 22 & 24, 1934. Tour program in possession of the author.

21. Labour MP Eric Heffer recalled that as a boy he and his friends "pretended we were actors from the film and trooped along the paths in the wood chanting I-EE-O-KO." Eric Heffer, *Never a Yes Man. The Life and Politics of an Adopted Liverpudlian* (London: Verso, 1993), 8.

22. *Film Weekly*, May 2, September 19, 1936, and March 6, 1937; Bourne, *Black in the British Frame*, 28–29.

23. Ruth Dudley Edwards, *Victor Gollancz. A Biography* (London: Victor Gollancz, 1987), 273.

24. Colin Chambers, *The Story of Unity Theatre* (London: Lawrence & Wishart, 1989), 11, 107, 117, 137, 152, 158, 159; Noreen Branson and Margot Heinemann, *Britain in the Nineteen Thirties* (London: Panther, 1973), 300; For night classes see advertisement in *Challenge*, November 1, 1938, 7; "Why I Joined Labour Theatre," Interview with Philip Bolsover, *Daily Worker*, November 24, 1937; "Paul Robeson Tells Us Why," Interview by Sidney Cole, *The Cine-Technician*, September–October 1938, in Foner, *Paul Robeson Speakers*, 119–23. Unity Theatre was linked to the Left Book Club, and Robeson appeared at the third LBC annual rally in April 1939, Edwards, *Victor Gollancz*, 294.

25. *Challenge*, May 28, June 2, 9, & 16, 1938.

26. *Daily Herald* & *News Chronicle*, December 20, 1937; Duberman, 212.

27. Walter C. Thurston, Cable to the Secretary of State. State Department, January 28, 1938, reference provided by Marika Sherwood; *Daily Herald*, January 9, 1939; Branson & Heinemann, *Britain in the Thirties*, 343.

28. D. N. Pritt, *From Right to Left. Autobiography of D N Pritt. Part 1* (London: Lawrence & Wishart, 1965), 260. Khrisna Menon, the St. Pancras Labour Councillor, and later Foreign Minister for independent India, spoke at the Convention and Indira Nehru (later Gandhi) attended.

29. Programme, St. Andrews Hall, Glasgow in possession of author. *Sheffield Star*, March 16; *Sheffield Telegraph*, March 17; *Liverpool Daily Post*, March 25, 1949.

30. *Manchester Guardian*, May 11, 1949; Gordon Schaffer, *Baby in the Bathwater* (London: The Book Guild, 1996), 190–92. The original conviction was reversed in 1949; in a re-trial, two of the accused were found guilty, four innocent. The two convicted were sentenced to prison terms.

31. National Archives, Foreign Office, The World Congress of Partisans of Peace, Paris, April 20–25, 1949. FO1110/27; David King Dunaway, *How Can I Keep From Singing. Pete Seeger* (London: Harrap, 1985), Chapter 1; Duberman, *Paul Robeson*, 363–80.

32. National Archives, Foreign Office, FO1110/230, 6; Texts included in *Let Paul Robeson Sing Again*, Brochure issued by Manchester Committee to Restore Paul Robeson's Passport, in Foner, *Paul Robeson Speaks*, 409–12; Diana Loesser, *Let Paul Robeson Sing*, Working Class Movement Library Bulletin no. 5.

33. *Here I Stand*, 64–67.

34. Duberman, *Paul Robeson*, 464; *The News Chronicle*, July 12, 1958.

35. For a personal reminiscence see Tony Benn, *The Gaitskell Years. 1955–60*, 284–85; *Labour Monthly*, September 1958, 398–402; *Daily Mail*, October 13, 1958.

36. See for example *Southampton Daily Echo*, September 23 & 24; *Birmingham Post*, September 25; *Hull Daily News*, October 18; *Blackburn Evening Telegraph*, October 22; *Sheffield Star*, October 28; *Dundee Courier and Advertiser*, November 10; *Liverpool Post*, November 20 & 21, 1958; *Newcastle Evening Chronicle*, January 24, 1976; *Sheffield Telegraph*, October 29, 1958; Concert, November 13, 1958, copy of programme in Newcastle City Library Local History.

37. Alan Bush Music Trust (www.alanbushtrust.org.uk/music/compositions); *News Chronicle*, June 29, 1959; on the tour see for example *Hull Daily Mail*, April 25 & 26, 1960; Harry Pollitt's Funeral. ETV Ltd 1960, details listed in Communist Party and related films held in ETV Ltd. Communist History Newsletter On-Line, no. 4, 1997 (http://les1.man.ac.uk/chnn/CHNN04CPF.html).

38. David King Dunaway, *How Can I Keep From Singing*, 209. Seeger was allowed to tour Britain in the autumn of 1961.

39. *Daily Sketch* and *The Times*, August 26, 1963.

40. *New York Amsterdam News*, April 20, 1968. Thanks to Marika Sherwood for this reference; *Irish News*, April 5, 1968; e.g., *Newcastle Evening Chronicle*, January 24, 1976.

41. Sean Creighton, *John Archer. Battersea's Black Progressive and Labour Activist 1863–1932* (London: Agenda Services, 1999).

42. Wadsworth, *Comrade Sak Shapurji Saklatvala MP*; Mike Squires, *Saklatvala: A Political Biography* (London: Lawrence & Wishart, 1990); Sheri Saklatvala, *The Fifth Commandmen: Biography of Shapurji Saklatvala* (London: Miranda Press, 1991); Sean Creighton, *John Archer*, Talk to Labour Heritage AGM 2004 Conference *Labour & Race*. AGM 2004 page of www.labourheritage.com. Jonathan Wood, *William Miller: Black Activist in the Plymouth Labour Movement*, History & Social Action Publications, 2006: see www.seancreighton.co.uk.

43. *The Stage*, April 14, 1955; Herbert Marshall and Mildred Stock, *Ira Aldridge: The Negro Tragedian* (London: Rockcliff, 1958), 2.

44. Marika Sherwood, "Peter Blackman (1909–1993)," *Black & Asian Studies Association Newsletter* 6, September 1993, 28; "Robert Broadhurst (1864–1948)," ibid. 15, April 1996, 32; and re-Milliard *Three Black professionals in the Manchester area 60 or more years ago*, ibid. 20, January 1998, 22–23.

45. *The Keys: The official organ of the League of Coloured Peoples*, vol. 2, no. 3 (January–March 1935): 62; *World Affairs*, December 8, 1934, p. 1395, Report on page 1453. Thanks to Marika Sherwood for this reference; *The Keys*, vol. 2, no. 3 (January–March 1935): 62, and vol. 2, no. 4 (April–June 1935): 69; *Challenge*, June 16, 1938, and June 30, 1938.

46. Stephen Bourne, "In Memoriam. Elizabeth Welch 1904–2003," *Black & Asian Studies Association Newsletter* 37, September 2003, 24–25; *The Keys*, reported "a large company of Africans and West Indians resident in London and Cardiff are supporting," vol. 2, no. 3 (January–March 1935). For details of many of those who were in the films see Bourne, *Black in the British Frame*, 43–65.

47. Bourne, *Black in the British Frame*, 20–21, 47; *The Keys*, vol. 2, no. 4 (April–June 1935): 83.

48. *The Era*, September 16, 1936; *Challenge*, March 1938; Ron Ramdin, *Reimaging Britain. 500 Years of Black and Asian History* (London: Pluto Press, 1999), 184.

49. *The Observer*, April 28, 1935.

50. C. L. R. James, "Paul Robeson: Black Star," *Black World*, November 1970; *The Spectator*, June 15, 1934; Anthony Bogues, *Caliban's Freedom. The Early Political Thought of C. L. R. James* (London: Pluto Press, 1997), 46; Paul Buhle, ed., *C. L. R. James: His Life and Work* (London: Alison & Busby, 1986), 73–74.

51. Colin Chambers, *The Story of Unity Theatre*, 182, 270, 358–59; Stephen Bourne, *Black in the British Frame*, 84–91, 98–99. For Nadia Cattouse see Stephen Bourne and Marika Sherwood, *Claudia Jones. A Life in Exile* (London: Lawrence & Wishart, 1999).

52. National Archives, Foreign Office, Review of Communism in the Colonies. FO371/77570; Visit of Paul Robeson, Noted American Singer, to Jamaica. American Consulate General. Kingston, Jamaica, to the Secretary of State, Washington, December 7, 1949; National Archives. Fo371/77570, piece N611/1018/38G; Foner, *Paul Robeson Speak*, 193–94.

53. Hakim Adi, *West Africans in Britain. 1900–1960: Nationalism, Pan-Africanism and Communism* (London: Lawrence & Wishart, 1998), 161.

54. Marika Sherwood, op. cit. 105; Duberman, *Paul Robeson*, 479.

55. *Here I Stand*, 75.

56. "Children's party," Undated press cutting; Telegram New Delhi to Secretary of State, State Department, December 9, 1958. Thanks to Marika Sherwood for this reference.

57. Foner, *Paul Robeson Speaks*, 477; Sherwood, op. cit. 25, 35, 44–46, 138–39, 165, 167, 199.

58. *Here I Stand*, 33.

59. *Here I Stand*, 123.

60. See various articles reprinted in Foner, ed., *Paul Robeson Speaks*.

61. *Here I Stand*, 52.

62. *Here I Stand*, 122.

63. *Here I Stand*, Appendix C, A Universal Body of Folk Music—A Technical Argument by the Author, 123–25.

64. *Here I Stand*, 90.

9

Preaching the Gospel of the Blues

BLUES EVANGELISTS IN BRITAIN

—ROBERTA FREUND SCHWARTZ

Before World War II only a handful of blues records were available in Britain, and these had been swept in with the rising tide of American jazz releases in the late 1930s. Parlophone and Brunswick, the two largest record companies of the day, released few contemporary blues discs. The few Bessie Smith songs that appeared on their labels were perhaps initially issued (and subsequently purchased) because of the noted jazz musicians that accompanied her, but her rich contralto voice and expressive style of delivery soon earned her many devoted followers. James Asman advised, "Learn to enjoy Bessie Smith's kind of jazz, for it is the only kind there is!"[1] Other recordings by classic blues singers could occasionally be found in a Hot Jazz or Rhythm-Style series; while these performers inspired less devotion, they nonetheless introduced a number of jazz record buyers to the blues for the first time.

Boogie-woogie records lingered in an uncertain categorical domain between jazz and the blues, though they were usually lumped together with Fats Waller and Jelly Roll Morton under the heading of "jazz piano."

These were particular favorites of the younger fans who attended the group listening sessions, called rhythm clubs, which met throughout the country. Boogie-woogie discs were somewhat rarer than the classic blues but arguably more potent, considering that blues fans like Chris Barber and Alexis Korner claimed Jimmy Yancy and Little Brother Montgomery as their earliest favorites.[2] There were also a few guitar duets by Eddie Lang and Lonnie Johnson[3] that were wholly anchored in the jazz idiom but were also strongly flavored by the blues. Lastly, there was English Brunswick 3562, "Drop Down Mama" b/w "Married Woman Blues" by Sleepy John Estes, a recording so far removed from jazz that no one knew quite what to make of it. According to Paul Oliver, it was the subject of intense speculation:

> None seemed rarer nor more strange . . . the broken voice, the wailing accompaniment . . . and the compulsive rhythm which produced vague references to Africa all confounded criticism. The twelve-bar blues had been accepted as a traditional pattern, and the three-line standard verse accepted as the traditional blues stanza. But at the time when Bunk Johnson was talking of playing the "twenty-four bar blues," here was issued a blues from a decade before which was on a loose twenty-four measure structure and sung in verse and refrain of a quite a-typical form.[4]

It wasn't much, but these few discs were enough to catch the ears of a select group of listeners who then became interested in American race music. Female blues singers—especially Ma Rainey and Bessie Smith—had a relatively wide appeal among jazz collectors, but this other kind of blues was "the subject of an esoteric cult, a backwater of interest in 'pure' jazz" that was "valued for its ethnicity, its authenticity and its historic importance rather than for its merits as a music."[5] It might have remained the isolated passion of a few interested souls had it not been for a small but growing number of jazz critics, collectors, and discographers who began to actively promote wider knowledge and circulation of the blues. All were devoted and vocal champions of African American music whose educational activities formed the foundation of the British blues revival. In the span of twenty years they transformed the blues from an odd musical novelty to a niche genre that was as popular in Britain in the 1960s as it was in its native land.

It wasn't until after the War that serious interest in the blues started to spread. There was some interest in the genre before that, but it was only after a different war, the one between the revivalists and the modernists, heated up that the active promotion of the blues began. It did so through a combination of factors, but all were tied, in one way or another, to revivalist jazz.

In January of 1948 *Melody Maker* ran a critique of the London swing scene by Ernest Borneman, a figure at the vanguard of blues proselytism. Granted, he wasn't British, but he was a regular commentator on jazz, as well as a temporary resident of the country, and his evangelical fervor was unquestionable. In a follow-up article entitled "Where does that smell come from?" he opined that the protectionist policies of the Musician's Union policies that shut out performances by foreign artists—"American bands in general and the great Negro musicians in particular"—were dooming British dance music to sterility. He felt that the only hope for her musicians was exposure to jazz played by African American artists, and a healthy dose of the blues. "If any single factor was responsible for the decline of all those other factors which had once made a powerful force out of the jazz idiom, then that factor was the gradual alienation of the idiom from the one and only source that can ever revitalize it—the flux of native Afro-American folk music."[6]

By this date Borneman had completed two monographs on African American music[7] and knew a good deal about the blues. Like most other writers of the time he held an expansive view of the genre. The blues were what Bessie Smith sang, but "blues" was also a catch-all term for African American music that wasn't a spiritual or jazz, and could describe "the whole store of Negro folk musics, from spirituals and folk songs, to hollers, street cries, play party songs, and nursery rhymes."[8] This general, or inclusive, use was employed in the book *Jazzmen*, which became the bible of the revivalist movement in both the United States and Britain. The chapter on the blues by E. Simms Campbell, one of the earliest treatments of the genre in any respect, discusses both the Classic blues and black folk song, and the term is applied in the rest of the text to boogie-woogie, swing, and jazz based on the twelve-bar blues form.[9]

Until the 1930s most black folk music was inaccessible outside of the African American community; no radio stations in the United States broadcast black music on a regular basis and "race records" were marketed almost exclusively to black consumers. The activities of John and Alan Lomax were crucial in enhancing the audience for this music. The Lomaxes were interested in studying folk music of all kinds, and their attention to the older repertoire of performers of traditional material—material that had no particular commercial value—in the early thirties started to bring blues and ballads to a new audience: scholars and folk song collectors.

At the time it was generally accepted that the blues was the parent idiom of jazz whose sole vestigial remains were the twelve-bar chorus, blue notes, and the output of the classic blues singers. In fact, an enormously influential pamphlet entitled *Jazz in Perspective: The Background of the Blues* asserted that "the blues is not the whole of jazz, but the *whole of the blues is jazz, having no existence apart from this idiom.* It forms a bridge between southern folk music—work songs and gospel songs—and the organized harmonic and rhythmic complexities of the improvising band."[10] This posited relationship of jazz and black folk music encouraged the consideration of early jazz as a sort of instrumental folk music, one that was "expressively honest and culturally rebellious," and had existed independently from the pressures of the marketplace.[11] Such a view also implied that to really understand jazz it was necessary to know something of its roots.

In the early years of the revival the blues "was the subject of an esoteric cult, a backwater of interest in 'pure' jazz"[12] shared by only a handful of the truly faithful. The most devoted began to actively promote wider familiarity with the blues. Knowledge of American race music was probably first disseminated through record recitals, which were still presented by many of the rhythm and hot jazz clubs that met throughout Britain during and after the War. By 1948 Albert McCarthy had established a strong reputation as a recitalist; Ernest Borneman cited his presentation featuring a "fine selection of blues records" for the Hot Club of London as the high point of the entire New-Year's-Swing Scene in 1947. At roughly the same time Paul Oliver began giving presentations on the blues to any groups that would have him, lugging his crate of rare Paramounts and Vocalions wherever he went.[13] Rex Harris and Max Jones—the latter a host of BBC's Radio Rhythm Club and the author of the first major article on the blues published in Britain[14]—were also respected recitalists who were much in demand. It is difficult to gauge the impact of these activities from surviving sources, but it would be reasonable to surmise that some of the earliest blues lovers in Britain discovered the music in this way.

In 1946 Sinclair Traill, one of the most outspoken proponents of the nascent British traditional jazz movement, founded a publication called

Pick-Up. By 1948 the periodical, retitled *Jazz Journal,* was the unofficial home of serious jazz criticism in Britain. It also featured a column entitled "Preachin' the Blues" by Derrick Stewart-Baxter, a well-known collector who had served as secretary of the Leamington Spa Rhythm Club in the 1930s. Therein he dispensed information on blues artists and styles, discussed his latest "junking" finds, and reviewed any record that could justifiably be categorized as blues. He also had an enormous impact on fledgling blues fans. "For years," Paul Oliver recalls, "his was the only column on the subject ... and his enthusiasm was projected to a lot of young readers. ... He used to hold court in an upstairs room of a Hove record shop, a gathering place for blues enthusiasts who were prepared to brave the smoke of his pipe to share in the sounds and discussion on jazz and blues."[15] In a column from early 1949, Stewart-Baxter expressed his puzzlement that there were not more collectors interested in the blues, as "blues shouting goes straight to the basic root of jazz." For those who regarded the blues as "unmusical" and full of "sentiments that are always the same" he recommended an educational listening program of recordings by Bessie Smith, Leroy Carr, Tommy McClennan, Blind Lemon Jefferson, Big Bill Broonzy, Leadbelly, and "the more sophisticated but equally wonderful" Josh White.[16]

"Preachin' the Blues" was a haven for British blues fans, and regularly featured profiles and discographies of both prominent artists and relatively obscure blues men like Bumblebee Slim and Barbecue Bob, as well as Stewart-Baxter's "casual ramblings on the blues and its various byways and footpaths."[17] *Jazz Journal* itself became a major advocate of African American folk music, and throughout the 1960s it devoted substantial coverage to the blues.

Only a few years before, Albert McCarthy and Max Jones had founded *Jazz Music,* one of the first British publications devoted to increasing knowledge and circulation of African American music including, but not limited to, jazz. The editorials and content focused on the superiority of black musicians, their importance as the originators of jazz, black folk styles, and the influence of racism and poverty on African American music. The last, an essentially Marxist viewpoint, was common in contemporary folk-song scholarship in the United States, but represented a radical shift in the dialogue about black music in Britain. The blues were part of *Jazz Music* from the beginning; the first issue included an article on Bessie Smith, and also "A Note on Spirituals."

Jazz Music was published only irregularly until the end of the War due to paper rationing, but it did produce individual pamphlets on jazz-related subjects. Of particular note were those written by Jones and McCarthy: *Piano Jazz* and (for the Jazz Appreciation Society) *A Tribute to Huddie Ledbetter*, their first proselytizing on behalf of an artist who would shortly have an enormous impact on music in Britain. *Jazz Music* endured until 1953, and established high standards of content. A short while later McCarthy founded *Jazz Monthly*, "The Magazine of Intelligent Jazz Appreciation." Its stated intention was good, solid jazz writing free of stylistic bias, but *Jazz Monthly* also consistently made space for blues reviews and featured articles on artists, meaning in the blues, and stylistic developments. It also, beginning in June 1955, published segments of Big Bill Broonzy's autobiography. In fact, so much of the journal was being devoted to the blues that by 1960 the editor was receiving letters of protest; one, in particular, groused about the frequency of "ten page day by day life histories of Blind Sammy Peasticks who died of TB in 1897."[18]

Another early journal involved in the promotion of the blues was the Jazz Appreciation Society publication *Jazz Records*, founded by James Asman and Bill Kinnell and edited by Graham Boatfield, Kennedy Brown, and Stanley Dance. An anti-authoritarian publication from the start, the journal not only featured articles that focused on non-commercial jazz and African American folk music, but also criticized British record companies for their neglect of the idiom.

Though the specialist publications developed a small but loyal British following in the late forties and early fifties, *Melody Maker*, one of only two national music weeklies, had the potential to spread the gospel of the blues far beyond the congregation of the faithful.[19] While it maintained its devotion to more mainstream jazz, pop, and swing bands, the blues evangelists asserted their influence through "Collector's Corner." The "Corner" column had been inaugurated in 1941 by rhythm club founder Bill Elliott as a way to facilitate the exchange of discographical information between serious jazz record collectors. After editorship of the column passed to Max Jones and Rex Harris in 1946 the occasional "Corner" was devoted to American "race" records, and discographies of blues artists like Barbecue Bob, Charlie Jackson, and Blind Blake appeared next to those of Bunk Johnson, George Lewis, and Jelly Roll Morton. This happened with more frequency when Sinclair Traill took over for Harris in 1949.

From an early date the pair held that any true understanding of jazz entailed accepting other kinds of African American music. "Swing music, Harlem 'jive,' ragtime, piano blues, and sundry types of Negro singing find ready acceptance by some among collectors. And often the Negro singing comes near in emotional content to the true jazz that is the collector's first consideration."[20] Thus, the authors reviewed new and re-releases of blues, folk, and gospel artists, often combining their commentary with artist biography, stylistic history, and social background; in short, the column served as a tutorial on African American music. One constant thrust of the feature was to reinforce the notion that the blues was the foundation for all "real" jazz, and was therefore relevant to jazz collectors and fans. Max Jones opined, "To understand the blues is to hold the key to jazz appreciation. Blues is the essence of jazz, and few enthusiasts who listen long and seriously fail to end up blues lovers. Most often jazz interest begins with an instrumental style, then, as taste matures, the vocal and piano blues idioms occupy more and more of the listener's attention."[21] He also felt that an interest in the blues was the hallmark of the truly sophisticated listener, as it was "the most difficult branch of jazz."[22]

Though not associated with the "Corner" after 1949, Rex Harris continued to promote jazz and blues appreciation through his writings and radio broadcasts. In 1952 he authored a paperback volume for Penguin Books, simply entitled *Jazz*. Its stated purpose was to trace the roots of jazz, as "after the long and wearisome years of 'swing' which overlaid the traditions of jazz there has arisen a new generation which is anxious to learn of the roots and growth of this fascinating folk music." *Jazz* was a succinct and articulate statement of the revivalist viewpoint; as such, it devoted significant attention to the musical precursors of jazz, including the blues. The author approached the subject carefully, as he believed that "there are many hazy ideas about what constitutes a blues number; many people imagine that it is any attendant lyric full of lachrymose bleatings. The public can hardly be blamed for its lack of discrimination, for it has had so many ersatz versions foisted upon it during the past thirty years that it is in the position of a man who, having been condemned to a diet of tinned salmon for many years, views the real thing with suspicion and a certain conservative alarm."[23]

Harris focused primarily on the lyrical content of the blues, though he did discuss the harmonic foundations of the twelve-bar blues and stress the importance of improvisation to the genre. Unlike most other jazz histories, he included no information on classic blues singers, as "they were influenced by jazz, but they did not influence the course of jazz. Blues singing ran (and runs) a parallel course." The simplicity of this statement belies its significance, for it was the first articulation of an idea that would not fully take root for several years: the blues was an autonomous musical genre that, despite its relationship to jazz, was not subsumed by it.

The promotion of the blues by its evangelists, collectors, and critics was not entirely dispassionate. Paul Oliver has commented, "there was an evangelical element in my talking about blues, I realize now, an urgent need to get the message across to as many people as I could in as many ways as I could. Like any enthusiast for a subject who feels passionately about it and about its neglect, I wanted the blues to be recognized and enjoyed."[24]

There was also a hope that as appreciation for the music grew record buyers would demand more blues releases. Immediately after the war it was difficult for most jazz fans to find blues recordings, even in the record shops that specialized in American imports. "When I first became interested," recalled Albert McCarthy, "I used to order them from the USA without much idea of what I was likely to get. The exotic array of names in the current lists meant nothing to me, but I tried to get an example of most of the artists."[25] In the depressive economic climate of the postwar years, ordering records from the U.S. was prohibitively expensive for most blues aficionados, and due to limitations on luxury goods and currency restrictions, it was technically illegal between 1949 and 1960.[26] The truly devoted blues aficionados prowled junk shops and thrift emporia, looking for the odd race record that had made its way to Britain. Others secured discs from American military personnel; black servicemen, in particular, were often willing to sell blues records or trade them for recordings of English jazz bands.[27] British seamen who regularly visited the States, called "Cunard Yanks" after their Liverpudlian brethren who worked for the Cunard shipping line, were generally quite knowledgeable about black American music, and were a reputedly reliable source of blues and R&B records. Thus, while many revivalist jazz fans were learning more about the blues and their significant performers, they only heard their music when the records were released in Britain.

Collective attempts to pressure the major record companies into releasing or re-releasing significant recordings date back to the Federation of

Rhythm Clubs in the 1930s; it did not take long for the revivalists and blues aficionados to mobilize in the same way. Perhaps their largest postwar successes were through the auspices of the National Federation of Jazz Organizations (henceforth the NFJO), formed under the sponsorship of *Melody Maker* in June 1948 "to protect and further jazz interests in Britain." Truth be told, the NFJO did not represent any actual jazz organizations, but its officers, who included Rex Harris, Max Jones, and Sinclair Traill, collectively served as the "spokesman of organized jazz opinion (read Trad jazz) in this country."[28]

In March 1949 the NFJO secured a promise from the major record labels in Britain to make every effort to re-issue items for which there was a demand; Jones and Traill made sure that some of the records requested were by blues artists. These discs were advertised as "recommended by the National Federation of Jazz Organizations," which naturally assured significant coverage of their release in those publications edited by its officers. Due to an onslaught of publicity and positive reviews, Leadbelly's "T. B. Blues" and "Alberta" finished quite well in the 1949 NFJO poll for that year, encouraging further blues releases. Likewise, the release of Bessie Smith's "Empty Bed Blues" by Columbia Records in January 1951 received nearly a page of related coverage in *Melody Maker*, including a testimonial establishing its importance: "To listen to a good record—and this is a very good one—by Bessie Smith is the finest training I known to help you really hear those things that are the important things to hear in jazz and the blues."[29] Even records not enjoying NJFO sanction were aggressively plugged; for example, "Up Above My Head" b/w "Journey to the Sky," by gospel singer and guitarist Sister Rosetta Tharpe was actively championed by the critics, and Max Jones concluded his review by stating "you will need two copies of this record, for it can be enjoyed by everyone."[30]

However, the record-buying public no longer had to rely on the major labels. After the War small, independent labels began to spring up across the United Kingdom, and by 1950 there were so many that *Melody Maker* felt compelled to print a guide describing their standard repertoire and distribution centers. These new labels mostly catered to niche markets that were not being served by Decca and EMI, and many specialized in jazz and the blues. Outfits like Jazz Collector, Ristic, Tempo, and Melodisc entered into licensing arrangements with the small, independent labels that catered to the American race market and pressed records only ninety-nine copies of each release in order to circumvent the Purchase Tax (P.T.) of 33.3 percent applied to larger batches of records intended for commercial sale.

Although the trickle of British blues releases by independent labels was a positive sign, it did not make the recordings more accessible to the average listener. The prices were steep—7s 6d (approximately £7.88 in today's currency) for a ten-inch 78 rpm disc, nearly double the cost of a popular record on a major label—and they were sold only in the handful of specialty jazz shops that were springing up throughout Britain. Perhaps the most famous was Dobell's Record Shop in London, which is still remembered fondly by blues collectors and aging rock stars who spent many happy hours sifting through the bins. Dobell's enjoyed such a reputation that by the late fifties the saying was, "Every jazz fan was born within the sound of Do Bells."[31]

The shop's owner, Doug Dobell, stocked a number of American jazz and blues releases and re-releases, both legitimate and pirated, as well as a smattering of 78s obtained by junk shopping or from other collectors. Dobell's main competitors were shops run by his fellow collectors: Dave Carey's Swing Shop in the suburbs of London, and James Asman's London Jazz Club (82 St. John's Wood, High Street), which served as an outlet for all of the British independent labels as well as American imports and rarities. Though London was unquestionably the most reliable source for rare jazz and blues records, there were outposts in other major British cities. Hessey's in Liverpool was reputedly a dependable source for records of all kinds, as was Messrs. Hime and Addison in Manchester, and several dealers in Birmingham and Bristol stocked jazz and blues discs, both imported and native.[32]

These specialist dealers also absorbed some of the function of the rhythm clubs. Fans of the still largely underground blues scene met while poking through the bins looking for the odd, rare Charlie Patton or Robert Johnson disc that had made its way to Britain. Records were shared, traded, and discussed, styles were analyzed, and fans with similar listening preferences soon formed alliances and friendships.

The number of British jazz fans who appreciated the blues, as well as the availability of blues records, had increased steadily since the beginning of the New Orleans revival, but appreciation of the blues really took off when, beginning in 1949, African American artists connected to the folk music scene in the United States began touring in Europe, bringing a taste of the "living blues" to the British Isles.

Given his eventual influence on British popular music, it is somewhat ironic that Huddie Ledbetter—better known as Leadbelly, his *nom de disque*—never performed there. A popular figure of the burgeoning New York folk music scene, Leadbelly was in many respects the perfect artist to introduce the blues to Europe; his biography fulfilled the most extravagantly romanticized expectations about southern black life, and his extensive repertoire circumscribed the entire body of African American folk music. His 1949 concert at City University Theater on the outskirts of Paris generated substantial interest in Britain due to the efforts of Sinclair Traill and Max Jones, who "had been propagating the Lead Belly doctrine for some years." The pair attended the recital in Paris, and upon their return devoted a number of "Collector's Corners" to the singer. Most were partially dedicated to reviewing the records that had been released in Britain in the wake of the event and stressing their importance to the average collector. "True, he is not singing jazz, but his material is related to it, and his style has been much influenced by it. . . . I hope everyone who has any interest in blues singing will get one at least."[33]

Even more excitement surrounded the visits of Josh White and Big Bill Broonzy in the following years. The former was the first folk blues artist to tour the country, and his were also the first commercially available recordings in the genre. His personal charisma and media exposure made Josh White a nationally recognized entertainer, and for many he served as their first introduction to African American folk music. He lost some of his audience, particularly the jazz cognoscenti devoted to the "authentic" and "non-commercial" blues, to Big Bill Broonzy, who altered the landscape of British popular music as surely as the Beatles did a decade later. More than any other American artist, he served as an ambassador of the blues, in equal parts sage, songster, teacher, and touchstone to what was believed to be a fading tradition.

The two concerts that Broonzy played at Kingsway Hall, Holborn, in September of 1951 were aggressively promoted by the blues evangelists; during the months of August and September the jazz press featured articles about the blues in general, and Broonzy in particular. His appearances were emceed by Alan Lomax, who not only introduced the singer but also drew him into discussions about the songs and their social import, making the audience feel "as if they had wandered more or less by accident into one of those fabulous jazz parties of which the books are full."[34] The critical response was unanimously positive. Ernest Borneman declared it one of the most memorable concerts

of the last four years. Individual reviewers like McCarthy and Traill commented on the beauty of Broonzy's guitar playing, the emotionalism of his
vocals, and his remarkable artistry. Their commentary indicates that the
blues evangelists were beginning to regard the repertoire as something more
than just primitive jazz, as the justifications and projected relationships to
jazz styles that marked earlier blues writing are absent from these reviews.

It is reasonable to question whether these early efforts to popularize
the blues through radio broadcasts, articles, columns, and record reviews
yielded significant results. However, the letters in *Melody Maker*'s "Corner
Forum" indicate that the average reader was beginning to think about and
listen to the blues. One wrote, "I want to thank Max Jones and colleagues
for the weekly 'Corner.' Each week I learn something new. . . . I am grateful
to the record companies for the Broonzy discs." Another said, "my non-jazz
friends and relations all pan 'noisy jazz' but have all become blues addicts via
Josh White and Big Bill. Yessir, there are thousands of potential blues collectors. . . ." Still another wrote, "I was very interested in Max Jones' article on
the blues. I like this kind of music very much, and have bought all the Blind
Lemon, Leadbelly, and Josh White releases, and also some Lonnie Johnson
and Big Bill records."[35] Thus, it is evident that, by mid-1952, the gospel of the
blues was slowly beginning to disseminate.

On rare occasion the blues even made it onto the radio. Given the BBC's
ambivalent attitude toward jazz it is not surprising that the blues did not
become a priority for programmers. However, the contemporary perspective
of the blues as African American folk music gave it a scholarly credibility that
its instrumental sibling lacked. The music of foreign cultures was, after all,
educational.

During his 1951 tour of England Josh White was featured in the BBC
Easter special "Walk Together Chillun," a program of black religious music
that proved so popular with listeners that the following year producer Charles
Chilton arranged for White to record six more programs for a *Negro Anthology*.
The series, eventually retitled *The Glory Road*, proved so popular that the
network was amenable to other programs of this type. Later that year Alan
Lomax, at that time resident in London, presented a series called *The Art
of the Negro* on the BBC Third Programme. The last of the three episodes
was "Blues in the Mississippi Night," which featured recordings by Sleepy
John Estes, Robert Johnson, John Lee Hooker, and Muddy Waters, as well as

commentary on black life by John Lee "Sonny Boy" Williamson, Memphis Slim, and Big Bill Broonzy, albeit under pseudonyms. The series was incredibly well received by the critics and public alike; not only was the British public exposed to many superb blues recordings, they were also given an illuminating look at the hard realities of racism that were the crucible of the genre. Many remember the broadcast as their first glimmer of a deeper understanding of the blues, if not their first introduction to the genre.

The following year Max Jones hosted the program "Jazz Club," presenting a recital of "Town and Country Blues" that introduced the music of Waters, Williamson, Tommy McClennan, Bumble Bee Slim, and Bukka White, along with generous helpings of Leadbelly and Big Bill Broonzy, to thousands of listeners across the country.[36] Guest critic Ernest Borneman called the program a "masterly illustration of the kind of music that no British band, no British singer, no British accompanist could have furnished for any amount of money."[37] Such series and special broadcasts may have been extremely important elements in the wider distribution of the blues; save for recordings, they were virtually the only aural introduction the average Briton would have to the genre.

There were occasional visits by visiting blues artists. The driving force behind much of the early British blues scene was Chris Barber, whose contribution to the dissemination of the blues in Britain is often overlooked. Although he played in a number of sweet dance bands in his teens and formed his own Trad jazz group in 1949, Barber was, at heart, a blues fan. He recalls buying his first blues record in 1945—either Sleepy John Estes or Cow Cow Davenport—and scuffling with Alexis Korner, a guitarist and fellow collector, over the rights to rare Robert Johnson finds.[38] Beginning in 1954 Barber arranged and sponsored tours by American blues artists; his guests included Big Bill Broonzy, Brownie McGhee and Sonny Terry (in 1957), Sister Rosetta Tharpe (also in '57), Muddy Waters (in 1958), Champion Jack Dupree, Memphis Slim, Little Brother Montgomery, and Sonny Boy Williamson. In order to circumvent the British Musician's Union's ban on American jazz musicians the blues singers had to be billed as "variety performers," and Barber and his band frequently served as both accompanist and opening act for their guests.

From the beginning the Chris Barber Band had included a short set of blues in their concerts; the rhythm section and a vocalist performed "race blues" songs they'd learned from Tampa Red and Big Bill Broonzy records at the intermission. Barber called this small ensemble the "skiffle" group, though he wasn't really sure what the word meant.[39] Likewise, Barber didn't give much thought to a track included on his *New Orleans Joys* LP, the skiffle group's version of Leadbelly's "Rock Island Line" featuring banjo player Lonnie Donegan, which would ultimately kick off the skiffle craze.

A good deal of ink was spilled debating the pros and cons of skiffle, an unlikely mixture of American folk music, country blues, and revivalist jazz played on inexpensive or home-made instruments that enjoyed phenomenal popularity in Britain in 1957–58. The music was influenced primarily by black folk artists like Leadbelly and Josh White, and African American folk songs comprised the central repertoire. Brian Bird, an Anglican vicar who wrote a popular "how-to" manual on skiffle, advised that potential vocalists "should have a fair knowledge of Blues style singing [sic], as many of the old Negro spirituals, work-songs, ballads, and Blues are some of the best material for a skiffle group."[40] While many jazz musicians believed skiffle to be a corruption of the revivalist impulse, most blues evangelists were generally more optimistic. The genre ultimately did, as hoped and predicted, create a larger audience for the blues as hoards of young, eager skiffle musicians absorbed potential repertoire from increasingly available anthologies of folk and country blues.

Chris Barber also founded the National Jazz League "in part to encourage and disseminate the 'blues' message," and for a time he served as the co-director of the National Jazz Federation. In 1958 he and Harold Pendleton established the Marquee Club, which served as a venue for Trad jazz and blues bands and, beginning in 1963, was ground zero of the British R&B/blues rock movement.[41]

One of the most influential of the blues evangelists is Paul Oliver. Oliver discovered the blues when he heard some black GIs stationed in Suffolk singing blues songs, and—via boogie-woogie piano—developed a life-long interest in the genre. He began promoting the blues in the early 1950s by contributing articles to jazz periodicals and giving record recitals. His groundbreaking original research into the stylistic history and cultural background of the blues unfolded in the pages of *Jazz Journal* alongside essays on the genre by Albert McCarthy, Charles Edward Smith, Derrick Stewart-Baxter, Charles Fox, and Tony Standish. Slowly a new picture of the blues began to emerge, one that not only highlighted past performers but also considered newer artists and styles as continuations of the tradition, rather than commercialized corruptions of an authentic and dying art. Oliver's semi-regular column in *Jazz Monthly*, "Screening the Blues," was the first step toward an autonomous appreciation of the music. Early on it had been his wish to "disengage the blues from jazz, to release it from its subordinate position to the better-known music . . ."[42] and recognize it as a living tradition with its own independent identity.

The idea of the blues as a contemporary and developing music was a relatively new one. The artists and repertoire that were familiar to critics and audiences in the early 1950s represented only the "folk" or country blues traditions. Most British jazz and blues fans knew something about discrimination and its effects in the United States; "Blues in the Mississippi Night" had presented powerful testimonials about racism in the rural south, and any number of record reviews had delved into the causes of the blues: exploitation, privation, and hopelessness in a land of plenty. However, there is little evidence that the average listener understood the African American experience to be anything but monolithic. There seemed to be little appreciation at this time of the effects of urban migration and musical cross-fertilization on blues styles. Between 1952 and 1956 postwar blues and rhythm & blues began to arrive in the Britain, music that challenged established ideas about what constituted the blues. Alongside rhythm & blues there were "plenty of recordings in the old style . . . by such artists as Country Paul, Muddy Waters, Smokey Hogg, and the ubiquitous John Lee Hooker. . . . [S]uch recordings are referred to as 'country' or 'Southern' blues and sell mainly in the Deep South."[43] However, this "old style" was not the familiar folk blues; though most of these "down-home" artists hailed from the rural southeast few had remained there, and both the musical style and lyrics conformed to their now largely urban existence.

Oliver was recognized for his efforts in documenting the changing face of the blues, balancing a desire to understand the history of the genre with respect for the music as it actually existed in the African American community. This dual impulse has shaped much of his writing. His search for meaning in the blues led to *Blues Fell This Morning*, still the fundamental reference for comprehending the highly referential language of the country blues within a sociological context. The book, along with Samuel Charters's *The Country Blues*, served as a primer for young blues and R&B fans who had discovered the music through skiffle, rock 'n' roll, and Trad jazz.

The necessity of capturing a portrait of the blues in its native environment led Oliver to undertake a collecting trip to the American south in the summer of 1960, under the auspices of the Foreign Specialist Program of the Bureau of Educational and Cultural Affairs of the United States Department of State. He was determined to compensate his subjects for their time—an ethical stance based on the collective disgust many collectors felt toward the past exploitation of artists—but lacked the funds to do so. The BBC provided the funds to pay the artists, and Robert M. W. Dixon—along with Trevor Benwell (Vintage Jazz Mart), Derek Coller, Tony Standish, and Derrick Stewart-Baxter—initiated the Blues Research and Recording Project with the intention of creating a fund to issue the recordings from Oliver's trip and to encourage the recording of artists overlooked by the major record companies.[44] The journey also yielded material for a score of essays and the influential *Conversation with the Blues*, a compilation of first-person narratives by blues musicians from a number of stylistic traditions, which documented the process of learning and the significance of the blues to its native audience over time and geographical distance. It remains a rare document in its willingness to let the musicians speak for themselves. In her review of the monograph Val Wilmer eloquently explained the significance of both the author and his output: "Paul's thorough, scholarly approach to blues criticism dispenses with damaging, cheap nostalgia. He is a serious individual yet highly successful in his conversations with the people who make and live the blues."[45]

Appreciation for the living tradition led Oliver and other blues evangelists to bemoan increasingly frequent attempts to force contemporary artists to play acoustic folk blues for the collector's market. Albert McCarthy opined,

> it should be no secret to readers of this magazine that most of the outstanding contemporary blues singers prefer using an electric guitar and featuring a backing that is sometimes classified as rock and roll. I am now hearing of instances where signers are being asked to record . . . on condition that they use an acoustic guitar and cut down the backing to one considered more "genuine." I am sure that if these blues followers were to hear Howlin' Wolf or Muddy Waters playing to their own audiences in Chicago night clubs they would consider them renegades.[46]

In fact, Oliver, McCarthy, and most other blues evangelists were important champions of postwar, urban blues and R&B, often in direct opposition to younger fans who considered anything except acoustic country blues a commercial bastardization of the idiom. Many of the true evangelists, regardless of their personal preferences—McCarthy, for example, thought R&B was a "music of gimmick and cheap excitement,"[47] and all held that most skiffle was really quite awful—defended and encouraged any kind of blues-based music that might created a wider audience for the "real thing." Exceptions, such as Sinclair Traill and Derrick Stewart-Baxter, feared that commercial pressure and overexposure would lead to a degradation of musical quality. Both, however, praised artists like Bo Diddley and Ray Charles whose work was commercially popular yet still rooted in the blues idiom.[48]

Their tolerance would be tested by the emergence of a native blues tradition spearheaded by their fellow evangelist Alexis Korner. Korner discovered the blues through boogie-woogie piano discs but shortly thereafter was seduced by the guitar work of country blues artists like Blind Lemon Jefferson. He worked for the Melodisc label for a time and served as an assistant to Sinclair Traill before joining the Chris Barber/Ken Colyer Skiffle Group in 1954. He eventually quit, as he felt the band was too commercially oriented, and the brief skiffle sets did nothing to satisfy his desire to play the blues. He teamed up with Cyril Davies, a blue-collar, hard-core country blues guitar and harmonica player who was, by his own admission, "fixated" with Leadbelly, and began an intensive, performance-oriented exploration of the blues. Korner was by this point also contributing articles on African American folk music and country blues to *Jazz Monthly* and *Jazz Journal* and developing blues-oriented programming for the General Overseas Service of the BBC.

By 1956 Korner and Davies were running the London Skiffle Club, which met every Thursday, but they grew tired of the endeavor when skiffle became the most popular music of the land. They shut down the club and re-opened as the Barrelhouse and Blues Club. Though an audience did not materialize immediately, within a short time the club became a gathering place for youngsters who were discovering the blues. Harry Shapiro recalled that the club was "an elongated upstairs room holding about 125 people, although on some nights there were more people waiting to play than pay." After hours the pair would hold master-classes for guitar players, and also did so at Ballad and Blues Club above the Princess Louise pub in Holborn, the first British folk club.[49]

After performing with Chris Barber on the BBC's "Trad Tavern," Davies and Korner began sitting in with the Barber band at the Marquee Club to try playing some American R&B numbers. The experience soon led to formation of Blues Incorporated, the first British rhythm & blues band.[50] The group opened at the Marquee in May of 1962 to scant audiences, but within a month picked up a strong following that continued to grow with every passing week.[51] Blues Incorporated was ostensibly comprised of Korner, Davies, Dick Heckstall-Smith (tenor sax), Keith Scott (piano), Charlie Watts (drums), Andy Hoogenboom (bass), and Art Wood (vocals), but Korner maintained a liberal policy toward sitting in with the band, and anyone with the passion or guts to give it a try was welcome. Mick Jagger recalls waiting in line with other aspirants to sing with the band. "We'd all sing the same bloody songs; we'd all have a turn singing 'Got My Mojo Working' or whatever it was. It was the Muddy Waters that went down best."[52]

The departure of Davies in late 1962 established a pattern of fluctuating membership that endured for much of the decade; it also made Blues Incorporated something of a nursery for young musicians who wanted to play the blues. Korner was interested in cultivating new talent, and served as mentor to the vanguard of the British blues-rock movement. His house was the hub of a blues "community," where young musicians could gather to grab a meal, listen to Korner's extensive record collection, or discuss the blues. By early 1964 his progeny—beginning with the Rolling Stones and the Yardbirds but also including Eric Burdon, Jimmy Page, Rod Stewart, and Jack Bruce—were fronting a popular rhythm & blues boom. "This," counseled Albert McCarthy, "has led to a genuine concern with the more authentic performers to a degree that was never true of the average follower of the [Trad] bands. The musical level of the British R-and-B bands may be as derivative and non-creative as that of Trad bands but their success gives us the opportunity of hearing such first-rate artists as John Lee Hooker and Muddy Waters, not to mention such entirely non-commercial figures as Blind Gary Davis and Lonnie Johnson."[53]

The earliest British R&B bands tended to be quite vocal about their influences and heroes. Both Keith Richards and Mick Jagger felt the purpose of the Rolling Stones "was to turn other people on to Muddy Waters. . . . We just wanted to get a few people interested in listening to the shit we thought they ought to listen to . . . to turn people on to the blues. If we could turn

people on to Muddy and Jimmy Reed and Howlin' Wolf and John Lee
Hooker, then our job was done."[54] By promoting the blues artists who had
influenced their style, these groups created more demand for blues records
and literature.

Additionally, larger audiences developed for touring blues artists, who
began to visit the country with more frequency. The American Folk Blues
Festival, founded by Horst Lippmann and Fritz Rau in 1962, featured perfor-
mances by luminaries like John Lee Hooker, T-Bone Walker, Muddy Waters,
Memphis Slim, and Willie Dixon and drew sellout crowds and rave reviews.
Many of the artists found they were far more popular in Britain than in the
United States, where audiences for the blues were diminishing. Several emi-
grated, and others seized the new commercial opportunities presented by the
British blues boom by recording extensively for the European market and
touring the blues club circuit with bands comprised of their young devotees.
By 1965 "British R&B" had become the dominant paradigm of popular music
and was spreading the gospel of the blues to the youth of Britain and beyond.

Far from remaining an "esoteric cult" and "mere backwater of jazz
interest," thanks to the efforts of a small group of devoted promoters, the
blues developed into a mainstream popular music with international appeal
through a series of incremental steps that cultivated greater familiarity with
the genre, in turn creating increased demand for recordings and live performances, which widened the audience for the blues, and so on. Other important figures spread the gospel of the blues in Britain: Peter Tanner, Graham
Boatfield, Simon Napier (who founded *Blues Unlimited*, the first periodical
in English devoted to the genre), Bob Groom (who established the compet-
ing *Blues World* in 1965), G. E. Lambert, and many more. The last recognized
the importance of the evangelists to the state of the blues in a 1960 article in
Jazz Monthly.

> Praise be to Max Jones, Albert McCarthy, Iain Laing, Paul Oliver, and the other
> good people who have helped bring about this state of affairs, a small but
> increasing stream of blues releases. Again it is easy to pass off this increasing
> popularity of the real blues by observing that the most popular blues singers in
> this country are those who have the fortune to travel with Chris Barber's band,
> or to comment that, after all, Lonnie Donegan still outsells Leadbelly by quite
> a fantastic margin. But the process of creating an audience for blues must be a

slow one . . . but the fact remains that we are faced with what is, in part at least, a genuine movement of understanding of, and love for, the blues.[55]

NOTES

1. Ron Staley, "Empress of the Blues," *Jazz Journal* 5/9 (September 1952): 12.

2. Harry Shapiro, *Alexis Korner: the Biography*, discography and additional research by Mark Troster (London: Bloomsbury Publishing, 1996), 13, 40.

3. Lonnie Johnson and Eddie Lang, *Two Tone Stomp* [R1195] and *Handful of Riffs/Bull Frog Moan* [R1496], were included in the Parlophone "Rhythm Style" catalogue. The flip side of R1195 is a classic blues by Ma Rainey. The UK release date is unknown, though the catalogue numbers suggest 1930 or 1931.

4. Paul Oliver, "Crazy Crying Blues: Sleepy John Estes," in *Blues Off the Record* (Tunbridge Wells, Kent: Baton Press; New York: Hippocrene Books, 1984), 224.

5. Oliver, "Blue-Eyed Blues," in Ibid., 230.

6. Ernest Borneman, "Where does that smell come from?" *Melody Maker*, February 14, 1948, 4.

7. "A Bibliography of American Negro Music with a short introduction on African Native Music" (1938–40) and "American Negro Music: A Preliminary Inquiry into the Origin of Ring Shouts, Spirituals, Work Songs, Blues, Minstrelsy, Ragtime, Jazz, and Swing Music" (1945–46). Both remain unpublished.

8. Borneman, "The Anthropologist Looks at Jazz," *Record Changer*, May 1944, 5, 38–39; and Krin Gabbard, "The Jazz Canon and its Consequences," in *Jazz Among the Discourses* (Durham, NC, and London: Duke University Press, 1995), 15.

9. Charles Edward Smith and Frederick Ramsey, Jr., *Jazzmen* (New York: Harcourt Brace & Co., 1939).

10. Iain Lang, *Jazz in Perspective: The Background of the Blues* (London: Hutchinson & Co., 1947), 102. Emphasis mine.

11. Bernard Gendron, "'Moldy figs' and Modernists," in *Jazz Among the Discourses*, 39; Iain Chambers, *Urban Rhythms: Pop Music and Popular Culture* (London: Macmillan, 1985), 47; and Richard Middleton, "The 'Problem' of Popular Music," in *The Blackwell History of Music in Britain*, vol. 6 (Oxford: Blackwell, 1995), 35.

12. Paul Oliver, "Blue-Eyed Blues: The Impact of Blues on European Popular Culture," in *Approaches to Popular Culture*, ed. C. W. E. Bigsby (Bowling Green, OH: Bowling Green University Popular Press, 1976), 230.

13. Tom Mazzolini, "A Conversation with Paul Oliver," *Living Blues* 54 (1982): 24.

14. In the *PL Yearbook of Jazz*.

15. Paul Oliver, "Moaners and Shouters," in *Blues Off the Record*, 124.

16. Derrick Stewart-Baxter, "Talkin' from the Heart," *Jazz Journal* 2/1 (January 1949): 3.

17. Derrick Stewart-Baxter, "Blues on Record (and other matters)," *Jazz Journal* 7/9 (September 1954): 8

18. "Letter to the editor," *Jazz Monthly* 6/7 (September 1960): 2.

19. The other, *The New Musical Express*, was devoted almost exclusively to popular music.

20. Rex Harris and Max Jones, "Collectors' Corner," *Melody Maker*, January 11, 1947, 5. The specific author is not listed (as would be the case in later columns), but the prose and evangelical bent suggest Jones.

21. Max Jones, "Collectors' Corner," *Melody Maker*, January 13, 1951, 7.

22. Max Jones, "I am not a Roberts fan," *Melody Maker*, July 16, 1949, 5.

23. Rex Harris, *Jazz*, 5th ed. (Harmondsworth, Middlesex: Penguin Books, 1957), introduction.

24. Oliver, "Talking Blues," in *Blues Off the Record*, 208.

25. Albert McCarthy, "Record Reviews," *Jazz Journal* 4/12 (February 1959): 22.

26. Bob Groom recalled in an interview by the author that the import tariff on records from the United States was often greater than the purchase price (Gloucester, England, July 24, 2004). Personal imports were generally ignored, but occasionally specialist record dealers were raided and fined.

27. Paul Oliver, interview by author (Gloucester, England, July 23, 2004).

28. "NFJO Clinches Big Record Release Tie Up," *Melody Maker*, March 5, 1949, 1.

29. Max Jones, review of "Empty Bed Blues" by Bessie Smith, *Melody Maker*, January 20, 1951, 9.

30. Max Jones, "Jazz Reviews: Hot gospel singing from the Holy Rollers," *Melody Maker*, December 30, 1950, 9.

31. Oliver, interview with author.

32. My thanks to Paul Oliver, Bob Groom, and John Cowley for confirming that these shops, which advertised in *Jazz Journal* and *Jazz Monthly*, were major outlets for jazz and blues discs.

33. Max Jones, review of "New Black Snake Moan" b/w "Four Day [sic] Worry Blues" and "Becky Deem, She Was a Gamblin' Gal" b/w "Pig Meat Papa" by Huddie Ledbetter, *Melody Maker*, December 3, 1949, 7.

34. Ernest Borneman, "Big Bill Talkin'," *Melody Maker*, September 29, 1951, 2. Other critics, particularly Max Harrison and George Melly, found Lomax's comments embarrassingly paternalistic.

35. "Corner Forum," *Melody Maker*, May 17, 1952, 3; June 14, 1952, 9; and May 24, 1952, 9.

36. "Collectors' Corner," *Melody Maker*, September 6, 1952, 9.

37. Ernest Borneman, "Radio Review," *Melody Maker*, August 30, 1952, 2.

38. Shapiro, *Korner*, 40.

39. It is alternately claimed that Bill Colyer coined the term "skiffle." Though neither claimed to have employed the word as a particular reference, the term appeared on the 1929 Paramount disc "Hometown Skiffle" [12806], a novelty "house party" record featuring Blind Lemon Jefferson, Blind Blake, Will Ezell, Charlie Spand, the Hokum Boys, and Papa Charlie Jackson. "Skiffle" was also used to describe a 1948 jam session by the Dan Burley Skiffle Boys: Burley, Brownie and "Stick" McGhee, Pops Foster, Sidney Bechet, and Kid Ory.

40. Brian Bird, *Skiffle: The Story of Folk Song with a Jazz Beat* (London: Robert Hale, 1958), 62.

41. "Biography," <http://www.chrisbarber.net/biography.html>, September 12, 2003, last update September 12, 2003.

42. Paul Oliver, *Conversation with the Blues*, 2d ed. (Cambridge: Cambridge University Press, 1997), xiv.

43. Doug Whitton, "Will the '53 Bubble become the '54 Boiler? MM puts the spotlight on R&B," *Melody Maker*, January 2, 1954, 3.

44. Albert McCarthy, "Comment," *Jazz Monthly* 5/9 (November 1959): 1.

45. Val Wilmer, "Review," *Jazzbeat* 2/7 (July 1965): 28.

46. Albert McCarthy, "Comment," *Jazz Monthly* 6/11 (January 1961): 30.

47. Albert McCarthy, "Rhythm and Blues," *Jazzbook '55* (London: Cassell, 1958), 84.

48. Both expressed these views repeatedly in columns and essays written between 1960 and 1965.

49. Harry Shapiro, Alexis *Korner*, 56–62.

50. Peter Clayton, "Ten Years After," *Jazzbeat* 1/6 (June 1964): 5.

51. *Jazz Today: Marquee Club Newsletter* (May 1962): 1.

52. Shapiro, *Korner*, 111.

53. Andrew McCarthy, *Jazz Monthly* 10/5 (July 1964): 2.

54. Keith Richards, "Muddy, Wolf & Me," interview by Jas Obrecht, *Guitar Player* 27/9 (September 1993): 90.

55. G. E. Lambert, "Bad Luck Blues," *Jazz Monthly* 6/4 (June 1960): 22.

10

Whose "Rock Island Line"?

ORIGINALITY IN THE COMPOSITION
OF BLUES AND BRITISH SKIFFLE

—BOB GROOM

Airplay has always been the major key to creating a hit record, particularly in the era before television exposure, celebrity reputations, and wider media coverage became significant. Over the years DJs have made hits out of the most unlikely records—David Seville's "Witch Doctor" and Chipmunks' records in America, "Happy Wanderer" by the Obernkirchen Children's choir and three hits by the Royal Scots Dragoon Guards Military Band in Britain are just a few examples that spring to mind. Surely at the time it first became popular, before it spearheaded a whole popular music phenomenon, "Rock Island Line" must have been seen in this novelty category. Despite the seemingly exotic nature of the lyrics, something about it appealed to British disc jockey Eamonn Andrews,[1] who was credited with "discovering" Lonnie Donegan's recording for BBC radio's *Pied Piper* series. With repetition, listeners also became intrigued with this railroad saga from the Deep South. (Jack Train's version of "The Runaway Train," originally a hit by Vernon Dalhart, was another BBC favorite at this time.) Not that they would be entirely unfamiliar with genuine American folk music, thanks to the efforts of Alistair Cooke, whose pioneering BBC radio series *I Hear America Singing* in 1938 contained an appreciable element of jazz and black music, drawn from commercial recordings and the Library of Congress Archive of folk song, folklorist Alan Lomax (resident in the United Kingdom in the 1950s), and BBC producer/presenter Charles Chilton, perhaps better known for the sci-fi thriller series *Journey into Space*. When Lonnie Donegan's "Rock Island Line" was first broadcast, it was simply one track of a popular eight-track ten-inch LP by Chris Barber's Jazz Band[2] on Decca (*New Orleans Joys*), but such was its popularity on air that Decca eventually issued it as a single (Decca F-J 10647) with "John Henry" on the B-side. It was also later made available on a Decca EP (DFE 6345) and so was available in all vinyl formats then in commercial use.

Record charts based on sales rankings had been introduced in Britain in 1952 by the *New Musical Express*, the "Hit Parade" having previously been constructed from sheet music sales (which still continued to be important for some years). By the autumn of 1955 all the major music papers featured record charts and "Rock Island Line" quickly made an appearance in them, climbing rapidly through January 1956 to reach its highest position at No. 8 during the first week of February. However, quite different from the "shooting star" path of most pop singles today—zooming to the top, and then quickly dropping off the chart—records often spent months on the charts, selling steadily. "Rock Island Line" spent twenty-two weeks on the chart, and when the Top 20 was extended to become a Top 30 in April 1956, it was back in at No. 16 and was listed at No. 19 the week before its last placing in June. (By which time Lonnie was at No. 2 with his first Pye-Nixa single, "Lost John.") Even more improbably, "Rock Island Line" became a major hit in America. Its raw excitement, a quiet opening, followed by acceleration to a fast and furious climax, hit the spot with U.S. record buyers. Lonnie himself was astonished by the record's huge popularity.[3] Ironically he derived no direct income from its sales (just a session fee as a member of the band when the recordings were made back in July 1954), although it gave him a seven-year career as a major pop star. While Decca shilly-shallied (instead of offering royalties and putting Lonnie on contract), Pye-Nixa signed up the new young sensation. Suddenly Donegan the jazzman was a pop star.

Those in the know felt that Lonnie had ripped off a composition of Leadbelly (Huddie Ledbetter) by claiming authorship of the song. "New words and music by Lonnie Donegan" was the credit, but neither element of this claim was correct. Essex Music first credited the song to Donegan on the sheet music, later changing it to "words and new music" by Donegan. On recent CD issues Ledbetter, J. and A. Lomax, and Donegan are co-credited with a song that none of them composed! Only later (long after the skiffle craze had died) did it come to light that Leadbelly himself had acquired the song from prisoners (Kelly Pace leading a group of seven axemen cutting pine logs) at the Cummins State Farm, Arkansas, when he was chauffeuring and acting as intermediary for John Lomax during a 1934 field recording trip for the Library of Congress. The prisoners sang about a train running from Memphis, Tennessee, to Little Rock, Arkansas, on a railroad line,[4] also celebrated in unrelated blues by Furry Lewis ("Rock Island Blues," Vocalion, 1927), Lonnie Coleman ("Old Rock Island Blues," Columbia, 1929), and Leroy Ervin ("Rock Island Blues," Gold Star 628, 1947), among others.[5] The chorus ran:

> Well the Rock Island Line is a mighty good road,
> Said the Rock Island Line is a road to ride
> If you want to ride you got to ride it like you find it,
> Buy your ticket at the station on the Rock Island Line

After the commercial comes a two-line religious verse, also repeated as verse four. Only verse three describes an actual train schedule on the railroad. Several times through the recording a hoot is heard, simulating the warning note of the engine approaching a crossing or halt.

Although the October 5, 1934, version by Kelly Pace and his fellow convicts (248-A-1) is the only one that has been issued, other group versions were recorded. According to the standard discography one was made only a few days earlier (236-A-1) by a different convict group at Little Rock, Arkansas. A text different from the lyrics heard on 248-A-1 was reproduced on page 474 of *Long Steel Rail* by Norm Cohen,[6] and it may be that this is from the earlier recording; if so its seeming lack of coherence may have prompted John Lomax to seek another version at Cummins Prison Farm.[7] On May 21, 1939, John Lomax, with son Alan, was back at Cummins Prison Farm, Gould, Arkansas, for the Library of Congress and while there recorded another version of "Rock Island Line" (2671-A-1) from a group of convicts led by Joe Battle. This has not yet been made available on vinyl or CD.

By this time Leadbelly had made his first recording of the song, for the Library of Congress in June 1937. Over the next twelve years he recorded it at least a dozen times. At first he referred to the song's work song origins[8] in a spoken introduction. Later he replaced this with an introduction to the action in the song as he developed this for dramatic effect. Realizing that it was parochial, he deleted the verse mentioning Memphis and Little Rock and substituted a story about an engine driver and a tollbooth official. The changes he made certainly were enough to entitle him to part-composer credit. Whether the credits accorded John and Alan Lomax represented any contribution to the lyrics by them is open to question.

A variety of artists covered the Donegan hit, including a then unknown Bobby Darin, who sang it on his first national television appearance in 1956, having just recorded it for American Decca. Established hit-maker Don Cornell's "cover" version for Coral at first threatened to outsell Lonnie's (issued on London Records in the United States), but it was Donegan who took it into the American Top Ten (No. 8 or No. 10, depending which chart you consult) in May 1956. A spoof version by master satirist Stan Freberg (on Capitol) made the lower reaches of the British Top 30 in July/August 1956. British actor/comedian Peter Sellers recorded a clever parody of Donegan's hits (including "Rock Island Line") called "Puttin' on the Smile"; Donegan hated it (although he had apparently been amused by the Freberg skit).

Blues artist Snooks Eaglin recorded "Rock Island Line" for Swedish Radio in 1964 and the great Little Richard performed it in a late 1980s film *A Vision Shared*, a tribute to Leadbelly and Woody Guthrie. Johnny Cash recorded "Rock Island Line" at Sun in 1956 and claimed ownership of the song. Cash may well have heard a Leadbelly version, or one by the Weavers (from 1951), but most likely his recording was a Sam Phillips–promoted "cover" of Donegan's. Cash inserts two "Casey Jones"–type verses to differentiate his from the Donegan version. Country hit maker Johnny Horton cut a version for Columbia, folksinger Ramblin' Jack Elliott recorded it for Prestige, and even smooth pop balladeer Brian Hyland included it in his *Rockin' Folk* album. The folk revival sparked numerous versions by groups like the Tarriers, the Brothers Four, and the Rooftop Singers. Inevitably Donegan eventually recorded "Rock Island Line" for Pye-Nixa, to complete his catalogue of hits, but by this time (August 1956) he must have performed it "live" at least a hundred times, and the re-cut lacks the raw excitement of the earlier Decca version.

With "Rock Island Line" red hot on the U.S. charts, Donegan was invited to do a ten-week American tour, commencing in June 1956 and including appearances on major television shows with Perry Como (who had him do a sketch with future American president, Ronald Reagan), Bill Randle, Howard Miller, and Paul Winchell, and package show performances with the likes of Chuck Berry, Clyde McPhatter, LaVern Baker, and Frankie Lymon and the Teenagers. The tour was a great success (at one point he was backed by the Rock and Roll Trio—Johnny and Dorsey Burnette and lead guitarist Paul Burlison!), but in August he made a swift return to the United Kingdom when his record company cabled that "Lost John" was No. 2 in the charts and he was needed for TV and concert dates. (Oddly "Lost John" was only a minor chart record in the United States, and Donegan had to wait until 1961 for his only other major American hit with a revival of the 1924 vaudeville song "Does Your Chewing Gum Lose Its Flavour on the Bedpost Overnight?")

Donegan's interest in black blues and gospel song dates back to his teen-age years. Born Anthony (Tony) Donegan in Glasgow, Scotland, on April 29, 1931, he moved to London with his parents two years later and by the time he was fifteen he had developed an interest in American folk music. Donegan discovered jazz in 1947 and during National Service in the Army (1949–51) became an amateur jazz musician. In London he saw Josh White perform and gained access to blues, gospel, and old-time country records at the American Embassy (he later confessed to permanently "borrowing" their copy of the Muddy Waters Library of Congress 78!), Collet's Bookshop and elsewhere. Lonnie Johnson and Leadbelly were his favorites. The story, possibly apocryphal, of how Tony became Lonnie Donegan is that he, with his little jazz band of the day, appeared on the same bill as Tony's musical hero, Lonnie Johnson, at the Royal Festival Hall in 1952. The compere got the two mixed up and introduced Tony as Lonnie Donegan.

Donegan's success triggered a nationwide British enthusiasm for skiffle groups and spasm bands, usually consisting of washboard, guitar, washtub or tea-chest bass, and sometimes harmonica and banjo. In skiffle's peak year of 1957 there were thousands of amateur skiffle groups in Britain, many of them in big cities like London and Liverpool, where the Quarrymen skiffle group would later emerge as the Beatles. Many famous beat groups and solo artists of the 1960s evolved from skiffle groups. Hank Marvin of the Shadows started as a skiffler, as did Adam Faith and Cliff Richard. Donegan had a string of hits in Britain with songs like "Cumberland Gap" (1957), "Battle of

New Orleans" (1959), and vaudeville/music hall numbers like "Does Your Chewing Gum Lose Its Flavour" and "My Old Man's a Dustman" (1960). His success was fairly short—he had little sympathy with the music of the rock 'n' rollers. His preference was for jazz, blues, and folk music, and when skiffle faded, he moved to country music and vaudeville songs. He had a brief revival of fame in the late 1990s when he recorded with Van Morrison and he was still performing when he died in November 2002.

The actual origins of skiffle are not entirely clear. The term seems to be a derivative of "scuffle," commonly used by African Americans in the sense of "scuffling for a living" or to describe a rough-and-ready party, or rent party, and by extension, impromptu music utilizing basic, often homemade or improvised instruments, performed at such gatherings. However, before 1900 the Razzy Dazzy Spasm Band with harmonica, cowbells, bullfiddle, pebble gourd, etc., played on the streets of Storyville in New Orleans. In the Windy City Jimmy O'Bryant and group recorded their "Chicago Skiffle" in 1925. In 1929 Paramount Records recorded (it was issued in 1930) a two-sided sampler of their blues hits under the generic title *Hometown Skiffle*. Folkways issued an LP titled *American Skiffle Bands* in 1957. This featured field recordings made by Sam Charters, including the Mobile (Alabama) Strugglers in 1957. Hokum blues, rent party music, and goodtime jazz have all been described as "skiffle." In 1940s Harlem, newspaper editor Dan Burley formed a skiffle group which made a number of recordings. Musically these little resemble what Lonnie Donegan et al. were to popularize as skiffle a decade later. So how did the British version get its name? Bill Colyer, brother of Ken and sometime musician, tells how he named the British music phenomenon, prior to a BBC broadcast. When pressed to find a less awkward name than "breakdown group music," he remembered a 1947 record by Dan Burley and his Skiffle Boys, coupling "Chicken Shack Shuffle" and "Skiffle Blues" (Arkay 1001/Exclusive 77) and dubbed the "new" music "skiffle." (Burley's group was also recorded live in 1951 performing a "Skiffle Jam.") Previously it had simply been the music of the "breakdown group" within a jazz band, a sparer, string band unit without brass instruments. British skiffle was born in 1953, named by October 1954, and became a musical phenomenon in 1956/7. At first, enthusiasm for it was mostly in jazz venues, but as its popularity mushroomed, it could be found in both coffeehouses and concert halls. Criticism in the press tended to dwell on the fact that most skiffle group guitarists didn't venture much beyond the three chord progression (C, F, G7) provided by a basic tutor. There was even a deliberate "dumbing-down" by some professional musicians. Washboards tended to be standard and can be heard on most records by McDevitt, the Vipers, et al. Oddly only Donegan's first hit featured washboard (by Beryl Bryden, a well-respected member of the jazz community), and when he went on the road in the United Kingdom he was quick to include drums in his line-up, giving a stronger, meatier sound than his rivals had.

What is the measure of originality? Was Leadbelly's "Rock Island Line" original? Not in the sense that the song already existed when he learnt it, but over a period of twelve years, beginning in 1937, Leadbelly re-shaped the song, effectively making it "his own," that is, personalized within his large repertoire. He gave it a preamble, describing the work gang that performed it for John Lomax at the Arkansas prison farm. As he worked on the song he extended the introduction to include a little story about the engineer (train driver) outwitting the tollgate keeper by pretending that the train is carrying "all livestock" when in fact he is hauling chargeable freight—"I fooled you, I fooled you, I got all pig iron . . ." he calls back. The chorus is retained from the "original" performance and Leadbelly also uses the "Jesus died to save our sins" and "I may be right, I may be wrong" verses from it, adding the always mysterious "Cat's in the cupboard" verse.

Later the preamble about the work gang was omitted, and a dozen recorded performances of "Rock Island Line" by Leadbelly were made between 1942 and 1949, the year of Leadbelly's death. Probably the most widely heard of these was one made with Paul Mason Howard on zither at an October 1944 session for Capitol when the (self-styled) "King of the Twelve-String Guitar" was trying his luck in Hollywood. The version that inspired Donegan may, however, have been a February 1945 version made in San Francisco and later issued by Folkways. Donegan had therefore inherited a fully-formed piece, developed by Leadbelly, transforming a work song (as Leadbelly first recorded it unaccompanied, for the Library of Congress in June 1937, and again at a June 1940 commercial session with the Golden Gate Quartet for Victor, which the company chose not to issue at the time) into a concert performance piece.

Although the songbooks of Leadbelly and Woody Guthrie were central to the repertoires of most skiffle groups, songs were acquired from a wide variety of sources, some homegrown such as the Vipers' splendid version of the Liverpool streetwalker song "Maggie May" ("and she'll never walk down Lime Street anymore"). Skiffle wasn't really a song genre, it was a particular approach to the instrumentation that gave it its distinctiveness, and when the novelty of that eventually wore off it spelled the end of skiffle as a commercial music phenomenon. The music industry has never really been comfortable with the do-it-yourself approach, and it is revealing to hear how many rock groups and performers had session musicians pressed on them at recording sessions by companies anxious to achieve the required standard. Out on the road there would be so much audience noise that a few fluffs wouldn't matter!

In the formative period of British skiffle, a traditional song from Texas became a favorite, and it was performed (and recorded) at a Copenhagen concert in 1953 with Lonnie Donegan and Ken Colyer duetting, and Lonnie, Dickie Bishop, and Chris Barber later did a studio recording of it (issued on Polygon) in May 1955. The overnight train to San Antonio, Texas, used to roll out of the Houston depot a few minutes past 11:00 every night. The Southern Pacific Railroad called it "The Alamo Special," but as it crossed the Brazos River Bottoms, twenty-five miles from the city and near the small town of Sugarland, an hour later, it passed close to Central Unit 2, part of the Texas prison farm system. The black prisoners there called it "The Midnight Special," a howl of noise, a stabbing core of light, and a glimpse of freedom, vanishing quickly into the night.[9] Inmates James Baker (known as "Iron Head"), Moses Platt ("Clear Rock") and Huddie Ledbetter ("Leadbelly," also sometimes "Lead Belly"), who was incarcerated at Sugarland between 1920 and 1925, all recorded a song about it for the Library of Congress.

> If you ever go to Houston, you better walk right,
> You better not stagger, and you better not fight.
> Oh let the Midnight Special shine its light on me,
> Oh let the Midnight Special shine its everlovin' light on me.

Mack McCormick has explained the origins of the title verse and some other elements of the song as probably deriving from an earlier song about Cowboy Jack Smith's unsuccessful jailbreak in Houston. The melody and the shape of the chorus may derive from an old spiritual.

At least two African American recordings of "The Midnight Special" were made up to 1930 (although a recording of that title, by Sodarisa Miller on Paramount dating to 1925 is unrelated). Southern blues singer and guitarist Sam Collins recorded "The Midnight Special" for Gennett in 1927. By the time Chicago pianist Romeo Nelson made his final recording in February 1930, "11.29 Blues," subtitled "The Midnight Special" (Vocalion 1494), the theme had become one of universal applicability:

When you come to Chicago,
said you better walk straight
and you better not stumble,
and you better not wait
or the police will arrest you. . .

Big Bill Broonzy and the State Street Boys recorded "Midnight Special" (Okeh 8964/Vocalion 03004) in January 1935. In a somewhat tongue-in-cheek version, Broonzy places the action in Tennessee's Bluff City:

Now if you ever go to Memphis, said you better walk right,
The police will arrest you and carry you down,
And take you to the station with the gun in his hand,
Then the judge will tell you, you have been a naughty man.

Rosie, who comes to get her man out jail, becomes Mary in this variant.

There have been numerous recorded versions of "The Midnight Special" by white country and folk artists starting with a 1926 version by Dave Cutrell with McGinty's Oklahoma Cowboy Band ("Pistol Pete's Midnight Special," Okeh 45057), and the song was also included in a 1927 song collection by Carl Sandburg published as *The American Songbag*. Woody Guthrie recorded the song on several occasions, but it was almost certainly Huddie Ledbetter who inspired its popularity with skifflers. Leadbelly recorded it for the Library of Congress in 1934 and again in 1935. In June 1940 he recorded it with the Golden Gate Quartet for Victor (27266). Amongst later versions of "Midnight Special," possibly the best is the 1948 recording for Fred Ramsey included in *Leadbelly's Last Sessions* (now available on Smithsonian/Folkways CD 40068/71). Notable among the other hundred plus commercially recorded versions are those by organist Jimmy Smith, Harry Belafonte (on his RCA-Victor album actually titled *Midnight Special*), blues shouter Big Joe Turner (Atlantic 1122), and Josh White (Elektra LP 114).

In his autobiography W. C. Handy recalls his youth in Florence, Alabama, when he heard old-time fiddle players like Uncle Whit Walker (born 1800) play a tune called "Sally Got a Meatskin Laid Away."[10] (As "Johnny Got a Meatskin Laid Away" it was recorded by black singer/guitarist Arthur "Brother-in-Law" Armstrong for the Library of Congress in Jasper, Texas, in October 1940.) "Sail Away Ladies," which was also performed by Walker, utilized the same tune. Popular white country artist Uncle Dave Macon recorded his excellent "Sail Away Ladies" for Vocalion (5155) in 1927. (Born in 1870, Macon was an exceptional musician with a huge repertoire, in some ways perhaps a white equivalent of Leadbelly.) The chorus includes the phrase "don't you rock me, daddy-o," repeated four times. Thirty years after this commercial recording was made, it was revived and partially rewritten by Wally Whyton to provide his skiffle group the Vipers with a UK Top Ten hit, "Don't You Rock Me Daddy-O," in February 1957. (Lonnie Donegan "covered" their version and took his version to No. 4 in the same month. It sold strongly for the following two months.)

Following "Daddy-O" the Vipers had several other hits, including "Cumberland Gap," which also reached the UK Top Ten but was overtaken by a bigger-selling Donegan "cover," which went on to No. 1, and a "skifflization" of the Red Nelson/Cripple Clarence Lofton classic "Streamline Train," that had been issued in Britain on a Brunswick 78. As skiffle faded the Vipers dropped the skiffle group title, but their transition to rock 'n' roll produced no hits.

Hot on the heels of the Vipers came the Chas McDevitt Skiffle Group. McDevitt had already been performing traditional music pre-skiffle and had discovered a potential hit song. Already fifty years old, the song about a freight train was about to leap up the charts. Elizabeth Cotten was a maid in the household of the folk-singing Seeger family in Washington, D.C., when her talents as a singer and guitarist were discovered. A compelling skiffle version by McDevitt of her song "Freight Train" was a top ten hit in the United Kingdom (peeking at No. 5 at the beginning of June 1957) and also made the American charts, although a cover version by Rusty Draper stole the biggest sales there. This led to a U.S. tour for the Chas McDevitt Skiffle

Group, featuring singer Nancy Whiskey. (They had another, smaller hit with "Greenback Dollar," before Nancy left the group to go solo.) McDevitt has continued to be active in music and participated in several skiffle revivals. Elizabeth Cotten made a series of recordings issued on Moses Asch's Folkways label which became very influential in folk circles. Born near Chapel Hill, North Carolina, in 1893, she claimed the words and music of "Freight Train" as her own, composed in her youth, around 1910. The McDevitt hit record, enhanced by whistling, changes the perspective of the song from the first person to observer, perhaps justifying a co-composer credit. The standard discography gives the Cotten recording as ca. 1958, but that was when it was released in the United States on her first album *Negro Folk Songs\ And\ Tunes* (FG 3526). It was probably recorded in 1952 and brought to Britain by Peggy Seeger in 1956. (Seeger herself recorded "Freight Train" for Pye-Nixa around November, 1957, and this was issued on an EP entitled *Origins of Skiffle.*) Later versions included one by blues duo Brownie McGhee and Sonny Terry (Bluesville BV 1002), quite a number of country versions (e.g., Chet Atkins, Dave Dudley, Jimmy Dean), several folk recordings (Pete Seeger; Peter, Paul, and Mary), and even a jazz version (Bud Shank on *Folk 'n' Flute*), as well as popular versions by acts like Dick and Deedee, Margie Rayburn, and the Johnny Mann Singers.

Johnny Duncan, an American by birth, replaced Lonnie Donegan in the skiffle unit within Chris Barber's Jazz Band. In 1957 Duncan went solo and, with his Blue Grass Boys, scored a massive UK hit, "Last Train to San Fernando," which reached No. 2 on the charts. Although classified as skiffle it sounded more like country music, but surprisingly enough it started life as a 1950 Trinidadian road march, composed by calypsonian Dictator (Kenneth St. Bernard)! It was about the last train to run from Port of Spain, the island's capital, to its second city, San Fernando, before the railway line was closed. A later recording, made in New York by another calypso singer, the Duke of Iron (Cecil Anderson), changed the lyrics somewhat, recounting how a lady wanted a last fling on the night before her wedding and the singer was happy to oblige: "You better beat this iron while it's hot!" The Duke of Iron 78 was issued in the United Kingdom (Melodisc 1316) and was the inspiration for the pop hit by Johnny Duncan, which was first credited to Randolph Padmore/Sylvester DeVere, before the Mighty Dictator was added on the sheet music and reissue credits.

Why did skiffle falter and fail while rock 'n' roll triumphed in the charts? I can offer some possible reasons. Firstly, it didn't produce marketable teen-age idols like Elvis, Ricky Nelson, and Cliff Richard. Without doubt Lonnie Donegan was a major star, but hardly a teenage idol! Like Bill Haley before him, when Lonnie passed age thirty his chart success quickly came to an end. Secondly, skiffle was branded as home-made, anyone-can-do-it music, whereas rock relied on guitar wizardry or skilful sax work. Thirdly, the music industry was more comfortable with the adolescent lyrics and tamer sounds that tended to dominate the charts as the fifties gave way to the sixties. Songs about racehorses, like "Stewball," or murder ballads like "Frankie and Johnny," didn't really fit the bill. The traditional jazz boom of the early six-ties also tended to favor softer material, and it was British blues that emerged as the next underground movement.

Although it spawned several records that became hits in America, the British pop skiffle craze was not repeated across the Atlantic. It was a peculiarly British phenomenon, although it also caught on in several other European countries. The do-it-yourself nature of the music, while not totally confined to working-class youth, was certainly at odds with the glamour of American culture in the mid-1950s. The smoldering rebellion represented by Marlon Brando and James Dean on film and Elvis Presley on TV in the affluence of America was light years away from spotty kids twanging guitars and play-ing washboards with thimbles in British coffee bars. But somehow skiffle seemed to fill a social need, channeling the restless energy of the young into popular music as Britain emerged from wartime and postwar austerity and social conformity. More recently there have been brief skiffle revivals in Britain, Germany, and elsewhere, probably as part of the general nostalgia for the music of the fifties.

So what of originality? A song whose origins predate the recording of black music is variously known as "Easy Rider," "See See Rider," or "C.C. Rider." Blues singer Ma Rainey recorded it for Paramount as "See See Rider Blues" in 1924. Blind Lemon Jefferson and Leadbelly also recorded it com-mercially. Big Bill Broonzy even claimed to have known its composer, an itinerant blues singer who probably called himself "C.C. Rider" after the song. Postwar it provided pop and R&B hits for Chuck Willis (1957), LaVern Baker, and Elvis Presley. It was also recorded by skifflers and traditional jazz bands. More recently it has been transmogrified into "Kootchie Rider" by a group called Freaky Realistic. The process of remolding and retreading songs continues. . . . It's a case of putting the song elements together in a different way to produce a "new" performance.

The $64,000 question is at what point does added value (a new arrangement; a change to the lyric; performing/recasting a song in a different style) constitute new or co-authorship? Several legal battles have been fought on this point, with variable outcomes. Did George Harrison plagiarize the Chiffons' "He's So Fine" by unconsciously borrowing the melody for his song "My Sweet Lord"? He lost the case, but lots of artists have got away with putting new lyrics to familiar tunes, from Woody Guthrie (whose "Grand Coulee Dam," later a Lonnie Donegan hit, put a new set of lyrics to the tune of the vintage song "Wabash Cannonball") to Chuck Berry (who borrowed the same tune for his "Promised Land" hit) to Bob Dylan. Judging the "added value" that renders a reshaping of a song original enough to merit a part-credit is certainly a matter of personal assessment and subjectivity. Ultimately our ears will judge the achievement of the artist in producing a new sound. A dictionary definition of "original" as "novel in character and style" would certainly fit Leadbelly's "Rock Island Line," and on that basis I would answer the question "Whose 'Rock Island Line'?" as "very definitely Leadbelly's"!

Appendix One

The well-established Chicago, Rock Island and Pacific Railroad Company took over the Choctaw, Oklahoma and Gulf Railroad in 1902, giving them control of a railroad line that crossed Arkansas, via Little Rock into the city of Memphis, Tennessee, a major Southern hub. This became known locally as the Rock Island Line.

The significance of Rock Island, a small town in Illinois across the river from Davenport, Iowa (where Bix Beiderbecke was born) is that it was here that the first bridge to span the Mississippi River was built in 1855, for the Chicago and Rock Island railroad, which had taken just two years (1852–54) to reach that point. Two weeks after the locomotive "Des Moines" crossed the long, wooden bridge (on April 21, 1855) a steamboat hit it, setting fire to itself and the bridge, which burned down but was later replaced as future president Abraham Lincoln, then the lawyer for the railroad, successfully defended an action by the steamboat company for damages and a nuisance to navigation. The case ended up in the Supreme Court, which held that building railroad bridges across navigable rovers was lawful.

Appendix Two

In 1933 Huddie Ledbetter, (later known as Leadbelly), then incarcerated in the Louisiana prison farm was recorded by John Lomax for the Library of Congress Archive of folk song. Lomax was excited at the discovery of a major black songster, with a huge repertoire, much of which would later be recorded. Following Leadbelly's release from Angola in 1934, Lomax agreed to Leadbelly becoming his chauffeur (and intermediary with black prisoners) on further field trips through the South. In October 1934 Leadbelly was present at the Cummins Prison Farm recordings, which included "Rock Island Line," and presumably learned the song there. (He may have also later heard the actual disc recording played.) Considerable publicity came from a nationally shown "March of Time" newsreel film, recreating Leadbelly's time on Angola and meeting with John Lomax.

In 1935 Leadbelly began performing for small white audiences. With encouragement from John Lomax and his son Alan, Leadbelly developed his natural flair for the dramatic to work up stories about and introductions to some of his songs. After falling out with John Lomax, Leadbelly tried for the big time, first in New York, later in California, but Hollywood humiliated and rejected him. He returned to the more modest career of entertaining white audiences and recording frequently, mostly for Moses Asch in New York. (Alan Lomax continued to document Leadbelly's repertoire for the Library of Congress.) A projected European tour was, due to illness, limited to one concert in Paris, France, before he was forced to return home. Leadbelly died in New York December 6, 1949, a victim of lateral sclerosis, and was buried in the Shiloh Baptist Churchyard.

Within months of his death, the Weavers folk group scored a massive international hit with "Goodnight Irene," a song that Leadbelly had made his own after learning it from his Uncle Terrell. (It originally derived from an 1886 published composition "Irene, Goodnight.") Nineteen fifty could have been Leadbelly's year, although it's doubtful if he could have achieved the huge sales of the smoother Weavers' version. Instead he didn't really become recognized until Lonnie Donegan made hits out of several of his best numbers—"Rock Island Line," "Bring a Little Water, Sylvie," "Take a Whiff on Me" (as "Have a Drink on Me"), and Donegan's last skiffle hit, "Pick a Bale of Cotton." (Film exists of Leadbelly performing this, impressive both musically and physically.) Donegan recorded at least fifteen other Leadbelly songs for albums or as "B" sides. His "The Cotton Song" became a major hit (as "Cotton Fields") for the Highwayman in 1962, while Leadbelly's adapted "Hawaiian Song" became an American Top Ten hit (as "Hula Love") for Buddy Knox. The same year Jimmie Rodgers hit the Top Twenty with "Kisses Sweeter Than Wine," earlier a hit for the Weavers, using the melody of Leadbelly's "If It Wasn't for Dicky." A 1976 film of Leadbelly's life, starring blues singer/guitarist Hi-Tide Harris only had limited release, and the importance of this great American songster is still underestimated today.

NOTES

1. Who had his own hit (in Britain) with "The Shifting, Whispering Sands," a 1955 American Top Ten entry for both Rusty Draper and the Billy Vaughn Orchestra.

2. Chris Barber, apart from leading a first-rate jazz band with a wide-ranging repertoire (for over fifty years), was largely responsible for bringing a number of major blues artists to the United Kingdom to tour successfully in the late 1950s and early 1960s, thereby helping lay the foundation for the sixties' Blues Boom that flourished in Britain and in turn sparked a Blues Revival in the music's homeland.

3. Donegan commenting about the success of "Rock Island Line" in interview with Michael Pointon (quoted in the notes to "More than Pye in the Sky").

4. See Appendix One on the significance of Rock Island. The Kelly Pace group recording is available on "Field Recordings Vol. 2," Document DOCD-5576.

5. In his 1936 "Mr. So and So Blues" (Bluebird B-6983) Arkansas Shorty sings "Well, I feel like ridin' on some Rock Island train."

6. I would suggest that this is from 236-A-1.

7. This version was supposedly issued on Document DOCD-5659, *Too Late, Too Late*, vol. 12, but the recording included turned out to be identical to 248-A-1, i.e., it is the Kelly Pace Group's version.

8. There is, of course, an outside chance that it was composed outside the prison system and then adapted as a work song at a later date. See Appendix Two for a brief outline of Leadbelly's career.

9. "A Who's Who of the Midnight Special" by Mack McCormick, "Caravan" no. 19, January 1960.

10. *Father of the Blues* (London: Sidgwick and Jackson, 1941), 6 and 139.

BIBLIOGRAPHY

Booklet notes to *Leadbelly's Last Sessions*, originally issued on 4 LP records in 1994, re-issued in a 4-CD box set. Smithsonian/Folkways SF CD 40068/71.

Booklet notes to *More than Pye in the Sky*, Lonnie Donegan 8-CD box set. Bear Family Records BCD 15700, 1993.

Cohen, Norm. *Long Steel Rail: the Railroad in American Folksong.* Urbana: University of Illinois Press, 1981 ed.

Dewe, Michael. *The Skiffle Craze.* Aberystwyth: Planet, 1998.

Dixon, Robert M. W., and John Godrich, comps. *Blues and Gospel Records, 1902–1943.* Chigwell, Essex: Storyville Publications, 3rd edition, 1982.

Groom, Bob. *The Blues Revival.* London: Studio Vista, 1971.

Henry, Robert Selph. *Trains.* Indianapolis: The Bobbs-Merrill Company, 1934.

Leigh, Spencer. *Puttin' on the Style: The Lonnie Donegan Story.* Folkestone, Kent: Finbarr International, 2003.

McDevitt, Chas. *Skiffle: The Definitive Inside Story.* Robson Books, 1998.

Rees, D., B. Lazell, and R. Osborne. *40 years of NME CHARTS.* London: Box Tree, 1992.

Whitburn, Joel. *The Billboard Book of USA Top 40 Hits.* New York, 1989.

Wolfe, Charles, and Kip Lornell. *The Life and Legend of Leadbelly.* London: Secker and Warburg, 1993.

11

The Blues Blueprint

THE BLUES IN THE MUSIC OF THE BEATLES,
THE ROLLING STONES, AND LED ZEPPELIN

— RUPERT TILL

Contemporary British popular music owes much to the blues. Within blues a blueprint developed for pop and rock musicians in England, that has become integrated into Western popular music in general and British pop music in particular. Musicians like Charlie Patton, Blind Lemon Jefferson, Leadbelly, B.B. King, Muddy Waters, Big Joe Turner, Sonny Boy Williamson, and Robert Johnson created this blueprint. British popular music today often features a group of musicians focused around a singer and a guitarist with a drum kit and bass player playing a lesser role. Sometimes this includes a keyboard player, a brass section, and occasionally harmonica. These musicians usually learn orally from others or are self-taught by listening to other music or musicians rather than being formally trained. They play material written by the band themselves, and this material is often written by using another piece of music as a source. These are all formats for musical activity that originate in blues or rhythm & blues, and that were absorbed from blues into popular music. There are many other musical elements that migrated from blues forms.

Blues-influenced popular music features dance rhythms and blues-scale-based bass lines and is sometimes focused around riffs and/or grooves, which are always important. The music often employs a scale similar to the mixolydian mode, that is usually called the blues scale, and is constructed using flattened notes (especially the third and seventh) in addition to the pitches of the major scale. It uses chords whose root notes are notes of the blues scale including these flattened pitches. Rhythmically the music features syncopation and implied multiple time signatures, with an emphasis on the offbeats as well as downbeats. This has the effect of implying compound time signatures with divisions of three, five, seven, and nine quavers and semi-quavers, which coexist with and pull against the regular pulse that normally features four beats in the bar. Bars with three or five beats are often produced by adding or dropping a beat, and there is a confusion of duple and triple time inferred by the use of triplets, of varying degrees of swing, syncopation, and rubato (varying the tempo). The music includes improvisation, and it focuses on recordings and performances. It is within these latter two elements that the text of the music is defined rather than in a notated score.[1]

The guitarist or guitarists play electric guitar, and often have a more important role than the other musicians accompanying the singer. They sometimes use open tunings and metal and glass slides, and regularly use glissandi and microtonal string bending. The singer also uses microtonal sliding notes, ornamentation, and complex syncopated rhythms also influenced by blues. Guitarists utilize intricate melodic structures, use irregular phrasing, jazz licks, and frequent guitar solos or fills, with an emotional approach. They sometimes play with the guitar between their legs[2] or behind their heads[3] and play the strings with their lips or tongue, while doing splits or spins.[4] Sexual posturing is featured in the music's performance and overt sexuality in its lyrics.[5] It presents itself as oppositional to city authorities and mainstream culture by association with womanizing, substance abuse, and drinking, or with vampire-like imagery of capes or coffins,[6] occult, or even demonic imagery.

Blues created a template that British popular music adopted and developed. All the elements of blues discussed above became integrated into the work of British popular music groups, and have become the predominant forms or techniques within many genres of popular music. Firstly, this black musical form migrated into white culture, in the United States and then in England. It was when black blues artists were recorded, their music commodified, transmitted on the radio and sold on record, that business-men decided that it was a form that could generate substantial incomes for themselves. In the long term, this commodification brought recognition to the original blues artists, but it would also boost the careers and fortunes of a generation of white British pop musicians, and change the face of British popular music forever: "Popular music as we have known it in the twentieth century is inconceivable without the massive injections of these black idioms which have sustained it."[7] The music industry has regularly been dominated by artists who have adopted elements of the style of one or other musical scene[8] or genre, without actually being part of it.

White American artists such as Elvis Presley took their musical and movement style, as well as their songs, from black artists like Charlie Burse, Wynonie Harris, T-Bone Walker, Big Joe Turner, and Arthur Crudup.[9] Elvis Presley was to become the spearhead of rock 'n' roll, which saw mainstream culture selling blues-based music, with the U.S. music business and allied media documenting, promoting, accelerating, and expanding the process. His international fame and record sales were unprecedented, and no other rock 'n' roll, blues, or jazz artists have had anything like his success.[10] Advances in television, film, recording, and PA system technology helped Presley to become a singing superstar, following on from famous crooners like Bing Crosby and Frank Sinatra, and achieving a level of fame, sales, and longevity above and beyond even the most successful of black artists such as Louis Armstrong and Nat "King" Cole.

Presley led a crowd of artists playing blues-based music that became hugely successful and influential in Britain. According to Tosches, "Good Rockin' Tonight," his second single, was learned from Wynonie Harris's version, which had been a big rhythm & blues hit in 1948. "Elvis learned more than songs from Wynonie Harris. The pelvic jab-and-parry, the petulant curlings of his lip, the evangelical wavings of his arms and hands—these were not the spontaneities of Elvis, but a style deftly learned from watching Wynonie Harris perform in Memphis in the early 1950s. Henry Glover, who produced most of Wynonie's records, told me when I spoke to him in the summer of 1977, 'When you saw Elvis, you were seeing a mild version of Wynonie.'"[11]

Roy Brown, who originally wrote and recorded "Good Rockin' Tonight," explains the attitude of Presley's manager Colonel Tom Parker: "I remember Colonel Parker making the statement, 'I believe the white kids want to hear rock 'n' roll, but I'm gonna have a white boy do it.' In other words: If you want to hear 'Good Rockin' Tonight,' I'm gonna have Elvis Presley do it. A lot of those guys did those things and copied the arrangements note for note, but that way it was accepted."[12]

Many British musicians, including Cliff Richard, the Beatles, the Rolling Stones, and Led Zeppelin, copied Presley's example of how a white musician could be successful performing the blues. In England Cliff Richard was presented by the music industry as the British Elvis and became hugely successful. Richard also moved on to make films (as did Presley) and to develop a more mainstream and commercial style.

As with Cliff Richard, it is easy to see the influence of blues in the early recordings of the Beatles, although to begin with this was through secondary sources such as Lonnie Donegan and rock 'n' roll artists, rather than earlier blues precursors. The Beatles began their career performing songs by black artists live to club audiences in Liverpool and Hamburg, and this experience had a huge influence on their musical style. Their earlier albums feature cover versions of rhythm & blues hits such as "Roll Over Beethoven" by Chuck Berry. This is especially true on the *Beatles for Sale* album that was rushed out due to contractual obligations, the band reverting to playing covers of songs by artists who had influenced them, including "Rock and Roll Music" by Chuck Berry; "Everybody's Trying to Be My Baby" and "Honey Don't" by Carl Perkins; the Little Richard–inspired medley of "Kansas City" and "Hey, Hey, Hey, Hey"; and "Mr. Moonlight" originally recorded by Piano Red/Dr. Feelgood. George Harrison's friend Eric Clapton plays blues guitar on later recordings such as "While My Guitar Gently Weeps," and many other songs use blues chord sequences. "Please Please Me" uses a characteristic blues chord sequence using major E G A and B chords (chords one, four and five along with a chord with a blue note, the flattened third of the scale, as its root). "Yer Blues" has a typical blues structure, the first line repeating followed by a different third line that rhymes with the first, and uses standard blues chord progressions. Of course the title implies that the Beatles are writing blues-based material. The mix of blues and elements of traditional British song-writing give this song, and much of the Beatles' early music, its characteristic style.

The idea of a band writing their own music was very novel at the time in England, and caused much consternation amongst the Musicians' Union (MU). Generally pop stars were not the writers of their own songs, professional songwriters were employed, and MU members could read and write music. Lennon and McCartney could not, and in this way they were musically illiterate. They had copied the behavior of their blues influences, by writing their own material. They wrote in a traditional blues fashion as well, often copying sections or sequences from blues songs, using them as a formula and template for their own creations, and sometimes passing material from other peoples' songs off as their own. Whether this is stealing, adapting, or fair use is, as we shall see, a complex issue with no simple answer.

The Beatles' song "Come Together" has lyrics from the Chuck Berry song "You Can't Catch Me." The words "Here come a flattop" are used, but more than this, the type of slang, style of lyric, the style of word use, melody, harmony, and rhythm are all taken from or heavily influenced by the Berry number.[13] Chuck Berry was a major influence on Presley and the Beach Boys in the United States, and on the Beatles as well. Generally the Beatles were more careful about avoiding obvious uses of existing material.

However this is not the only example of the Beatles using elements of African American music in their composition and arrangement. In a fascinating analysis of the records John Lennon kept on his own personal jukebox, the British television program *The South Bank Show* investigated the Beatles' early influences, and revealed to what extent the band incorporated aspects of African American musical culture. The characteristic "Wooh" often sung by the Beatles (in songs such as "Help," "She Loves You," and "I Saw Her Standing There") was taken from soul band the Isley Brothers, picked up when the band recorded the Isley Brothers' "Twist and Shout," and also from Little Richard, who himself copied the idea from gospel singer Alex Bradford. Lennon is heard in the documentary saying that they put that "Wooh" all over their music.

The song "I Feel Fine" is based on "Watch Your Step" by Bobby Parker, with the melody and lyrics changed but the blues chords and guitar riff the same. The main guitar riff on this song also features on "Day Tripper." Discussing these songs in the documentary, Lennon is heard candidly explaining how important African American musical styles were to him, describing how he would use the music from existing songs to write his own, adding new lyrics and melody[14]: "In the early days, I would often write a melody, a lyric in my head to some other song because I can't write music. So I would carry it around as somebody else's song and then change it when putting it down on paper, or down on tape—consciously change it because I knew somebody's going to sue me or everybody's going to say 'What a rip off.'"[15]

Parker's "Watch Your Step" was itself based on Dizzy Gillespie's "Manteca." Parker altered the riff turning it into a blues. Unknowingly the Beatles (and later Led Zeppelin) were taking from Dizzy Gillespie as well as from Parker.

The Beatles' backbeat drum sound was taken from rhythm & blues and Motown music, and the whole Merseybeat sound was at the very least heavily influenced by these styles. The harmonica playing on the Beatles' "Love Me Do" was copied from Delbert McClinton, who played harmonica on the Bruce Channel hit "Hey Baby," in a style taken from blues player Sonny Boy Williamson.

In comparison to the Beatles, the Rolling Stones more specifically referenced blues artists. They began as a band that played rhythm & blues covers. Their first three albums included versions of "I Just Want to Make Love to You" and "Little Red Rooster" by Willie Dixon, "Mona" by Bo Diddley, "Everybody Needs Somebody to Love" by Solomon Burke, "Carol," "You Can't Catch Me," "Around and Around," and "Talkin' 'Bout You" by Chuck Berry. They credited artists like Willie Dixon and Chuck Berry properly, moving on to write their own songs as their career and song-writing skills developed.[16]

The Rolling Stones' musical roots are somewhat different from those of the Beatles, and are linked to the later group Led Zeppelin via the spread of the blues in London in the 1960s. British musicians Alexis Korner and Cyril Davies had seen Muddy Waters on tour and were converted to become "life-long disciples of the blues."[17] Korner and Davies created Blues Incorporated, the first blues band to be formed in the 1960s London's blues explosion, and a band that was to be very influential. By May 1962 Mick Jagger and Charlie Watts (who were soon to form the Rolling Stones) and Jack Bruce (who would eventually join blues guitarist Eric Clapton as a member of Cream), were members of Blues Incorporated, and it quickly became a popular band, developing a surrounding blues scene in London that contrasted with the Merseybeat sound that spawned the Beatles. Schoolboy friends Jeff Beck and Jimmy Page took up the guitar, influenced by Chuck Berry and Bo Diddley, inspired by this new blues scene. The pair started to host regular blues jams and were to become significant figures in the London blues scene. Page played with Cyril Davies's interval band at the Marquee club, one night supporting Muddy Waters. Jagger and Watts left and went on to form the Rolling Stones, who began to perform as support act to Blues Incorporated. The Rolling Stones exploded into the charts in 1963 (a year after the more commercial sound of the Beatles had done the same), left their weekly residency at the Marquee, and were replaced by Eric Clapton's experimental blues band the Yardbirds.[18]

The Yardbirds' lead guitarist Eric Clapton left to form Cream (with former Blues Incorporated member Jack Bruce), and went on to play with the Beatles and become perhaps the best-known British blues guitarist, doing much to popularize older American blues artists, but outselling them considerably. He was replaced in the Yardbirds by another guitarist from the London blues scene, Jeff Beck, the schoolboy friend of Jimmy Page (who had been offered and turned down the role). Page would go on to form Led Zeppelin. Like the Rolling Stones, the Yardbirds went on to record in Chess Records' studios, making their own pilgrimage to the source of many of their influences. Eventually Jimmy Page was asked again to join the Yardbirds, and this time said "yes." Page had spent a number of years playing on huge numbers of pop hits as a session musician for groups such as the Who, the Kinks, Them, and others. In 1965, blues original Sonny Boy Williamson came to the United Kingdom to tour, and played a session with a number of British blues musicians including Jimmy Page.[19] Williamson was eventually to record with the Animals and Chris Barber's band as well as with the Yardbirds. The Yardbirds eventually fell apart. Page decided to complete a tour booked for the band, and found new musicians to perform the Yardbirds' remaining gigs. After the tour the new group changed its name to Led Zeppelin.[20]

Led Zeppelin in particular became hugely successful with a style that overtly and consciously took from blues music. Page recruited a session musician called John Paul Jones to play bass guitar and keyboards, and two up-and-coming musicians, blues singer Robert Plant and drummer John Bonham.[21] Singer Robert Plant was hugely influenced by the blues, having seen Sonny Boy Williamson perform in Birmingham in 1965, been influenced by Bukka White's vocal style, and played in numerous Midlands blues groups and also with Alexis Korner.

Allan Moore, and also Hatch and Millward, claims Led Zeppelin's music relates little to the blues.[22] However, Susan Fast disagrees, and like her I cannot see how one can ignore the band's blues influences. "Lyrically, Plant leaned very heavily on blues songs, often combining sections from several sources into a single song."[23] Of guitarist Page, Fast says, "Page's guitar style throughout Led Zeppelin draws extensively on blues licks derived primarily from the Delta blues scale, and even a late song such as 'In My Time of Dying' utilizes bottleneck guitar playing derived from the blues."[24]

In fact this song is a variation of "Jesus Make Up My Dying Bed," a gospel blues recorded in 1927 by Blind Willie Johnson, recorded in 1929 by Charlie Patton as "Jesus Is a Dying Bed Maker," and in 1933 by Josh White as "In My Time of Dying." Bob Dylan performed "In My Time of Dying" on his debut album in 1961. Led Zeppelin credit the song as if they had written the words and music themselves. The band also covers Robert Johnson's "Nobody's Fault but Mine" (also without crediting it). Fast describes Plant's "trademark of stringing together fragments of text from existing blues songs."[25] Bass player John Paul Jones says that, "Robert would sing along using lyrics from blues songs that he already knew in order to get a melody and/or phrasing and would then rewrite them later (or not!)."[26] Like Page, bass player John Paul Jones had been a successful session musician.[27] John Bonham was a successful young drummer with interests in blues and soul. The band also borrowed from British folk music and other styles, all integrated into their own electrified heavy style, and were undoubtedly innovators turning blues into a massively commercially successful form by playing it louder, faster, and more carefully produced than ever before.[28]

It is interesting to investigate the degree to which Led Zeppelin were influenced by blues music. Led Zeppelin's first album included versions of "I Can't Quit You Baby" and "You Shook Me" by Chess Records' songwriter Willie Dixon. On "I Can't Quit You Baby," Page plays some note-for-note quotes, guitar lines from the Willie Dixon version (which features more guitar solos than Otis Rush's version of the song). Plant sings higher and wilder than either version, but with similar slides and syncopation. "You Shook Me" was a song Jeff Beck (Page's school-friend and ex-Yardbirds bandmate) had included on his recently released (at the time) album *Truth*. Without the detail of the original Willie Dixon version, without the rhythmic syncopation and inflection, Beck's version lacked blues authenticity, with organ chords layed straight on the beat and Rod Stewart also singing the lyrics on the first beat of the bar instead of anticipating or weaving around the beat. The Led Zeppelin version is far more authentic, quoting the guitar part from the original, showing the influence of years of blues scholarship and a deep understanding of the music.[29] However, despite Jeff Beck, Muddy Waters, Otis Rush, and John Mayall's Bluesbreakers all crediting the song correctly to Dixon in previous recordings, Led Zeppelin failed to credit him and were sued, with Dixon receiving a substantial settlement.

"Babe I'm Gonna Leave You" credits Anne Bredon, also known as Anne Briggs, after Led Zeppelin was sued for not having credited her. The only available previous recording of the Bredon track is by Joan Baez on her *In Concert* album. Baez regards the song as a blues, and as a modern composition, and says of the song, "One of the favorite themes in Blues is that of 'traveling on,' moving from one place to another, finding new loves and new experiences. This restlessness is rarely expressed so well in modern urban blues."[30]

Bob Dylan, Baez, and others had revived an interest in acoustic blues via the U.S. folk revival, and acoustic blues had become popular with folk musicians in the United Kingdom, influencing British folk musicians, many of whom mixed U.S. blues music in with traditional British folk music in their live performances.

The last track on the first Led Zeppelin album is titled "How Many More Times" (HMMT). This seems to be derived from a number of sources. According to Page, "That has the kitchen sink on it, doesn't it? It was made up of little pieces I developed when I was with the Yardbirds, as were other numbers such as 'Dazed and Confused.' ... I initiated most of the changes and riffs, but if something was derived from the blues, I tried to split the credit between band members."[31]

Howling Wolf recorded a very similar song, "How Many More Years" (HMMY), and another called "No Place to Go" (NPTG). HMMT begins, "How many more times, treat me the way you wanna do," NPTG includes the lyrics, "How many more times you gonna treat me like you do" with a similar melody line and a harmonica part which is also featured in the Zeppelin tune. HMMY begins, "How many more years, have I got to let you dog me around," lyrics that are similar if not identical to NPTG, but this song has clearly the same tune, and is the source of the Zeppelin melody.

In the middle of the track the song goes into an obvious cover of the Albert King song "The Hunter." Some of the lyrics, the melody, chord sequence, rhythm, and tempo are the same, and this is obviously a quote from the King song. Zeppelin guitarist Page even takes one of the guitar riffs from the beginning of the song and integrates it. Led Zeppelin's use of "The Hunter" is very different to the approach of their contemporaries Free, who cover the same song but credit King. HMMT's bass guitar line on the song is taken from the Yardbirds' cover of the Howling Wolf song "Smokestack Lightning." Page originally played bass in the Yardbirds, so it is possible that the bassline was his creation. This bassline is the main driving riff for HMMT on which the arrangement is based. Just over three minutes into the song, the band begins a quote from a tune by Jeff Beck, "Beck's Bolero," on which Page had played. It takes the rhythm guitar part as well as the solo part from the Beck tune. This and the use of "You Shook Me" created bad feeling between the two childhood-friend guitarists. HMMT is a song that is pieced together out of other blues songs, and yet it is credited to Page, Bonham, and Jones. It is very clear that the band are a blues band, growing out of the blues explosion and playing largely blues music at first, and this collage style song-writing technique is a traditional blues one.[32]

The band's use of traditional tunes from British and African American sources is a complex issue as it was for the Beatles and the Rolling Stones. Rights and ownership were not as well defined, understood, or controlled as they are today; it was common to record other people's music without crediting it. Considering that Elvis Presley, the Beatles, the Beach Boys, and blues artists themselves often took material from other blues artists, it is not surprising that Led Zeppelin did the same. It is perhaps because they so overtly used blues material, they were so specifically a blues group and that their sales and fame became so large, that their use of blues material is so well documented. This first album was made in three weeks and so was rather rushed, using any material to hand, much of which Page knew from his days in the Yardbirds. It is also clear that this first album is a Yardbirds album with a changed band name, using material that the Yardbirds performed, but with new personnel apart from Page.[33] In this way, the band is very much a part of the blues explosion of the 1960s. Their later albums featured less music that was not either original or at least better disguised, and yet like the Beatles and Stones they continue to profit from passing the uncredited use of copyright and traditional materials off as their own.

On their second album, *Led Zeppelin II*, the band recorded Willie Dixon's "Bring It On Home" but failed to credit him. In 1972 Arc music sued Led

Zeppelin, claiming that they had plagiarized Dixon, and a settlement was reached out of court. On an early version of this second album one track is "Killing Floor," credited to Chester Burnett, better known as Howlin' Wolf. Later vinyl and recent CD versions are titled "The Lemon Song" and are credited to the members of Led Zeppelin. The song is by Burnett, and his publishers sued in the early 1970s and settled out of court. Albert King and the Electric Flag had recorded previous versions, both credited correctly to Burnett.

The album also includes the song "Whole Lotta Love." This song was originally credited only to the band, but eventually they were forced to change the credits to include Willie Dixon, after being sued by Dixon and settling out of court. "You Need Lovin'" is a version of the Dixon song (also not correctly attributed) by the Small Faces. Steve Marriott discusses how Led Zeppelin came to play it, referring in particular to Robert "Percy" Plant:

> "'Whole Lotta Love' by Led Zeppelin was nicked off that album," Marriott
> pointed out. "Percy Plant was a big fan. He used to be at all the Small Faces gigs.
> We did a gig with The Yardbirds which he was at and Jimmy Page asked me
> what that number was we did. '"You Need Lovin',"' I said, 'It's a Muddy Waters
> thing,' which it really is, so they both knew it, and Percy used to come to the
> gigs whenever we played in Kidderminster or Stourbridge, where he came from.
> He was always saying he was going to get this group together. He was another
> nuisance. He kept coming into the dressing room, just another little mod kid.
> We used to say, 'That kid's here again.' Anyway we used to play this number and
> it became a stock opener after that album. After we broke up they took it and
> revamped it. Good luck to them. It was only old Percy who'd had his eyes on
> it. He sang it the same, phrased it the same, even the stops at the end were the
> same, they just put a different rhythm to it."[34]

Plant discussed the sources of "Whole Lotta Love" in an interview: "Page's riff was Page's riff. It was there before anything else. I just thought, 'Well, what am I going to sing?' That was it, a nick. Now happily paid for . . . you only get caught when you're successful. That's the game."[35]

Dixon used the settlement from "Whole Lotta Love" to start The Blues Heaven Foundation. It aims to promote the blues, but also "a long-term goal is providing for blues artists and/or their heirs who suffered from the lack of financial safeguards in writing and recording their music."[36] Alexis Korner's

CCS (Collective Consciousness Society) released a version that became even more famous when it became the theme music for UK chart TV show *Top of the Pops*.

Also on the *Led Zeppelin II* album is "Moby Dick," an instrumental track based on "The Girl I Love She Got Long Curly Hair" by Sleepy John Estes and Bobby Parker's "Watch Your Step," the track the Beatles used as a source for "Day Tripper" and "I Feel Fine." As discussed earlier, Parker had based his tune on a Dizzy Gillespie track, "Manteca." An early live version released by the BBC recently features Plant singing Estes's lyrics and uses Estes's title. "Moby Dick" is credited to Page, Jones, and Bonham.

Led Zeppelin went on to record a third album which featured "Gallis Pole," (a blues version of a folk song recorded by Leadbelly), renamed and arranged as "Gallows Pole," and "Hats Off to (Roy) Harper" is adapted from Bukka White's "Shake 'Em On Down" and credited as a joke to "Traditional Arr. Charles Obscure," not so funny for White. "Since I've Been Loving You" is an original blues track. On their fourth album they recorded Memphis Minnie's "When the Levee Breaks,"[37] and continued to be blues-influenced, but also brought more influences in from other styles such as funk and reggae. They also recorded a song called "Rock and Roll." It begins with the drum introduction to "Keep a Knockin'" by Little Richard. "We were recording something else—I can't remember what it was at the time and John Bonham just started playing the opening bars of 'Keep A Knockin',' by Little Richard—the drum intro. I heard that and just started playing what you know as the riff of 'Rock and Roll.' We got through the first twelve bars and said, 'Let's stop and listen to this.' The other song just got totally forgotten about and we did 'Rock and Roll,' all in a matter of minutes."[38] This is a good illustration of how the band developed but still kept their blues roots, taking less material from existing music and creating their own instead.

In an interview, Jimmy Page discussed the band's use of blues material:

> As far as my end of it goes, I always tried to bring something fresh to anything that I used. I always made sure to come up with some variation. In fact, I think in most cases, you would never know what the original source could be. . . . So most of the comparisons rest on the lyrics. And Robert was supposed to change the lyrics, and he didn't always do that—which is what brought on most of the grief.

We did, however, take some liberties, I must say [laughs]. But never mind; we did try to do the right thing, it blew up in our faces. . . . "Boogie With Stu" . . . was obviously a variation on "Ooh My Head" by the late Ritchie Valens, which itself was actually a variation of Little Richard's "Ooh My Soul." What we tried to do was give Ritchie's mother credit because we heard she never received any royalties from any of her son's hits, and Robert did lean on that lyric a bit. So what happens? They tried to sue us for all of the song!! We had to say bugger off. We could not believe it.[39]

Plant in particular has continued to perform blues music, still touring in 2006. In concert one cannot fail to note his knowledge of blues music, describing all his sources carefully and paying tribute to his sources and influences. Even so, Page's pride at the group's half-hearted attempt to do the right thing once is laughable, as Fast puts it, "Borrowings are common in other Zeppelin songs, a characteristic for which the group have been severely criticized as well as sued for royalties. . . . [T]here can be no excuse for denying black blues artists their share of royalties."[40]

To put this in perspective, it is important to appreciate the level of success that groups like the Rolling Stones, the Beatles, and Led Zeppelin have had. The Rolling Stones' more authentic approach has of course, brought them substantial success, selling 4.1 million albums in the United Kingdom alone. However UK sales are tiny compared to those in the United States, where the population offers the opportunity for huge sales. Recording Industry of America Association figures show that the Rolling Stones have sold 53.5 million records in the United States. In comparison, the Beatles have had at least 5.8 million sales in the United Kingdom, and they are the biggest selling artists in the United States of all time with 164.5 million sales. Led Zeppelin are the second-highest selling artists of all time in the United States, selling 105 million albums (and 200 million worldwide). In the United Kingdom they have had 3.9 million sales.[41] These are some of the most financially successful acts in the history of the music business. These figures give an indication of their levels of success, although sales figures are incomplete and do not include early sales in the 1960s, or substantial areas such as income from live performances, merchandising, cover versions by other groups, radio, television, and film.

Black artists did not find as much support and financial success in the music industry. Chuck Berry describes his lack of understanding of copyright. He didn't have a clear understanding of which elements of the music were owned by others and protected, and how copyright of his own music would work. Speaking of his first contract with Leonard Chess of Chess records and Arc (Chess Records' publishing arm), he tells us: "He gave me ... a publishing contract, a segment of the music business I was totally ignorant of. ... I didn't understand most of the terms and arrangements of publishing either. ... Some of the statements were beyond my knowledge of the record business, such as the 'Residuals from mechanical rights,' the 'Writer and producer's percentages,' and the 'Performance royalties and publisher's fees.' ... I was being railroaded ... Leonard knowing full well I'd sign the darn thing anyway."[42]

Willie Dixon also discusses Arc music (the company famous for adding label printer Fratto and deejay Freed to Chuck Berry's credits on his first single "Maybellene"). Dixon makes it clear that Arc made a lot of money for its owners and that the black artists making the music saw little of the income from their recordings.

> I think Chess took advantage of everybody because I don't know anybody
> they gave all their money to. ... I knew they were getting me but I didn't have
> another place to go. Chess had threatened other people in record companies ...
> that if they started recording me they were going to have problems out of them.
> Frankly Leonard (Chess) was a maneuverer. He was dealing with people who
> didn't know anything about the recording business. I call it swindling but most
> people call it smart business when you can take advantage of someone who
> don't know no better. I didn't know anything about copyright laws or anything
> like that. ... The law can take care of it if you can get enough money to get a
> lawyer to get justice. They felt like if they could keep you poor enough, you
> wouldn't have nothing to fight with and that's the truth.[43]

Dixon is critical of Chess and Arc, and yet Chess was a label that was groundbreaking at the time in its support of black artists and at least provided an avenue for them to gain exposure. Many musicians, both black and white, failed to be appropriately rewarded financially for their work during this era due to a lack of legal awareness and readily available information, allowing managers and record and publishing companies to take advantage of this situation for their own benefit.

We have seen how blues music created a blueprint that has become integrated into Western pop music in general and British pop music in particular. We saw particularly how the Beatles, the Rolling Stones, and Led Zeppelin became hugely successful by writing well-produced blues-soaked music that epitomized this blueprint, and exaggerated it. They were at the beginning of the development of rock music, a style that exemplified this blueprint and continues to exaggerate it. Led Zeppelin are a good example of what Frith calls "cock rock" which features many elements of this blueprint.[44] We have also seen how these groups went on to have huge UK record sales, and became some of the highest-selling recording artists in the United States, where they had more influence than the blues artists who first inspired them.

Led Zeppelin adopted the overt sexuality of blues lyricism and performance practice, Page adapting Chuck Berry's duck walk and the blues guitar hero image, Plant reflecting the sexuality common in blues music.[45] British culture reacted to the physicality and sexuality of blues culture by the moral panic[46] engendered by the gyrating pelvis of Elvis Presley and the reaction of British youth to rock 'n' roll, and a few years later by the hysteria that accompanied the Beatles. The influence of sexuality and physicality in blues music on British culture is an area that warrants more detailed investigation.

There are many reasons why this process of appropriation of black culture has happened. There are sound commercial reasons; having seen the success of Elvis Presley, others followed his example. The otherness and physicality of African American culture appealed to British musicians living in a culture where historically culture had split attitudes to mind and body, with the physical often seen in a negative light.[47] The dances that accompanied various musical styles also appealed. Despite not being African culture, African American culture still held attractive vestiges from it that were either actually present, or appeared to be in the minds of Europeans, in stark contrast to Western European cultural attitudes to dance and the body, where "style has become separated from cultural knowledge so that dance movements are rarely recognized as bearers of cultural values."[48] These nonwestern attitudes to physicality were present in blues music, and I believe this was part of the reason blues specifically, and African American music in general, was especially popular in Britain.

Some writers have claimed that British musical culture had become industrialized and McDonaldized, so that musical production was a process that could be calculated and controlled by industry.[49] Blues and African American culture appealed very strongly in Britain, seeming closer to a raw musical style that developed within a specific cultural setting, not homogenized and commercialized, with more of its rough edges unpolished, or at least appearing so to a white audience.

Musical cultures are different and not immediately comparable due to their mediation, and this is important to bear in mind.[50] However, what are interesting are these differences of culture, performance practice, and mediation, between these European and African/African American cultural, artistic, and musical worlds, and the way that they have attracted British audiences, influenced British music, British cultural practices, and therefore British culture. It was the mixture of African American and white European culture that was so successful, whether it was Berry or Presley mixing country and blues, or white Europeans playing African American blues music.

The success of the British bands that based their music on blues eventually benefited African American blues artists by making them more famous and financially successful. However, it does not seem that the black originators of this culture have benefited proportionately from it or been given credit to a level appropriate to their contribution. This is not just due to the choices of consumers, but also because of what has been offered to audiences, prioritized, and marketed to them. It has been caused by copyright laws that were written by, and designed to benefit, the wealthy and powerful within the music industry, and also by lack of opportunity and discrimination. It is also due in some cases to individuals very deliberately taking advantage of this situation in order to make themselves more wealthy, often at the expense of African American blues musicians. Thus it seems that while the lives of British and other European people have been enormously enriched by African American musical culture, it has often been as a continuation of the exploitative relationship first established with the transatlantic slave trade.

NOTES

1. See Cutler quoted in Bruce Horner and Thomas Swiss, *Key Terms in Popular Music and Culture* (London: Blackwell Publishers, 1999), 212, and Simon Frith, *Performing Rites—on the value of popular music* (Oxford: Oxford University Press, 1996), 227.

2. Charlie Patton played with his guitar between his legs and was known for jumping around while performing. He was a prototype for rock guitarists.

3. T-Bone Walker is probably the first to play electric (rather than acoustic) blues guitar in 1935/6, and adds splits and twists to Patton's stylings. Notes from CD booklet. *T-Bone Walker: The Original Source* (London: Proper Records, 2002).

4. Prince epitomizes how these elements of blues performance practice have become part of popular music. Many of these performance tricks can be seen in his film *Purple Rain.*

5. Wynonie Harris is a good example of a blues musician who deliberately sexualized his performances in order to attract audiences. See Nick Tosches, *Unsung Heroes of Rock 'n' Roll* (New York: Da Capo Press, 1999), 45–53.

6. Screamin' Jay Hawkins was a singer who wore stage make-up and capes, used coffins as props, and whose onstage theatrical flamboyance is a source for later artists like Little Richard, James Brown, and Ozzy Osbourne of Black Sabbath. Hawkins left the music industry, frustrated that his records didn't sell while covers by white artists became successful. "I got fed up. I went to Honolulu for ten years because I figured the world wasn't ready for me. In the meantime, all these people are recording my goddamn stuff. Nina Simone, Alan Price, the Animals, Creedence Clearwater Revival, the Who, Them, Manfred Mann, the Seekers, Arthur Brown. Melvin Van Peebles copied my whole act and put it on Broadway. . . . At one time or another, they've all taken a little something from me, and I get the impression that everybody's going places with what I was doing fifteen goddamn years ago. Everybody but me." Screamin' Jay Hawkins in Tosches, *Unsung Heroes of Rock 'n' Roll,* 162.

7. Paul Oliver, *Black Music in Britain* (Buckingham: Open University Press, 1999), 168.

8. Andy Bennett, *Popular Music and Youth Culture: Music, Identity and Place* (London: Macmillan, 2000).

9. Ibid., 194.

10. Presley is the only rock 'n' roll artist of the 1950s in the top 100 selling artists in the United States. There are no black blues or jazz artists in the top 100. Record Industry Association of America, *Top Artists,* www.riaa.com/gp/bestsellers/topartists.asp (October 7, 2006).

11. Tosches, *Unsung Heroes of Rock 'n' Roll,* 45–46.

12. Ibid., 77.

13. Lennon admitted "Come Together" was based on Berry's song, and in response Berry's publisher sued Lennon. After some wrangling Berry did not get credited on the Beatles' song, but in an out-of-court settlement, Lennon promised to record three tracks that belonged to the same publisher. On seeing how many of the publisher's songs he liked, Lennon decided to record a whole album of covers. The album emerged, called *Rock and Roll,* in 1975. It featured a cover of "You Can't Catch Me" by Chuck Berry alongside "Sweet Little Sixteen," a Berry song from which the Beach Boys copied the chords, structure, riffs, rhythm, melody, and arrangements for one of their first major hit singles, "Surfin' USA." Writing credits were changed on the Beach Boys' song after the threat of legal action to include Berry. The Beach Boys' "Fun Fun Fun" similarly is based on Berry's "Johnny B. Goode." Lennon's album also featured "Ain't That a Shame" by Fats Domino and music by Ben E. King, Sam Cooke, and Lee Dorsey, further showing Lennon's blues influences.

14. Chuck Berry's first Chess Records hit "Maybellene" was originally called "Ida May," based on the country song "Ida Red." It was Berry's heavily derivative attempt to mix blues and country. Leonard Chess shrewdly suggested changing the name of the title to disguise the similarities. Like other blues artists, Berry learned to write songs by adapting other people's material.

This way of composing was a common blues practice. Indeed Berry's song is also indebted to the Harlem Hamfats' 1936 single "Oh! Red."

15. Information on Lennon's Jukebox comes from a television documentary, produced by C. Walker, shown March 14, 2004, *John Lennon's Jukebox* on *The South Bank Show* (documentary) by Initial, Endemol UK, for ITV television, United Kingdom.

16. It is interesting to note that mid-career Lennon and the Beatles took musical material and lyrics from "You Can't Catch Me" for "Come Together" in 1969 without any attempt to credit the author, while in comparison the Rolling Stones cover and properly credit "You Can't Catch Me" as early as 1966.

17. Steven Davis, *Hammer of the Gods: Led Zeppelin Unauthorized* (Oxford: Pan Books, 2005), 15.

18. These developments are traced in Bob Brunning, *Blues: The British Connection* (London: Helter Skelter Publishing, 2002 ed.).

19. Davis, *Hammer of the Gods*, 19–20.

20. Ibid., 17.

21. Steve Winwood, Keith Moon, and John Entwhistle all discussed joining Page's new band.

22. Allan F. Moore, *Rock: The Primary Text* (Milton Keynes: Oxford University Press, 1993), 72; David Hatch and Stephen Millward, *From Blues to Rock: An Analytical History of Pop Music* (Manchester: Manchester University Press, 1987).

23. Susan Fast, *In the Houses of the Holy: Led Zeppelin and the Power of Rock Music* (Milton Keynes: Oxford University Press, 2001), 8.

24. Fast, *In the Houses of the Holy*, 8.

25. Ibid., 25.

26. Ibid., 26.

27. Andy Fyfe, *When the Levee Breaks: The Making of Led Zeppelin* (London: Unanimous Ltd., 2003), 23.

28. S. Pond, "The Song Remains the Same," in *Rolling Stone* (New York: 522 Wenner Media, 1988), 68–69.

29. The sources of Led Zeppelin's influences have been discussed at length in Dave Headlam, "Does the Song Remain the Same? Questions of Authorship and Identification in the Music of Led Zeppelin" in Elizabeth West Marvin and Richard Hermann, eds., *Concert Music, Rock and Jazz since 1945* (New York: University of Rochester Press, 1995), 313–64. I have also sourced some of this information from Will Shade, "The Thieving Magpies: Jimmy Page's Dubious Recording Legacy," *Perfect Sound Forever* www.furious.com/perfect/JimmyPage (June 26, 2006), and from Davis, *Hammer of the Gods*. I have also used two CDs "The Early Blues Roots of Led Zeppelin" (UK: Catfish Records, 2000) and "Led Zeppelin's Sources of Inspiration" (Stockholm: Jefferson Records/Scandanavian Blues Association, 1995). I also used comments from interviews, and in some cases the sources have been discovered through my own research. In each case I have found a recording of the original source and compared it with the relevant Led Zeppelin Recording. This is the case for the whole of the section relating to Led Zeppelin.

30. Joan Baez, *The Joan Baez Songbook* (New York: Amsco Publications, 1964), 178.

31. Jimmy Page interview in *Guitar World Magazine* (London: Future Publishing, December 1993), 91.

32. As discussed in David Evans, *Big Road Blues: Tradition and Creativity in the Folk Blues* (Berkeley: University of California Press, 1982).

33. "Dazed and Confused," which was to become a mainstay of Led Zeppelin's live show, had been performed with almost exactly the same arrangement by the Yardbirds, and was an uncredited arrangement of "I'm Confused" by Jake Holmes.

34. Paolo Hewitt, *Small Faces: The Young Mods' Forgotten Story* (London: Acid Jazz Books, 1995).

35. This Robert Plant quote is from http://www.iem.ac.ru/zeppelin/docs/FAQ.html#15 Roberto De Feo (July 1, 2006).

36. Willie Dixon and Don Snowden, *I Am the Blues* (London: Quartet Books, 1989), 222.

37. Credited to Memphis Minnie but actually written by her husband Kansas Joe McCoy. See Paul Garon and Beth Garon, *Woman With Guitar: Memphis Minnie's Blues* (Cambridge, MA: Da Capo Press, 1992).

38. Jimmy Page "Promotional Interview," *Led Zeppelin Official Website*, http://www.led-zeppelin.com/news-pageint12-99.html (January 17, 2000).

39. Page, *Guitar World Magazine*, 93.

40. Fast, *In the Houses of the Holy*, 25.

41. UK figures are from www.bpi.co.uk (British Phonographic Industry), U.S. figures are from www.riaa.com (Recording Industry Association of America) (both May 1, 2006).

42. Dixon and Snowden, *I Am the Blues*, 104.

43. Dixon and Snowden, *I Am the Blues*, 218.

44. "Cock Rock" is a term used to describe music that expresses an explicit, crude, and often aggressive male physicality and sexuality. See Simon Frith and Angela McRobbie "Rock and Sexuality," in Simon Frith and Andrew Goodwin, eds., *On Record: Rock, Pop and the Written Word* (New York: Pantheon Books, 1990), 371–89.

45. Fast, *In the Houses of the Holy*, 147.

46. Sarah Thornton, *Club Cultures. Music, Media and Subcultural Capital* (Cambridge: Polity Press, 1995).

47. J. Gilbert and E. Pearson, *Discographies: Dance Music, Culture and the Politics of Sound* (London: Routledge, 1999), 39.

48. Joyce Sherlock, "Dance and the Culture of the Body" in Sue Scott and David Morgan, eds., *Body Matters* (London: The Falmer Press, 1993), 35.

49. Brian Longhurst, *Popular Music and Society* (Cambridge: Polity Press, 1996), 15–19; D. Martindale and J. Reidel, "Introduction: Max Weber's Sociology of Music," in M. Weber, *The Rational and Social Foundation of Music* (Carbondale: Southern Illinois University Press, 1958), li.

50. Middleton refers to the problems of directly comparing in a simplistic fashion western European art music and African music. "Cultural specificity makes comparative interpretation of rhythmic styles dangerous. For instance to talk of twentieth-century popular music of Afro-American extraction—by comparison with, say, European 'art' music, or its pre-twentieth-century bourgeois popular derivatives—as more 'instinctive,' more 'rhythmic,' more body-orientated misses the point." Richard Middleton, *Studying Popular Music* (Milton Keynes: Open University Press, 1990), 227.

12

"The Blues Is the Truth"

THE BLUES, MODERNITY, AND
THE BRITISH BLUES BOOM

—LEIGHTON GRIST

Directed by Mike Figgis, *Red, White & Blues* is one of the seven, mainly documentary films that comprise the series *Martin Scorsese Presents the Blues: A Musical Journey* that was produced for the American Public Broadcasting Service as part of the United States' centenary celebration of the blues in 2003.[1] The series also enjoyed some theatrical exhibition, and was broadcast in the United Kingdom on the subscription channel BBC4 in 2004.[2] Combining interviews with relevant personages with archive material and footage of specially organized sessions held at London's Abbey Road studios, *Red, White & Blues* is concerned with and traces the 1960s British blues boom from its roots within the jazz revivalist movement through the influence of numerous American blues performers and the emergence of various British bands, singers, and musicians to the revisiting and revaluation of the blues within the United States attendant upon the success of certain of those bands, singers, and musicians. Central to the concerns of this article, however, are the definitions of the blues propounded within a sequence toward the end of the film. These encompass the formal, but more demonstrate a repeated recourse to that which exceeds strict musical or rational exactness, to an invocation of, in short, the emotive and the ineffable. For John Mayall the blues is "uplifting" and "energizing." For Bert Jansch it is music that comes from the "heart." For Georgie Fame the blues is "a feel . . . an emotion." For Steve Winwood it is "a plea . . . a way of expressing a need or a want." For Lonnie Donegan the blues is a "rather natural expression rather than a contrived one." For Peter Green blues music is "kind of like religion." Eric Burdon strikes a cosmic note, that the blues "has the magical structure of three chords which you can tie into earth, sun, moon, man, woman, God," while Jansch further contends that the blues seems to express "the truth," a position more forcibly asserted by Van Morrison, who concomitantly and somewhat problematically denies it any racial pertinence: "There's no black, no white. . . . The blues is the truth." The formal definitions given range from the comparatively detailed and sophisticated to the sweepingly simplistic, from Humphrey Lyttleton's outlining of "a twelve bar format with fairly simple chord progressions" and George Melly's description of blues verse structure to Burdon's "It's simple. Anybody can play it." Even so, such definitions are, as represented, effectively subsumed by the more inscrutable statements offered. Indeed, having described blues verse structure, that there are "two lines, which are the same, the first line more or less repeated, then a third one which completes the sense," Melly promptly declares the blues "more a feeling."

Interestingly, it is the definition proposed by the sole black and American performer interviewed, B.B. King, that comes closest to situating the blues in material, historical terms. For King, the blues is about "Life. Life as we live it today, life as we lived it in the past, and life as I believe we'll live it in the future. It has to do with people. . . . It has to do with people, places, and things."[3] This article will nevertheless argue that the a-materialist definitions of the blues that dominate the sequence provide a means of placing the influence of the blues on the generation that surfaced in the United Kingdom following World War II historically and culturally, and thus a means of explaining, at least to some degree, the influence of the blues and the 1960s British blues boom.

In pursuing this argument the blues have first to be located culturally and historically in relation to modernity and aesthetically in relation to modernism. The relation of the blues to modernity has, even when implicit, as in various historical accounts of the blues, been at best largely assumed rather than specifically addressed.[4] The relation of the blues to modernism has tended either to be somewhat allusive or simply overstated. For instance, Greil Marcus's comparison of the work of Robert Johnson to that of William Faulkner and Steven C. Tracy's positing that Ezra Pound's artistic project was "characteristic of the source and spirit of the blues" are suggestive, but not argued through, while Luc Sante's assertion that the country blues of the 1920s and 1930s were "as much an expression of modernism as anything hatched in Paris or Berlin or New York" and that its practitioners "could properly be considered avant-garde" is bold, but little else.[5] Again, there is a need for more specific, as well as in this matter more nuanced, address.

Certainly, the blues emerged and developed synchronously with what can be regarded as the main phase of modernist experimentation and innovation, which in the broadest terms can be considered as covering the period approximately 1880–1950.[6] Simplifying, modernism constitutes the aesthetic response to the tensions and contradictions implicit to modernity. Modernity as a cultural-cum-historical phenomenon is linked with the nineteenth-century rise of democratization and industrialization and the attendant shifts from craft to mass production, rural to urban life, and differentiated to mass culture. Taking a longer historical view, it can be seen as the liberal-humanist culmination of the Enlightenment. However, while modernity's explosion of long-standing and often oppressive norms and structures brought with it liberating opportunity, it also brought turmoil and uncertainty. To compound matters, the Enlightenment has been perceived within modernity to have taken a "dialectical turn" through which the establishment of an increasingly systematized, technocratic social order became the source of renewed, and near-totalizing, oppression.[7] Correspondingly, modernism—as it comprises numerous, quasi-discrete movements, crosses different media, and is marked by an emphasis on formal and stylistic newness and involution—may well express freeing possibility, but also characteristically articulates fragmentation, paradox, alienation, and anomie.

The blues can in turn be located in an historical context within which the contradictions fundamental to modernity attained a particularly acute reality. While it is now generally accepted that the blues began to coalesce as a recognizable musical form during the 1890s, it emerged out of the larger social changes wrought by Emancipation and Reconstruction; that is, in relation to a markedly "enlightened" and liberal, if not in this instance especially humanist, extension of liberty and rights.[8] But as the consequent freedoms were heightened by the preceding fact of slavery—as witness the freedom of movement, which contributed to an eventually massive, and typically "modern," urban migration first within the South and later to the more heavily industrialized North and West—so too were the associated uncertainties and dislocations, not least with regard to the new need to earn a living. To quote LeRoi Jones, "the more complicated social situation of self-reliance proposed multitudes of social and cultural problems" that the black population "never had to deal with as slaves."[9] These, moreover, were exacerbated by the presence of residual and renewed racism, whether in the South, where the collapse of Reconstruction and the introduction of Jim Crow legislation tacitly validated often violent prejudice, or in the North and West, where the possibilities of greater prospects and earnings were qualified by social marginalization.

We might here also consider the axiomatic notion that the blues is an intensely personal music, be this in terms of the significance granted a performer's individual style, vocal and/or instrumental, or the propensity of blues lyrics signally to personalize matters of wider social and political import. Once more this evokes the context of modernity: namely, the emphasis laid philosophically, economically, and politically on the putatively rational individual that was, again, both empowering and, in its tendency toward social fractionation, isolating and estranging. As Jones asserts, "the insistence of blues verse on the life of the individual and his individual trials and successes on the earth is a manifestation of the whole Western concept of man's life."[10]

With respect to how the blues gives voice to the black experience of modernity after slavery, a specific example: John Lee Hooker's "Boogie Chillen." Hooker was born near Clarksdale, in the Mississippi Delta, in 1917, and moved to Detroit, via spells in Memphis and Cincinnati, in the late 1930s. "Boogie Chillen" was, on its release in November 1948, Hooker's first—and first hit—record, a claimed million-seller upon which his subsequent career was founded. A highly distinctive blues stylist, Hooker was besides, and with particular pertinence to this article, an important figure in relation to the British blues boom. He first performed in the United Kingdom in 1962 as part of a one-off concert that was a late addition to the inaugural European tour of the American Folk Blues Festival, and made his first UK tour in June 1964, returning to play three further tours during 1964–65 alone.[11] The influence of his music on British blues bands and performers of the period was considerable.[12]

"Boogie Chillen"

Well my mama she didn't allow me just to stay out all night long
Oh Lord
Well my mama didn't allow me just to stay out all night long
I didn't care what she didn't allow, I would boogie-woogie anyhow

When I first come to town, people, I was walking down Hastings Street
I heard everybody talking about Henry's Swing Club
I decided I'd drop in there that night, and when I got there
I say yes, people, yes they were really having a ball
Yes I know

Boogie chillen

One night I was laying down, I heard Mama and Papa talking
I heard Papa tell Mama, "To let that boy boogie-woogie
'Cos it's in him, and it's got to come out"
Well I felt so good, and I went on boogie-woogieing just the same
Yes

"Boogie Chillen" could be regarded as a paean to the freedoms afforded by modernity. Given the singer's biography, the song tacitly describes a transition from the rural to the urban, from the South and Mississippi to the North and—as the reference to Hastings Street makes explicit—Detroit, that is reciprocally structured upon and underpinned by an implicit movement from restraint to defiance, childhood to adulthood, family to independence, restriction to liberty, and repression to release, all of which connotations are augmented by the familiar sexual double-meaning of the terms "boogie" and "boogie-woogie."[13] The general and the historical are thus characteristically expressed through the personal and the autobiographical—or, rather, the suggestively autobiographical: Hooker patently exemplifies Dennis Jarrett's notion of "the bluesman," of the assumption of a "blues persona" that enables the blues singer to perform the blues.[14] Nevertheless, if in "Boogie Chillen" the familial and the sexual further combine in the (themselves modern) Oedipal connotations of the paternal sanction eventually granted boogie-woogie, then these obtain biographical resonance from Hooker having acknowledged that his guitar style, his boogie, is derivative of that of his blues-playing stepfather, Will Moore.[15] It is, moreover, through the oft-noted hypnotic rhythmicity of Hooker's guitar playing—not to mention its interpolated crescendos and the brief, variation-as-solo that precedes the final verse—that much of the song's (again undeniably sexual) sense of release is conveyed. However, the reverberant, close-miked recording of Hooker's *acoustic* guitar also significantly relates such release to the technological and—indivisibly— the modern.[16]

But as "Boogie Chillen" declares a freedom that, as it emerges from and against restraint, bespeaks modernity, so it suggests an attendant, and likewise assignable, uncertainty. While defiant of his mother, the song's protagonist is somewhat uneasily so.[17] The line "I didn't care what she didn't allow, I would boogie-woogie anyhow" is sung with something less than brash defiance, being more an expression of rather sullen and adolescent, guilt-ridden determination that contrasts markedly with his final, paternally endorsed affirmation of like sentiments: "Well I felt so good, and I went on boogie-woogieing just the same."[18] Similarly, the protagonist's description of his first arriving in Detroit, of being on Hastings Street and seeking out Henry's Swing Club, implies a hesitancy, the unsureness of a young man from the country new to the city that enhances, gives a feeling of relief to, his excited observation on entering the club that "they were really having a ball."[19]

Yet if in "Boogie Chillen" the protagonist's enabling paternal sanction is implicitly doubled in Hooker's paternally ascribed guitar work, then the latter further invokes—in its rhythmicity, but also its drone-like tonality and preponderance of bent, flattened notes—a larger "parental" permission: that of the blues' acknowledged West African heritage.[20] Like notice can be made of the opening verse's AAB structure: namely, the arrangement of "two lines, which are the same, the first line more or less repeated, then a third one which completes the sense" that Melly describes in *Red, White & Blues*. It is a structure that can arguably be traced back, via its transmutations in field hollers, work songs, and spirituals, to African antiphonic, call-and-response patterns.[21] True, the structure is in "Boogie Chillen" abandoned after one verse, but subsequent lines largely approximate that verse's metre. Consequently, as the song's implication of liberation and uncertainty is set off and grounded by multiple parental referrals, so the contingencies of modernity are expressed through and mitigated by formal elements that call forth long-standingness and stability, whether their provenance is recognized or not. In this, "Boogie

Chillen" is in turn indicative of the correlation of the modern and the traditional that contrastingly shapes the blues in all of its historically determined
regional, individual, and stylistic incarnations.[22] Furthermore, not only does
the blues' particular concern with modernity intersect with that of modernism, but its formal mitigation of the dislocations of modernity invites specific comparison with a distinct strain of modernist mythopoeia; that is, the
evocation and/or creation of myths and of mythic structure that, as it analogously seeks to temper the apparent illogic and fragmentation of modernity
through the suggestion of supra-historical order, varyingly encompasses work
produced by, *inter alia*, T. S. Eliot, James Joyce, Thomas Mann, W. B. Yeats,
and, with due respect to Marcus and Tracy, Faulkner and Pound.[23]

Having listed such names, we need to pause. Although the blues is far
from lacking in knowing and intentional artistry, it operates on a different
aesthetic terrain to that of, say, *The Waste Land, Ulysses, Absalom, Absalom!*, or
the *Cantos*, all of which could be conceived of as explicitly and self-consciously
adducing and constructing that which in the blues is implicitly and intrinsically structuring. Moreover, for all its emphasis on personalization and individual style, and Sante's claims notwithstanding, the blues pales before the
"remarkably high degree of self-signature"[24] characteristic of the original and
often inimitable tendencies of many modernist texts. The allusiveness and
linguistic play of such works functions reflexively to foreground the con-
ditionality of representation, and thus of meaning, within modernity. The
no-less-familiar play with and allusive repetition of verbal and musical terms
and phrases within the blues can be similarly *read*, but this derives from and
largely persists within an "oral-formulaic" folk tradition of use and reuse,
appropriation and variation, wherein representation and meaning, if not
fixed, are much less malleable.[25] Nevertheless, while the blues is not a modernist mode per se, it can be regarded as sharing a modernist epistemology,
a common—if, in the blues, tacit and not reflected upon—conception of
modern existence, as being a—perhaps paradoxical—folk form that holds
and articulates a modernist *Weltanschaung*.

Better still, the blues is a perhaps paradoxical folk-popular hybrid. From
early in its development, the blues has been molded by a commercial imper-
ative, whether played on the streets, in juke joints, at house rent parties,
in clubs, in traveling shows, or, especially, for recording purposes. It was, moreover, its commodification and dissemination through records that eminently

enlarged its audience, and made the blues a popular music regionally, nationally, and internationally. Most of those involved in the British blues boom first engaged substantively with the music via records; *Red, White & Blues* includes a section titled "Vinyl" during which note is made of visiting record shops, of totemic discs and record labels, of Mayall's "massive collection" of records, of sending off for records to the United States, of people bringing records back from the United States, and of "record listening parties" that lasted "all the way through the night." This returns us to the questions of why the influence of the blues and why the British blues boom. Both can be related to the circumstances produced by the post–World War II domestic settlement in the United Kingdom. Informed by the radical policies of the 1945 Labour government, the period saw, among other things, the establishment of a modern welfare state, and most notably the National Health Service, greater educational opportunity, slum clearance and improved housing, the nationalization of services and of heavy industry, and, in part related to the last, increased worker strength and confidence. During the 1950s there was in addition the spread of available and affordable consumer durables and other products. But if it was a time of expanding possibility, it was similarly one of increasing bureaucratization and rationalization. There were also the uncertainties generated by change, and the residual limitations of a class-dominated society. It was, in short, a period redolent of the contradictions of modernity: hence, perhaps, the appeal of a music that expressed and mediated the same.

In turn, not only was it the working class that chiefly confronted the variously empowering and discomfiting changes of the postwar settlement, along with a comparatively intact class system, but as the British blues boom was dominated by those who had grown into adulthood after World War II, so it can be regarded as a primarily working—and, to a lesser extent, lower middle-class phenomenon.[26] Among the singers and musicians featured in *Red, White & Blues*, Donegan, Jansch, Burdon, Green, and Morrison, not to mention Jeff Beck, Tom Jones, Eric Clapton, Davy Graham, Chris Farlowe, Albert Lee, and Lulu, all embody this class background, although the same cannot be said of Mayall, Fame, Winwood, or Mick Fleetwood. Indeed, one would hardly claim an exclusive class pertinence to the British blues boom, as witness the involvement of performers such as Alexis Korner, Brian Jones, Paul Jones, and Dick Heckstall-Smith. However, the point respecting class

in general holds: further to which, those Britons included in *Red, White &*
Blues who belong to or are aligned with the preceding generation, such as
Lyttleton, Melly, and Chris Barber, belong likewise to a higher class.

The blues itself was (and is) also largely the music of the black American
lower class. We must nevertheless beware of suggesting too close or direct an
equivalence between the experience of the black American lower class after
slavery and that of the British working class after World War II. While not
denying the problems faced by the latter, there were unbridgeable differences
between their situation, and that of British blues performers, and those
of their black American counterparts in terms of opportunity, exclusion,
oppression, violence, or simply social mores.[27] Certain deficiencies implicit
to the British embrace of the blues only underscored such differences. Note,
for instance, the tendency toward the romanticization of the music and its
exponents—whether this took the form of an idealization of certain artists or of an often associated, purist conception of blues form and purpose:
positions that were often exploded upon contact with actual American blues
performers[28]—or the question of literal comprehension. As Fame states in
Red, White & Blues: "We couldn't understand a lot of the lyrics to what these
guys were singing." The difficulty was presumably not just that of enuncia-
tion, pronunciation, or vocabulary, and such terms as "mojo" and "black cat
bones," but that of meaning. Blues lyrics, while demotic, are frequently not
transparent, being suffused, as in the example of "boogie," with (regularly
sexual) double-meanings or even, arguably, heavily codified.[29]

Yet thus to worry over literal meaning is somewhat to deny the more
abstract meanings conveyed vocally and musically through, say, inflection,
emphasis, and intonation. For blues artist Corey Harris there is in the blues
"a distinction between the emotions of the singer and the words he or she is
singing," what he terms a "language of exclusion," within which the words
"don't contain the emotion, they're a vehicle for it."[30] Peter Guralnick similarly observes that while what blues singers sing is not "trivial exactly," "it
does not entirely reflect what they are singing about."[31] This would appear to
take us back exactly to where we started—Fame's comment about not understanding blues lyrics is made specifically in support of his contention that the
blues is "a feel." However, if the appeal of the blues to its British followers cannot be assigned easily to shared experience, neither can it be related to "universal" feelings or truth, would such fancies remotely exist. The issue is, again,

rather that of epistemology, with the modernist epistemology embedded in the blues not only having distinct resonance for the manifest disjunctions resultant upon the post–World War II UK settlement but being rendered available culturally for the predominantly working-class participants in the British blues boom through the music's folk-popular commodity form; those of the preceding British generation who had engaged with the blues had done so, by contrast, via the then more culturally respectable music of jazz.[32] In sum, what is in *Red, White & Blues* largely described as being a-material, outside clear rational definition, a matter of the emotive and the ineffable, is, precisely, material, explicable, a matter of history and culture.

There is nevertheless a little more to be said. At the risk of apparent self-contradiction, we might return briefly to some more general considerations regarding modernity and modernism, and to "Boogie Chillen." As modernity presents mutually the culmination and the contradictions of the Enlightenment, so modernism can further be read as expressing the return of the Enlightenment repressed—hence the recourse in numerous modernist movements and texts to the realm of the ambiguous, the undecidable, and/or the ineffable. In turn, as—once more—the blues partakes of a modernist epistemology, so we can correspondingly consider in "Boogie Chillen" the interjection "Oh Lord" that follows its first line. Apart from the potentially complex connotations of an appeal to the Lord in a song so concerned with boogieing, the words as voiced, while evocative, are in terms of meaning—as they indefinitely suggest frustration, weariness, culpability, and/or sorrow—ultimately irreducible. As such, while they contribute specifically to the shifting emotional intimations of "Boogie Chillen," they also maybe, in their emotive, *seeming* ineffability, condense the very fascination of the blues.[33]

Regarding the British blues boom itself, for many involved the blues became—in some instances, and within the accelerated culture of the 1960s, very quickly—a means rather than an end. The phenomenon is finally more significant for the music that it enabled than for that which it produced. There is, moreover, an undeniable historical and cultural rationale to the several elaborations and even deformations of the blues that surfaced during and subsequent to the British blues boom. No less than the different styles of American blues, whose influence it sometimes latently but inescapably bears, such music emerged from, and differently articulates a response to, a specific material context; that is, cosmopolitan, 1960s British modernity. Consider, for example, the variable combination of R&B, soul, and pop through which the Rolling Stones and the Kinks purvey their respective visions of swinging and not-so-swinging London; the jazz-informed, extended soloing and increasingly "paranoid" lyrical concerns of Cream; the psychedelic shadings of (at least the singles of) Fleetwood Mac; or the idiosyncratic fusion of blues, jazz, folk, and, pointedly, in terms of this article, modernist literature that structures the highly personal work of Van Morrison. Moreover, one might pause aesthetically and ideologically before the particular elaboration of certain blues tropes and boorish replication of ostensible blues misogyny that is heavy metal, but as a possibly dismaying consequence of the British blues boom it has a distinct musical, historical, and cultural logic.

Near exemplary of the development of 1960s British blues is the case of the Groundhogs. Led by guitarist Tony McPhee, the Groundhogs emerged as a straight blues band in London in 1963. Named after Hooker's "Ground Hog Blues," and calling themselves at one point John Lee's Groundhogs, they actually backed Hooker on his first UK tour in 1964, stepping in when initial backing band John Mayall's Bluesbreakers could not complete the itinerary. The Groundhogs subsequently became Hooker's British backing band of choice, and recorded an album with him in November 1964.[34] Upon the decline of the British blues boom, and following a failed attempt at self-transformation into a soul band, the Groundhogs went into a period of abeyance. They re-emerged in 1968, and, after again touring with Hooker in January 1969, transmuted into a successful "progressive" blues-rock band with an overtly contemporary agenda: their best-selling albums, *Thank Christ for the Bomb* (1970), *Split* (1971), and *Who Will Save the World?* (1972), center serially, in terms of their lyrics, upon alienation, schizophrenia, and the environment. Musically, they are dominated by lengthy, pounding instrumental sections that converge upon McPhee's involved, frequently discordant soloing. The albums correspondingly approach heavy metal, but in retrospect beside convey a sense of 1960s idealism crashing headlong into harsher realities.

Split, moreover, concludes with the band's reworking of "Ground Hog Blues." Furthermore, while what is retitled "Groundhog" is chiefly a showcase for McPhee's playing, not only does the latter incorporate extended, blues-inflected slide guitar work, but the track respects both the musical structure of Hooker's original and its lyrical concern with a (clearly metaphoric) "rootin" groundhog. It consequently bears late yet powerfully respectful testimony to the significance of the blues as an apposite and enabling means of expression for the generation that, emerging within post–World War II modernity, fostered the British blues boom. It thus brings us back also to the notion of the blues as a peculiarly modern, and implicitly modernist, musical form. All which stated, the last word can suitably be granted Hooker: "There's a lot of things that give you the blues, that give me the blues, that give any man the blues . . . when you gets the feelin' it's not only what happened to you—it's what happened to your fore-parents and other people . . . that's what makes the blues."[35]

NOTES

1. The centenary was conveniently dated from the year 1903 that composer W. C. Handy declared was when he first heard the music subsequently designated the blues while waiting at a railroad station in Tutwiler, Mississippi.

2. Apart from the films, the series spawned a five-CD set compilation of the blues, a single CD compilation, twelve CD compilations of the work of individual artists, individual soundtrack CDs of the seven films, and a companion book—Peter Guralnick, Robert Santelli, Holly George-Warren, and Christopher John Farley, eds., *Martin Scorsese Presents the Blues: A Musical Journey* (New York: Amistad/HarperCollins, 2003).

3. It is notable that while black blues performers and critics are no less likely to discuss the blues in terms of "feeling" and "truth" than white performers and critics, they have a much greater tendency to relate such "feeling" and "truth" to specific historical circumstance. For example, whereas Peter Guralnick contents himself with simply asserting that "blues after all is little more than a feeling" (*Feel Like Going Home: Portraits in Blues and Rock 'n' Roll* [revised edition, Harmondsworth: Penguin, 1992], 41), James H. Cone analogously declares "The blues and Truth are one reality of the black experience," but adds that "to sing the blues, it is necessary to experience the historical realities that created them," and that "Because the blues are rooted in the black perception of existence, they are historical" (*The Spirituals and the Blues: An Interpretation* [New York: Seabury Press, 1972]), extracted as "The Blues: A Secular Spiritual," in Steven C. Tracy, ed., *Write Me a Few of Your Lines: A Blues Reader* (Amherst: University of Massachusetts Press, 1999), 235, 237).

4. Note, for example, Paul Oliver's *The Story of the Blues* (Harmondsworth: Penguin, 1972), in which the history of the blues is referred constantly to a context of modernity that is nowhere explicitly acknowledged.

5. Greil Marcus, "When You Walk in the Room" (1986), in *The Dustbin of History* (London: Picador, 1996), 148–49, 153–54; Steven C. Tracy, "Prologue," in Tracy, ed., *Write Me a Few of Your Lines*, xii); Luc Sante, "The Blues Avant-Garde," in Guralnick, et al., eds., *Martin Scorsese Presents the Blues*, 74.

6. This is not to claim that significant modernist tendencies were not apparent before 1880 or that significant modernist work, depending on medium and/or context, has not been produced since 1950.

7. Richard Sheppard, "The Problematics of European Modernism," in Steve Giles, ed., *Theorizing Modernism: Essays in critical theory* (London: Routledge, 1993), 8. Sheppard is summarizing the argument made by Theodor W. Adorno and Max Horkheimer in *Dialectic of Enlightenment* (1947), translated by John Cumming (London: Verso, 1986).

8. The *locus classicus* regarding the relation of the blues to the post–Emancipation and Reconstruction period remains LeRoi Jones, *Blues People* (New York: William Morrow, 1963). See, in particular, 50–80.

9. *Blues People*, 62.

10. *Blues People*, 66.

11. The American Folk Blues Festival was an annual package tour of American blues artists. Subsequent to 1962, it toured the United Kingdom as well as mainland Europe. Hooker's second and last UK tour of 1965 was as part of that year's package.

12. In terms of Hooker's influence, consider Charles Shaar Murray's account of Hooker songs recorded by noteworthy British blues artists in and around 1964 alone:

> Eric Clapton's first-ever studio recording was a version of "Boom Boom" cut at the Yardbirds' first demo session; the Animals also recorded "Boom Boom" for *their* original demos. . . . The Animals reprised the song, albeit augmented with a few choruses of "Shake It Baby," for their first album—cut in early '64 . . . —and threw in "Dimples" and a bravura version of "I'm Mad Again". . . . The Spencer Davis Group, having gotten their Brummie selves into a studio in April '64 . . . essayed a version of "Dimples" which also incorporated large chunks of "Boom Boom", in *Boogie Man: The Adventures of John Lee Hooker in the American Twentieth Century* (Harmondsworth: Viking/Penguin, 1999), 295.

13. Hastings Street was, in Oliver's words, "the main artery of the black ghetto" (*The Story of the Blues*, 80), and was, like Memphis's Beale Street, Detroit's main site of black entertainment.

14. Dennis Jarrett, "The Singer and the Bluesman: Formulations of Personality in the Lyrics of the Blues," *Southern Folklore Quarterly*, 42, no. 1 (1978): 31–37, reprinted in Tracy, ed., *Write Me a Few of Your Lines*, pp. 195–200 (p. 195). Notably, Hooker's "I'm Bad Like Jesse James" is one of the examples Jarrett cites in his article (p. 199). In turn, Hooker has himself stated that "Boogie Chillen" presents less than strict autobiographical experience. With respect to the song's described parental exchange: "It could have been between my father and my mother, or my mother and her last husband. The song was '*mama and papa*,' but it would relate more to my real father, because mama said, '*Let that boy boogie-woogie.*' It could've been either one." (Murray, *Boogie Man*, 40).

15. See, for example, Murray, *Boogie Man*, 35–40.

16. For an account of the song's recording, the details of which have been a little contested, see Murray, 131–33.

17. Given the slippages implicit to the song's autobiographical connotations, it is probably best not to refer to its first-person narrator as "Hooker."

18. "Many of the thoughts termed 'lines' might actually be heard or transcribed as two 'lines' since a strong medial caesura is frequently characteristic in the vocal performance of the blues line" (Steven C. Tracy, "Introduction," in Tracy, ed., *Write Me a Few of Your Lines*, 4).

19. The implication of the protagonist's "new kid in town" uncertainty, and indeed callowness, is even more pronounced in the earlier versions of "Boogie Chillen" that Hooker recorded during the same session—"Johnny Lee's Original Boogie" and "Henry's Swing Club."

20. For a detailed account of this heritage, see Paul Oliver, "Savannah syncopators: African retentions in the blues" (1970), in Paul Oliver, Tony Russell, Robert M. W. Dixon, John Godrich, and Howard Rye, *Yonder Comes the Blues: The Evolution of a Genre* (Cambridge: Cambridge University Press, 2001), 11–142.

21. See, for example, Janheinz Jahn, *Muntu: African Culture and the Western World* (1958), translated by Marjorie Grene (New York: Grove Press, 1990), 220–25; Oliver, *The Story of the Blues*, 8–14; or Gerhard Kubik, *Africa and the Blues* (Jackson: University Press of Mississippi, 1999), 49–50.

22. The blues is not just indebted to African sources, but to those whose basis is European, such as the harmonic progressions of the folk ballad tradition; see Oliver, *The Story of the Blues*, 20–25. With respect to regional blues variations, Tracy outlines some of the possible material determinants thus: "the source in Africa of slaves brought to that area; the relations and interactions between blacks and whites in the area; the proximity and access to other kinds of music; the popularity and/or dominance of a particular area performer; and the access to commercial blues recordings" ("Introduction," 5).

23. For Eliot's much quoted, but still instructive, promulgation on behalf of modernist mythopoeia, see T. S. Eliot, "*Ulysses*, Order and Myth," *Dial*, 75 (November 1923), 481–83, reprinted in Frank Kermode, ed., *Selected Prose of T. S. Eliot* (London: Faber and Faber, 1975), 175–78.

24. Malcolm Bradbury and James McFarlane, "The Name and Nature of Modernism," in Malcolm Bradbury and James McFarlane, eds., *Modernism: 1890–1930*, Pelican Guides to European Literature (Harmondsworth: Penguin, 1976), 29.

25. The term "oral-formulaic" is in inverted commas because the strict relation of the blues to such mode of composition is a matter of some dispute. For more on this, and on how the blues lyrics relate to oral-formulaic composition, see Jarrett, "The Singer and the Bluesman" and John Barnie, "Oral Formulas in the Country Blues," *Southern Folklore Quarterly* 42, no. 1 (1978), 39–52, reprinted in Tracy, ed., *Write Me a Few of Your Lines*, 201–12.

26. For a more detailed discussion of the post–World War II UK settlement and its effect on the working class, see, for example, John Clarke, "Capital and culture: the post-war working class revisited," in John Clarke, Chas Critcher, and Richard Johnson, eds., *Working-Class Culture: Studies in History and Theory* (London: Hutchinson, 1979), 238–53.

27. With regard to the situation faced by black American blues artists, Oliver writes:

> Everyday conditions in the ghetto, which constantly recur in the blues, were shared by countless singers. But even the more extreme and dramatic circumstances were to be found in the lives of some of them: Leadbelly, Son House, Robert Pete Williams, Bukka White . . . are among those who have served sentences for homicide; Noah Lewis, Scrapper Blackwell, Charley Jordan, Pine Top Smith, Buster Pickens and Little Walter among those who died from stabbings, shootings, or "muggings." Blind Arvella Gray was blinded by being shot in the face, Blind Boy Fuller by lye water . . . Henry Brown was a policy racketeer, Kokomo Arnold was a bootlegger . . . [T]he lives of many blues singers bear the scars of indifference, suppression and segregation. (*The Story of the Blues*, 106)

28. For example, in *Red, White & Blues* Melly says of Big Bill Broonzy, with whom he toured, that he was both a "lovely man" and a "terrible liar," and that while he gave "the impression he'd come straight from the Delta, into a studio, and then into fame" the "real truth was that he'd came out of Chicago where he'd sung rhythm 'n' blues at one time." To be fair, however, Broonzy had, as Lyttleton points out, been booked on the understanding that he was "not to play electric guitar" and that he played "the old field blues, country blues." Indeed, when Waters and Otis Spann first visited the United Kingdom in 1958 they caused "major controversy with their rock-scaled levels of amplification" (Murray, *Boogie Man*, 288).

29. Argument has especially centered upon the possible further meaning—or otherwise—of the blues' thematic emphasis on the exigencies of heterosexual relations. Among other interpretations, this has been read as a conscious or unconscious displacement of pro-test (Paul Oliver, *Screening the Blues: Aspects of the Blues Tradition* (London: Cassell, 1968)), as being metonymic of blacks' compromised freedom post-Emancipation (Angela Y. Davis, *Blues Legacies and Black Feminism: Gertrude "Ma" Rainey, Bessie Smith, and Billie Holiday* (New York: Pantheon, 1998)), as figuring a desire for transcendent, mythic unity (Rod Gruver, "The Blues as a Secular Religion, Part Four," *Blues World*, 32, July 1970, 7–9), or as simply being reflective of male-female relations in the black community (Jeff Todd Titon, *Early Downhome Blues: A Musical and Cultural Analysis* (Urbana: University of Illinois Press, 1977)). Blues singer Willie King is, however, unequivocal on the matter: "They would use a lot of these songs, which they would talk about a woman, but they was telling you about the boss man. . . . 'Oh my baby she's so mean, she jus' won't treat me right, she take all my money': well you're telling about the boss man. But this was a way that they have to get the message undercover." (Willie King's comments are made in another film in the *Martin Scorsese Presents the Blues* series, that directed by Scorsese himself, *Feel Like Going Home*.)

30. Martin Scorsese, "Preface" in Guralnick, et al., eds., *Martin Scorsese Presents the Blues*, 6.

31. Guralnick, *Feel Like Going Home*, 41.

32. Of the British blues scene as he first encountered it, Clapton notes that "even if they were playing [the] blues, they would lean toward the jazz side of things to give it some respectability" (Peter Guralnick, "A Conversation with Eric Clapton [1990]," in Guralnick, et al., eds., *Martin Scorsese Presents the Blues*, 235).

33. With regard to such religious interjections in the blues, note the following passage:

> Blues performers so frequently invoke the names of God or Jesus (or the Lord) in blues songs that one wonders whether such invocation is merely an empty habit learned in childhood days proven hard to break, a blasphemous cry of exasperation devoid of serious religious connotation, a deliberate rejection of or challenge to the power and authority of the Christian God, or a serious reflection of the spiritual universe of a person caught with one foot in the street and one in the sanctuary, struggling to walk a straight and satisfying path in this world. (Steven C. Tracy, "The Blues and Religion," in Tracy, ed., *Write Me a Few of Your Lines*, 214)

34. In an interview with Max Jones of *Melody Maker* in November 1964, Hooker noted: "I'm bound to say that John Lee and his Groundhogs are the number one best blues group you have over here, and they fit in with my type of music perfectly. . . . John Mayall has a real good blues band too, but the Groundhogs, they fit better with what I do." Quoted in Bob Brunning,

Blues: The British Connection (Poole: Blandford Press, 1986), 98. The album recorded by Hooker with the Groundhogs suffered a checkered history. Originally released in the United States by Verve-Folkways in 1965 as . . . *And Seven Nights*, the record was quickly deleted and subsequently "bounced around from label to label . . . sometimes under the near-fraudulent billing of *John Lee Hooker With John Mayall And The Groundhogs*, sometimes—as on the 1969 Wand album *On The Waterfront*—with several tracks retitled and an actually-not-bad horn section overdubbed at some later date by person or persons unknown" (Murray, *Boogie Man*, 324).

35. Paul Oliver, *Conversation with the Blues*, second edition (Cambridge: Cambridge University Press, 1997), 21.

13

Lowland Blues

THE RECEPTION OF AFRICAN AMERICAN BLUES AND
GOSPEL MUSIC IN THE NETHERLANDS

— GUIDO VAN RIJN

In the 1950s European popular music was transformed by the rise of rock 'n' roll. The huge success in Europe of Elvis Presley, a white American boy who started out by covering black artists like Arthur "Big Boy" Crudup and "Big Mama" Thornton, led to the creation of a great many rock 'n' roll groups. Many of their fans became interested in the black artists that had inspired their heroes. As a result African American blues music became very popular in Europe in the sixties. The Beatles and the Rolling Stones were avid collectors of blues records and imitated the songs of their blues heroes like Chuck Berry, Little Richard, and Muddy Waters on their first records. Many hundreds of so-called "Beat groups" followed their example and the crossover result, "white blues," became very successful indeed. Britain was by far the most important of the blues-influenced European countries. One of the reasons for this may be the fact that English is the language of the blues, although African Americans practically transformed it into a language of their own. The blues became very popular in other Western European countries like Austria, Belgium, France, Germany, Italy, Sweden, and Switzerland, but the Netherlands were perhaps the second most important European blues country after the United Kingdom.

Although the history of the blues in Britain has been documented quite well, this is not the case with the Netherlands. An outline of the history of jazz in the Netherlands can be found in Wim van Eyle's excellent survey, *Jazz & Geïmproviseerde Muziek in Nederland*.[1] However, in this essay I will attempt to outline or chronicle the history of the blues in the Netherlands, and try to answer the difficult question why the blues became even more popular in Holland than in other European countries and what this reveals about the Netherlands.

As was the case in other countries, Dutch interest in black music was not new. A number of black American musical performers and groups visited the Netherlands from the 1870s on, and many achieved considerable success there. In late January 1877 the Fisk Jubilee Singers sailed from the United States for Holland. Their tour had been organized by a Dutch businessman, G. P. Ittman Jr. Ittman had enlisted the Dutch cleric Adama van Scheltema to translate Gustavus D. Pike's *The Jubilee Singers, and Their Campaign for Twenty Thousand Dollars* (1873) into Dutch to pave the way.[2] The Singers' arrival caused a sensation in Holland. Crowds of children in clogs prevented them from shopping on foot.

They first performed in Baron van Wassenaer de Catwijck's drawing room, which was scented by a servant with a hot ladle of perfume. At nine p.m. Queen Sophia swept in studded with diamonds. A hundred courtiers and diplomats in all their splendor followed her. The American consul introduced the Jubilee Singers and the Queen came forward and spoke to each of them. "What makes you so much lighter than the rest?" she asked Mabel Lewis. "Why are you so dark?" she asked the man next to her. The Queen was especially moved by "The Bells" in which the group imitated the tolling and echoing of church bells. She called for it twice. The performance was so successful that the group appeared before King William III of the Netherlands in his country retreat *Het Loo* a week later.[3] After only two months of performing in the Netherlands, the Fisks had raised another ten thousand dollars for their University. They were to return to the Netherlands within two years.[4]

Several other black American singers and entertainers were to visit the Netherlands in the late-nineteenth/early-twentieth centuries. In April 1877 a second Jubilee group visited, much to the chagrin of the Fisk Jubilee Singers.

They called themselves the Wilmington Jubilee Singers, and they claimed to be raising money to have a school built in Wilmington, North Carolina.[5] Rather different was the solo entertainer Edgar H. Jones, who played the xylophone and probably blew a jug,[6] and performed in Amsterdam in 1895, 1898, 1899, and 1905, in Scheveningen in 1895, in Rotterdam in 1901 and 1904, and in The Hague in 1905. He was billed as a "Negro musical eccentric," and one review shows that he could play two mandolins at the same time and that he worked with a violin made out of a cigar box, with bottles and a puppet.[7] The Black Troubadours, five men selected from the Original American Jubilee Singers, a group of Fisk Jubilee singers led by Maggie Porter Cole, performed in Rotterdam in 1898, 1901, 1905, 1906, and 1907, in Amsterdam in 1901 and 1906, and in The Hague in 1907 and 1911. One review, in language redolent of the attitudes of the day, says "the nigger quartette finds stormy applause with their serious and comic songs, first of all the frolicking cats' song."[8] Another group, the Louisiana Troupe, this time a quartet consisting of two ladies and two gentlemen, performed in Rotterdam in 1903 and in The Hague and Amsterdam in 1904. One advertisement claimed they were famous for their "high class vocal entertainment and famous cake-walk."[9]

In the first fortnight of 1902 "Miss Bella and Mr. James Fields, Amerikaansche Neger Duet" performed in the Rotterdam Casino. Bella—Arabella Fields, "The Black Nightingale"—was born in Philadelphia in 1879. She initially came to Europe as one half of the brother and sister act in 1889. She toured widely during the first two decades of the twentieth century and finally settled in Europe.[10] She was in Amsterdam in 1915, 1916, and 1917, and she made tours through the Netherlands in 1926, 1928, and 1931.[11]

At least two more African American women spent some time in the Netherlands. Singer, entertainer, choreographer, and directrice, Belle Davis, toured extensively in Europe from 1901 to 1929. She was born in New Orleans in 1873 or 1874, and she performed in Amsterdam and Rotterdam in 1905 and in The Hague in 1906. She appeared with her "precocious pick chicks," two or three little dancing comedians.[12] "Pick" is short for "pickaninny." Eva Taylor (1895–1977), the blues singer famous for being one of the first to perform on radio in the United States, performed under her real name of Irene Gibbons as a "pickaninny" in the troupe of Josephine Gassman in Carré in Amsterdam in 1906. On October 22, 1967, she returned to perform in de Blokhut in Amsterdam.[13]

Several African American singers were to take up permanent residence across the Atlantic. Elmer Spyglass (1877–1957) from Springfield, Ohio, came to Europe in 1906. He had classical ambitions, but managed to establish himself as a leading interpreter of Negro spirituals. After failing to build a career in England he traveled first to Frankfurt before coming to the Netherlands in 1909 where he was based for the next twenty years. There are reports of concerts in Rotterdam, Amsterdam, Scheveningen, and The Hague where, as the following report shows, they were especially fond of him:

> Café Chantant Central was packed each evening, waiting for the event. When
> Spyglass finally arrived the whole hall rose. They pushed each other aside,
> stood on the chairs or worked their way forward through the aisles. After a few
> quiet songs there was "Indianola" at last.[14] Spyglass sang, laughed, cried, beat
> his forehead and even jumped on the grand piano. In the end the audience
> applauded as long as was necessary for the bonus choruses. "For then he is really
> good," the regulars in Central said. After an extra refrain there was another and
> yet another. Louder Spyglass shouted, wilder he jumped on the grand piano and
> harder he hit his head with his fists, until at last, the poor fellow was allowed to
> go, bathed in sweat.[15]

Spyglass sang in eight different languages, including Dutch and wrote a song in the language entitled "Waardeering" (Appreciation).[16] He retired in 1930 and settled in Schwalbach, Germany, where he survived the Second World War, was made an honorary citizen of the town, and died in 1957. In 1995 Schwalbach named an award for contributions to intercultural relations in his honor.[17]

Among other black touring musicians were the Four Black Diamonds, an "American Song & Dance" group from San Francisco who performed in Rotterdam in 1907, in The Hague in 1912, in Amsterdam in 1914, and in The Hague again in 1919. They dressed up as Tirolers for a hilarious yodel act.[18] Minstrel player Will Garland performed in Rotterdam in 1908, in The Hague and Groningen in 1909, in Amsterdam and The Hague in 1910, and in Scheveningen in 1923. He led a company of eighteen artists whose "Trip to Coon Town" was a popular success.[19] One assumes that the titles, like the use of "pickaninny" by other performers, were direct importations from the United States, but they also suggest that common attitudes spanned the Atlantic.

The composer, performer and conductor Louis Douglas, who was born in Philadelphia in 1889, presented a rather different sort of musical style. He performed in The Hague, Haarlem, Rotterdam, and Amsterdam in 1926; in Rotterdam, The Hague, Arnhem, and Utrecht in 1928; in Utrecht, Zeist, Nijmegen, Hilversum, Amsterdam, The Hague, Zutphen, Arnhem, Deventer, Haarlem, Zwolle, Groningen, and Leeuwarden in 1931. One of his shows was *Black People*, a two-act revue with dancing and songs from Mississippi in Act I and from New York City in Act II.[20]

These early African American visitors to the Netherlands often played in the same halls, many of which no longer exist. A survey of them indicates the variety of towns and cities which, with the geographic spread across the country, suggests a wide audience for black performance:

Amsterdam	*Circus Carré, Flora, Panopticum, Taverne Grand Gala, Paleis voor Volksvlijt, Stadsschouwburg*
Deventer	*Buitensociéteit*
Groningen	*Stadsschouwburg*
Haarlem	*Stadsschouwburg*
Leeuwarden	*De Harmonie*
Nijmegen	*Concertgebouw*
Rotterdam	*Circus Pfläging, Casino Variété, Groote Schouwburg*
Scheveningen	*Seinpost*
The Hague	*Scala, Gebouw voor Kunsten & Wetenschappen*
Utrecht	*Stadsschouwburg*
Zeist	*Schouwburg Figi*
Zwolle	*Odeon*
Zutphen	*Stadsschouwburg*

Interest in African American music even when performed in the United States was evident when in 1926 a reporter from the Dutch daily *De Telegraaf* published a series of articles in his newspaper about his two-month stay in the United States. These were subsequently reprinted in the book *Amerikaansche Kunstindrukken* (*American Art Impressions*). One of these articles was a review of a concert for fifteen hundred African Americans by blues singer Clara Smith (c. 1894–1935) in Newark, New Jersey, in 1926: "The cry! From behind the wings it comes, loud and plaintive: the note of the blues.... Suddenly Clara is there, her body like a flame, in bright orange and black around the brown of her skin. The mouth is wide open, as in a trance the head is laid back. And loud, cruelly the blues note sounds like a cry of pain, driving all of us, and frightening. Loud, loud, deeply trembling, torn from the throat, the yell of a tormented, tortured animal."[21]

Very few blues performers crossed the Atlantic in the interwar years, but the celebrated jazz and blues singer Alberta Hunter (1895–1984) performed in Cabaret "La Gaité" in Amsterdam for several weeks in the middle of 1934. She was accompanied by Surinam-born alto sax player Lex van Spall's "Chocolate Kiddies."[22] Alberta returned to Holland in February 1938 when she played with Leon Abbey at the "Dancing Tabaris" in The Hague.[23]

Academic interest in the subject of black music was also evident in the Netherlands and in 1943, in the middle of the Second World War, Dutchman Frank Boom wrote a groundbreaking study with the title *The Blues, Satirical Songs of the North American Negro*. The work was never completed and became one of the most notorious "desk drawer manuscripts." An abortive attempt to publish the book in the Studio Vista series (c. 1971) was described by Tony Russell in *Juke Blues*.[24] Although this is the first interpretative book to study blues from commercial recordings, Boom's parents refused to give permission for publication. Over sixty years later Wim Verbei gathered the fragmented parts and reconstructed the work after an intensive search. Boom's work will now be published, first in Dutch, hopefully later in English as well.[25]

Tours of Europe by black performers resumed after the war had ended, some supported by the U.S. government. Elijah Wald, Josh White's biographer, wrote that Josh was in Holland in the summer of 1950, during his first visit to Europe in the company of Eleanor Roosevelt, but no reports of concerts have been traced so far. White toured in Europe extensively, especially in the period 1959–1963, but Wald has not been able to establish a tour schedule.[26]

One of the most successful postwar blues performers to tour the Netherlands was Big Bill Broonzy. The first time Broonzy came to Europe was on July 18, 1951, but he did not appear in the Netherlands until 1952, bringing pianist Blind John Davis (1913–1985) with him. Broonzy's first Dutch concert took place on November 7, 1952, in "Die Haghe" in The Hague and the next day in the "Kurhaus" in Scheveningen.[27] In 1953 Bill played in France, Spain, Belgium, the United Kingdom, and the Netherlands. The Dutch concerts were organized by photographer Wouter van Gool (1911–1990). The first concert took place on February 26 in "Ons Huis," in the Rozenstraat in Amsterdam. It was an afternoon performance and afterwards Big Bill was taken to a pub in old Amsterdam. When he was asked to sing a few more songs there he refused, to the surprise of his Dutch friends. When they asked for the reason he explained that he was afraid that he might be arrested for being black. After it had been explained to him that there was no reason to fear such a thing in the Netherlands, Bill played for an hour.

The next concerts were held on February 27, 1953 ("De Hooizolder" above cafe "De Kroon," Boschdijk 136 in Eindhoven), February 28 ("Ons Huis," Rozenstraat in Amsterdam), March 1 ("Lommerrijk," Straatweg 99 in Rotterdam and "Gebouw voor K&W," Singelgracht in The Hague), and March 2 ("De Waakzaamheid," Hoogstraat 4 in Koog aan de Zaan). On March 2, Broonzy also recorded for VPRO radio, and on April 19, performed in the Rotterdam Jazz Centre. All the concerts were sold out, except for the April 14, one in Rotterdam and the one in Eindhoven. The Eindhovense Jazz Club (EJC) suffered a loss of several hundred guilders. This was the consequence of forces of nature rather than lack of interest. The Eindhoven concert had originally been planned for February 5, but was postponed because of the Zeeland floods. In a review in the Eindhoven Jazz Club magazine *E.J.C. Flitsen* W. A. Eschauzier wrote, "A review in the ordinary meaning of the word is not really fitting here, for this is no cultural, artistic achievement, but it is untouched folk art, the typically elementary you either like or do not, but which cannot be reviewed."[28]

The 1953 Amsterdam concerts were organized by the Amsterdam Jazz Society and by Hans Rooduijn of "Le Canard" Foundation. Bill had just finished his tour in France. The two concerts were recorded by Louis van Gasteren (b. 1922), who had specialized as a film sound engineer. He later became a film producer and director and an artist in other fields, and is now one of the most acclaimed film makers in the Netherlands. In a local pub Louis told Bill how he had been brought up by his parents on Paul Robeson and his song "Ol' Man River," and how he was manipulated by Communism. Bill commented: "Politics, no good, man!" Broonzy gave his permission to record the concerts for two bottles of Dutch "oude jenever" (=old gin). Today van Gasteren still considers the dialogue with Bill as one of the most important conversations he ever had.[29] In 2006 the two Big Bill

Broonzy concerts that Louis van Gasteren recorded in Amsterdam in 1953 were finally issued by Munich Records.[30]

In 1954 Broonzy stayed in the States, but the following year he was back again for concerts in the United Kingdom, Belgium, and the Netherlands. In Holland he performed for the Haarlemse Jazz Club in Dansschool Schröder in Haarlem on November 25, 1955. The concert was reviewed by J. M. Baas in the magazine of the Haarlemse Jazz Club:

> Broonzy is not a musician, at least not in the generally accepted sense of the word and he does not pretend to be one. But here lies the attraction: what he has to say is not an exponent of sophistication, not the product of a thorough study lasting many years, not even a strictly personal view. Sorrow, hope, love, disappointment, humor, satire, they are all public property of a community of simple souls, of which this man is a prototypical representative. This made this performance acceptable, also for those issues which under different circumstances would not have made this acceptable for our western concepts, for example with regard to the shortcomings in accompaniment harmonies. However, an exception must be made for the lack of variation in tonal keys, which was not to the advantage of the desired variation necessary for "white ears."[31]

On November 26, 1955, Broonzy recorded for AVRO television's "Jazz Societeit" and AVRO radio's "Radioscoop." The radio program in which Bill sang "Lonesome Road Blues," "Willie Mae," "Louise," and "Keep Your Hands Off" has survived. It was presented by Michiel de Ruyter and broadcast on December 12, 1955.

On November 27, Broonzy was in concert in Rotterdam, and on November 28 and 29, he performed for the foundation "Le Canard" at the "Doelenzaal," Kloveniersburgwal 87 in Amsterdam. After the concert of November 29, Broonzy was a guest at the home of Michiel de Ruyter (1926–1994), the most famous Dutch jazz critic. Also present were Paul Breman, Gerrie Miga, Jos Acket, Paul Acket, Pim van Isveldt, and Jaap de Vries. The proceedings were recorded on tape. The next day, on November 30, he played in Amicitia, Westeinde 15 in The Hague. The 1955 tour was organized by promoter Paul Acket (1922–1992) of later North Sea Jazz Festival fame.

In 1956 Bill came to France, Belgium, Germany, Denmark, Italy, and the Netherlands. The only recordings made by Big Bill Broonzy in the

Netherlands that were issued commercially were made on February 17, 1956, in studio "Hoog Wolde" in Baarn. The results were issued on a deluxe album (Philips LP B 08012 L) that is very rare indeed now and for which blues collectors pay impressive prices. The recording session was experienced as a unique event by those present, album cover producer Leo Boudewijns remembers. Austrian artist Emmerich Weninger had come from Alkmaar to draw Broonzy, and his drawings are included with the album. Hans Buter took photographs. Theo van Dongen sat opposite the artist and began to talk to him about his life, the blues and finally about the recordings Broonzy had in mind. Broonzy then asked for a bottle of whiskey. The session ended late in the evening. When Columbia jazz producer George Avakian visited Baarn in December 1956, he assigned matrix numbers to the Broonzy songs and later reissued the Philips album on Columbia LP 111. The album was issued in Columbia's Golden Masterwork Series and was awarded five stars in a *Down Beat* review.

Before the concert in the Amsterdam "Doelenzaal" on November 29, 1955, Bill met a Dutch girl. Her name was Pim van Isveldt (born February 11, 1929) and she made costumes for the theater. Bill was bent over his guitar and when he looked up and saw her he said: "Jesus Christ." Pim was shy but it was love at first sight. She told Bill about her five-year-old son and he told her about his children, and showed her a photo of his mother, who was then more than a hundred years old. The couple corresponded, and Pim went to Antwerp or Paris whenever Bill was performing there. Once, on the train from Antwerp to Amsterdam, Bill was very nervous. Pim was going to introduce him to her parents. Although he was black, and older than her parents, the meeting was a success. Bill and Pim's son, Michael, was born on December 4, 1956. There was talk of marriage, but it was not possible to do that in the States with both a white and a black child. Whenever Bill brought a present for Pim's elder son, Jeroen, it was always a build-it-yourself airplane, for which the child was too young. Jeroen, who had been born in 1950, tragically died in a car accident in 1958.[32]

The Amsterdam Maria Austria Institute holds a unique collection of 165 photos of Big Bill Broonzy in Amsterdam shot from 1955 to 1957. In the dressing room (20), on stage (19), playing his guitar in an informal setting with Pim van Isveldt and Michiel de Ruyter (36), at home with Pim, Jeroen playing a children's drum and Michael in the baby chair (38), with Bill walking behind the pram in Amsterdam (20), with Michael and his guitar in Bill's lap (12), and with Michael in his arms next to Pim and Jeroen (20).

Sadly Pim van Isveldt died of cancer on March 13, 2005. She had a shoe-box full of more than fifty love letters from Big Bill, dating from December 29, 1955, to March 18, 1958. Pim's fondest memory of Bill was doing the dishes with him. They sang together then: "Goodnight Irene," and "The Bluetail Fly." Pim got sentimental when she thought of this. Michael wanted to be called Broonzy when he was eight, but the name change was too expensive. He never knew his father, who died when Michael was two and a half. For a while Michael corresponded with his half brothers and sisters in America, but this correspondence dried up. Michael often wondered what had moved Bill to start a relationship with a Dutch girl when he was hardly ever there. Michael has listened to his father's music and he once introduced himself as Big Bill's son to Muddy Waters when the latter was giving a concert in the Netherlands. Tears came to Muddy's eyes and he held Michael's hands for two minutes. At the concert he dedicated two songs to Bill's son.[33]

1957 was the year of Broonzy's final visit to Europe. He performed in the United Kingdom and France, and before leaving for America in April 1957 he said his last goodbye to Pim. Back in the States, Bill returned to his three-storey brick house on Chicago's South Side, where his wife Rose, five children, and seven grand children were awaiting him. He was operated on for cancer of his vocal cords in July 1957. Two benefit concerts were held for him in London that raised £ 1100. He was never to sing again. Big Bill Broonzy died in Chicago on August 15, 1958.[34]

After Broonzy's death the number of jazz-related blues artists appearing in the Netherlands continued to grow. In 1958 alone Big Joe Turner and Pete Johnson performed in Jazz at the Philharmonic, Jimmy Rushing with Benny Goodman, and Sammy Price appeared with J. C. Higginbotham. In the 1960s the American Folk Blues Festivals came to Europe. These concerts were orga-nized by the German promoters Lippmann and Rau and were immensely influential in the globalization of the blues. For the first time Europeans had the chance to hear and see not one, but a whole group of distinguished blues artists at first hand. The first AFBF to visit the Netherlands was number four in the series; the one in 1965 in which Fred McDowell, John Lee Hooker, Walter Horton, and J. B. Lenoir were the stars. In 1966 Big Joe Turner, Sippie

Wallace, Otis Rush, Buddy Guy, and Roosevelt Sykes conquered Holland. In 1967 the seminal country blues artists Bukka White, Son House, and Skip James were contrasted with the classic Chicago blues of Hound Dog Taylor and Little Walter. The same contrast between country and city blues permeated the 1968 edition with Big Joe Williams, Jimmy Reed, John Lee Hooker, T-Bone Walker, and Eddie Taylor.

The greatest blues opportunity missed in the Netherlands was the 1969 festival, for which we had to travel to Belgium. Dutch blues fans come in two shapes, those who are old enough to have seen Magic Sam and Earl Hooker in Belgium in 1969 and those who will forever regret that they were born too late. The AFBF continued intermittently until 1985, but the later concerts were far less influential because so many of the great blues artists had died by then.[35]

It was not just the blues that continued to have a Dutch audience— there was still an obvious interest in gospel and religious music by African Americans. In 1962 VPRO Television broadcast a concert by the Black Nativity gospel group in the Geertekerk in Utrecht. *Black Nativity* was a gospel musical, written by Langston Hughes, and was originally performed on stage in both the United States and Europe. The artists were Marion Williams and the Stars of Faith, Professor Alex Bradford and the Bradford Singers, Princess Stewart, Madeline Bell, Kitty Parham, and Henrietta Waddy.

On Ascension Day 1964 Mahalia Jackson came to the Irene Hall in Utrecht to sing at "Palaver '64," a religious gathering of twenty-three thousand young Christians to celebrate 150 years of the Dutch Bible Society. Three of the songs that Mahalia sang that day were recorded on a Dutch LP. Mahalia had been in the Netherlands in April 1961 as well.[36] In the latter half of the 1960s Europe was also visited by the "Spiritual + Gospel Festival." Only the second and the third of these annual shows came to the Netherlands. The second one was held on January 15, 1966, in the Amsterdam Concertgebouw. The artists were Bishop Samuel Kelsey, Rev. John I. Little, the Gospelaires, the Harmonizing Four with Gospel Joe Williams, and the Dorothy Norwood Singers. Sadly no recordings were made of this concert. The third one came to Amsterdam on November 18, 1967. The hall was only half full, although some very interesting gospel stars were featured: Rev. Cleophus Robinson, Sister Josephine James, organist Napoleon Brown, the Mighty Clouds of

Harmony, and the Robert Patterson Singers. The concert was recorded and issued on Fontana.[37]

The Dutch interest in the blues was also evident in the amount of written work devoted to the subject from the 1960s on. In 1960, the same year in which Paul Oliver published his ground breaking *Blues Fell This Morning: The Meaning of the Blues*, Hans Rookmaaker (1922–1977), a Dutchman who later became a Professor of the History of Arts, published his *Jazz—Blues—Spirituals*, a survey of contemporary black music in the United States.[38] It is now dated, but at the time it was an eye-opener for the Dutch, full of fascinating photos and references to the blues and gospel records of the period. In 1964 Rookmaaker began to edit the "Classic Jazz Masters" series for Riverside records, which eventually comprised twenty deluxe gatefold albums dedicated to classic prewar blues and jazz recordings, dubbed from 78s owned by Dutch collectors like Max Vreede, Jan Schoondergang, and Theo Kool.

In July 1965 a large format Dutch-language magazine called *Jazzwereld* was started, and ran for eight years, folding after issue #43 in June 1973. The blues reviews and articles in that magazine by Arend Jan Heerma van Voss educated a new generation of blues enthusiasts of which I am a member. Heerma van Voss was also the agent of the world's first specialist blues magazine, the British-based *Blues Unlimited*, founded by Simon Napier in April 1963. We all subscribed.

In 1967 Eddie Boyd recorded Philips album 655033 *Praise the Blues* in the Netherlands, accompanied by the Dutch blues band Cuby and the Blizzards. That same year Wim Verbei started the first Dutch blues magazine, *Mr. Blues*.

In 1969 Martin van Olderen and Guido van Rijn founded the Netherlands Blues and Boogie Organization (NBBO). In recognition for his influential writings on the blues Arend Jan Heerma van Voss was made an honorary member. After some concerts with Dutch blues artists, Memphis Slim was the first African American to be booked. The year was 1971, and the location was *The Bajes*, a former police station in Amstelveen, where Guido van Rijn grew up. That same year concerts by Jimmy Dawkins, Clarence "Gatemouth" Brown, and Big Joe Williams followed. For the rest of the seventies the NBBO organized a few concerts each year, thus providing the Dutch with opportunities to see great blues artists. The Netherlands became the envy of many

European countries and the number of foreign visitors to NBBO concerts was ever growing. There were a few hundred members and the concert halls became larger and larger. The NBBO published a blues magazine of its own, *The Boogie Woogie en Blues Collector*. It is still being published today, although it is now only a catalogue for Paul Duvivié's Amsterdam record shop.

Paramount Records was the most exciting of the American prewar blues and gospel labels. In 1971 Max Vreede, the most authoritative Paramount collector in the world, published a wonderful discography of the Paramount 12000 to 13000 series. The discographical details were presented on the right-hand pages with great accuracy, while the left-hand ones featured contemporary Paramount ads traced in the African American press by Laurie Wright, the editor of the British magazine *Storyville*.[39]

In 1972 *Mr. Blues* merged with the pop magazine *Oor*. In 1974 Martin van Olderen started his label Oldie Blues, a pun on his surname and old blues music, eventually issuing 46 LPs and 13 CDs.[40] Some of the NBBO concerts also resulted in long play albums. In 1972 Thomas Shaw recorded "Do Lord Remember Me" (Blues Beacon LP 1932-123) and Little Brother Montgomery cut "Bajes Copper Station" (Blues Beacon LP 1932-115). In 1973 Big Joe Williams made "Malvina My Sweet Woman" (Oldie Blues LP 2804) in Amstelveen. The album was issued in 1975 in a box that contained Leo Bruin's book on Big Joe, *Malvina My Sweet Woman*. In 1974 Blind John Davis recorded "The Incomparable Blind John Davis" (Oldie Blues LP 2803).

Black performers continued to come to the Netherlands in the 1970s. For example, on November 26, 1971, blues guitarist Freddie King played in the Amsterdam RAI building as part of a program around pop star Leon Russell. A few days later, on December 4, 1971, his colleague B.B. King gave a concert at the Amsterdam Concertgebouw. In 1976 concert promoter Paul Acket started the colossal *North Sea Jazz Festival* in The Hague. Each year the greatest jazz musicians travel there to perform in *Het Congresgebouw*, a huge building where jazz can be enjoyed in a large number of halls for three days. After thirty years in The Hague the *North Sea Festival* moved to Rotterdam in 2006.[41]

In 1979, three years after the first show of the *North Sea Jazz Festival*, the NBBO organized the first *Blues Estafette* in Vredenburg in Utrecht. Each year dozens of American blues artists were flown to Holland for the occasion, and performed on two stages for over twelve hours. The name "Estafette," which means "Relay" in English, was chosen because the artists alternate with each other at great speed. In this way the Dutch were able to see and hear the great blues heroes, many of whom have since died. For many artists this festival was their first chance to perform abroad, and very often their appearances started a new career. The *Blues Estafette*, which evolved into one of the most important blues festivals in the world, was held for the twenty-sixth time in 2004. Sadly lack of sponsors and changing tastes have now ended this annual treat.[42] After Jaap Hindriks took over the organization of the *Blues Estafette* from the NBBO, Martin van Olderen started his own *Amsterdam Blues Festival* in 1983. This Festival was held nineteen times, until 2001, when Martin fell ill. He died in 2002.

Several record labels producing and reproducing blues material have been established in the Netherlands. In 1979 Guido van Rijn started his Agram blues label, mainly reissuing pre-1943 blues. So far fifteen LPs and three CDs have been issued on Agram.[43] The name Agram is a combination of the first letter in the alphabet and "gramophone." This way the label heads each list. That same year Sundown, a postwar reissue label, was started by Gerard Robs, Kees van Wijngaarden, and Marcel Vos. It was renamed Black Cat in 1981 and Black Magic in 1982. Black Magic has issued fifty LPs and CDs so far.[44] In 1985 Marcel Vos left the company to start his own Double Trouble label. Twenty-eight LPs and CDs of modern black and white blues were issued. In 1980 Leo Bruin started his Swingmaster label, issuing recent recordings. His first release was LP 2101, recorded in Holland by R. L. Burnside. Swingmaster has issued seventeen LPs and seven CDs so far.[45]

Dutch interest in the blues was evident in the continued output and success of blues publications and academic studies. In 1974 Rien Wisse started a third Dutch blues magazine. He called it *Block*, a combination of blues and rock. More than thirty years later *Block* is still alive and well, and has reached issue 136. Among its most interesting features is Wim Verbei's column "De Blues Bibliotheek" ("The Blues Library"), in which he presents bibliographical details and reviews of all the blues books he can trace.[46]

In 1995 Guido van Rijn received a Ph.D. from Leiden University for his *Roosevelt's Blues*, in which he analyzed comment on FDR in contemporary blues and gospel recordings. The commercial edition of his dissertation was published by the University Press of Mississippi in 1997.[47] Its sequel, *The Truman and Eisenhower Blues* was published by Continuum in London and

New York in 2004.[48] *Kennedy's Blues* will be published by the University Press of Mississippi in 2007. In 2003 Alex van der Tuuk published *Paramount's Rise and Fall: A History of the Wisconsin Chair Company and its Recording Activities.*[49] Profusely illustrated by rare label shots and contemporary adverts and photos, the book is a noteworthy history of the label whose discography had been written by Max Vreede thirty-two years before.

Some black performers were to establish roots in the Netherlands just as Bill Broonzy had done. At the NBBO Blues Festival in Utrecht blues piano player Little Willie Littlefield (born in Texas in 1931) met and fell in love with a Dutch woman called Tonny. In 1981 they married, and Willie settled in the Netherlands, as other important blues pianists like Memphis Slim, Curtis Jones, Eddie Boyd, "Champion" Jack Dupree, and Willie Mabon had done elsewhere in Europe before him. In Europe they felt they were finally recognized as artists and less discriminated as human beings of a different color. Littlefield has retired now, but he is still alive and well in the Netherlands.

Most of the great blues artists have died now, and although the blues is still popular in the Netherlands, the times are changing. The demise of the *Blues Estafette*, the lack of blues artists at the *North Sea Festival* and low CD sales are evidence of a dying tradition. The purists cannot stand all the white imitation and the black soul blues and instead concentrate on the enlargement of their record collections. The CD age has opened up long-closed record archives providing access to recordings that were only dreamt of in the days of the gramophone. Similarly the rise of the DVD has released film footage the existence of which most collectors were not even aware of in the video era.

As this survey has shown, there was a considerable interest in black American music in a variety of different forms in Netherlands from the late-nineteenth century on, and clearly there was considerable postwar following for the blues. The question remains why so many Dutch people have been dedicated blues lovers for so long. Why were there more blues concerts and record releases in the Netherlands than in all the other European countries except for the United Kingdom? It could be argued that the Dutch simply have an excellent taste for high-quality music and that their relatively good command of English made the music more easily accessible than for some other Europeans. It is quite likely that some of the factors that applied in Britain were also an influence in the Netherlands. Whatever the reason, the musical journey of the Dutch through the world of the blues has been long and most rewarding, and the location of the Netherlands so far removed from the land of the blues has allowed us to have a good overall view.

NOTES

1. Utrecht: Het Spectrum, 1978.

2. For bibliographical details see Wim Verbei, "De Blues Bibliotheek," part 28 in *Block* 128 (Spring 2004): 25–26.

3. Andrew Ward, *Dark Midnight When I Rise: How Black Music Changed America and the World* (New York: Amistad, 2000), 331–36.

4. The Fisk Jubilee Singers were also in Holland in 1928. Cf. Wim van Eyle, *Jazz & Geïmproviseerde Muziek in Nederland* (Utrecht: Het Spectrum, 1978), 33.

5. Ward, 225 and 331.

6. Rainer E. Lotz, *Black People: Entertainers of African Descent in Europe, and Germany* (Bonn: Birgit Lotz Verlag, 1997), 152.

7. Ibid., 155–60.

8. Ibid., 173–82.

9. Ibid., 194.

10. Eileen Southern, *The Music of Black Americans: A History* (New York: W. W. Norton & Co, 1971; ed. 1997), 305–6.

11. Lotz, 240–44.

12. Ibid., 74–76.

13. See Van Eyle, 46, for a photo of the 1967 concert.

14. For the cover of the sheet music see: http://scriptorium.lib.duke.edu/sheetmusic/a/a59/a5908/

15. Alexander Coret, *Melodieën en Muzikanten: Cavalcade van de Lichte Muziek* (Zeist, the Netherlands: W.de Haan, 1965) 103 (my translation).

16. Lotz, *100 Jaar Amusement in Nederland* (Den Haag: Staatsuitgeverij, 1987), 146.

17. See C. Higman, "James Elmer Spyglass, Honorary Citizen of Schwalbach," at http://www.higman.de/spyglass.pdf

18. Ibid., 269–79.

19. Ibid., 209–16.

20. Ibid., 326–70.

21. L. M. G. Arntzenius, *Amerikaansche Kunstindrukken* (Amsterdam: Allert de Lange, not dated) 169–73. Cf. my English translation in "Clara Smith Eyewitness Account 1926," *Juke Blues* 46 (Spring 2000), 52–53.

22. Van Eyle, 35, and Frank C. Taylor, *Alberta Hunter: A Celebration in Blues* (New York: McGraw Hill, 1987), 120. Hunter, who had appeared opposite Paul Robeson in the London production of "Showboat" in 1928, spent most of the 1930s in Europe. Lex van Spall was born in 1903 and was one of Holland's earliest jazz musicians; see http://www.vjm.biz/newpage2.htm.

23. Van Eyle, 36, and Taylor, 138.

24. Tony Russell, "Famous Desk Drawer Manuscripts, Part 5: Laughing to Keep from Crying by Frank Boom," *Juke Blues* 25 (Spring 1992): 29.

25. See Wim Verbei, "De Blues Bibliotheek," Part 4, *Block* 103 (July/August/September 1997): 19.

26. Elijah Wald, *Josh White: Society Blues* (New York & London: Routledge, 2002), 172–74.

27. Leo Bruin, "Big Bill Broonzy in Nederland," *Block* 76 (October/November/December 1990): 25–27.

28. W. A. Eschauzier, "Big Bill Broonzy Zong voor de Eindhovense Jazz Club," review in *E.J.C. Flitsen*, third year, number 7, March 1953.

29. Personal communication to the author (2005).

30. Big Bill Broonzy, *Amsterdam Live Concerts 1953: Unissued Concerts Recorded by Louis van Gasteren*, Amsterdam, February 26 and 28, 1953; issued on Munich MRCD 275-1 and 275-2.

31. J. M. Baas, "Van de Bandstand," Haarlemse Jazz Club, December 1955.

32. Guido van Rijn, various interviews with Pim van Isveldt, Amsterdam, 2004 and 2005.

33. Ibid.

34. For some years now the American Robert Riesman has been working on a Big Bill Broonzy biography that will be published by Routledge in 2007 or 2008.

35. For an illustrated survey of the history of the American Folk Blues Festival see: http://www.wirz.de/music/afbffrm.htm

36. Mahalia Jackson (and other, non gospel artists), "Palaver '64," Utrecht, the Netherlands, May 7, 1964; issued on VR LP 030.

37. *Spiritual & Gospel Festival 1967*, Amsterdam, November 18, 1976; issued on Fontana LP 885.437.

38. H. R. R. Rookmaaker, *Jazz Blues Spirituals* (Wageningen, the Netherlands: Zomer & Keunings, 1960).

39. Max E. Vreede. *Paramount 12000/13000 Series.* London: Storyville, 1971.

40. http://www.munichrecords.com/

41. http://www.northseajazz.nl/

42. http://www.bluesworld.com/Estafette.html

43. http://www.ne.jp/asahi/ko-1/crossroads/label/agram/agram.htm

44. http://home.planet.nl/~blues.record.centre/bmagic.htm

45. http://www.swingmasterrecords.com/cgi-bin/s/swingmaster?qTzSYWhV;;10

46. http://home.planet.nl/~wisse225/

47. http://www.bluesworld.com/Guido.html

48. See: http://www.continuumbooks.com/book_details.cgi?bid=12542&ssid=OB1C3AGER F1416BWLZ165Z

49. Alex van der Tuuk, *Paramount's Rise and Fall: A History of the Wisconsin Chair Company and its Recording Activities* (Denver, Colorado: Mainspring Press, 2003).

14

The Blues in France

—ROBERT SPRINGER

France and African American music have had a relationship whose beginning has generally been placed at the end of World War I with the arrival of James Reese Europe and his military band, the Harlem Hellfighters.[1] During that war, France had acquired a reputation of freedom from racial prejudice among African American troops[2] and many of the soldiers in New York's 15th Heavy Foot Infantry Regiment "decided to remain ... after mustering out of the service. Other former soldiers, especially those who had been members of James Reese Europe's military band, returned" to Paris to meet the demand "for black musicians to fill the bandstands of the small nightclubs" in the Right Bank district of Montmartre.[3] It was this small yet significant community of expatriates that durably exposed France to African American syncopated sounds and ultimately paved the way for a genuine appreciation of jazz and blues. For the two genres, at least initially, were almost inextricably linked in the minds of French audiences, if not of the few early connoisseurs. The French, like other Europeans, discovered the blues through jazz, the former being viewed as the initial wellspring of the latter. This article is an attempt to trace the circumstances that made it possible for blues appreciation to take root in France; it will conclude with an examination of blues reception from the musicians' point of view.[4]

The Gradual Rise of Blues Appreciation in France before World War II

The earliest exposure of Europeans to the blues came through a small number of performers in concert and, mainly, club appearances. While England was fortunate enough to see jazz and blues guitarist Lonnie Johnson, who came over with a musical revue in 1917[5] and may have played blues on that occasion, the first blues performer ever to reach France was probably Alberta Hunter in 1927.[6] She was at the Palace Hotel in Nice late in the year, where she presumably sang the repertoire of vaudeville and blues songs she was used to offering in Harlem, remaining on the Riviera in early 1928 to sing in Monte Carlo, before traveling to England to perform at the London Pavilion, and going back to Paris in 1929 for engagements in Montmartre clubs like the Grand Ecart, Chez Florence, and the newly opened and soon to close (local) Cotton Club.[7] After returning to Harlem, she was in Paris again from 1933 to 1934, singing at Le Boeuf sur le Toit, and The Little Club, and even replacing Josephine Baker at the Casino de Paris. Also performing in Egypt, Turkey, Greece, and Italy, Hunter sailed back to New York for good when tensions in Europe seemed to be clearly edging toward war.[8]

In the same decade, American blues and jazz records became available via Columbia, when it acquired the French Pathé-Frères recording company in 1929.[9] The first encounter of French record buyers with a "classic blues singer" came the following year, though ironically Clara Smith sang no blues on "Get on Board"/"Livin' Humble."[10] This early exposure was complemented at the end of that year by the release of a film which was to have a lasting impact in France. King Vidor's *Hallelujah* acquainted Parisian moviegoers with blues singer Victoria Spivey though here again no blues songs were offered.

After the Great War, the blues had already begun to be defined and analyzed in French-language publications. As early as 1919, Swiss conductor Ernest Ansermet had singled out the blues as the genre where "the genius of the race is at its most powerful."[11] In 1926, the first book on jazz published in France, simply titled *Le Jazz*, contained a short section on blues in which one of the authors, ethnomusicologist André Schaeffner, quite correctly characterized the genre as the secular counterpart of the spirituals.[12]

Radio exposure to jazz and blues came later and was probably initiated by a program hosted weekly on Radio L.L. (the initials of owner Lucien Lévy) in 1931 and 1932 by Jacques Bureau, a future founding member of the Hot Club de France.[13] After this promising start, the airwaves, unfortunately, were rarely graced by the sounds of African American music. It was probably the paucity of jazz-related activity in those early years of the Depression that led to the advent of an association which was to have an immeasurable influence on jazz and blues knowledge in France.

The Hot Club de France and the Blues

The Hot Club de France was founded in 1932 by Hugues Panassié and a coterie of early French enthusiasts to promote jazz appreciation. It remains active today. Very soon, it had chapters throughout the country but also in other parts of Europe and in the United States. This was where then rare and expensive jazz and blues records could be heard, analyzed, bought, or exchanged. The first concerts were organized by the Club shortly after. Alberta Hunter, for one, sang to a full room at salle Pleyel in Paris in June 1933. She returned three years later, still under the aegis of the Hot Club.[14]

In 1935, the board of the Club decided to start a periodical, *Jazz Hot*, little more than a newsletter at first, to add to their pedagogical effort and, in 1937, launched Swing, the first record company in the world entirely devoted to jazz.[15] Panassié himself regularly lauded the blues for being not only the main pillar of jazz but also a manifestation of what he saw as the true spirit of black Americans. He wrote many articles on the blues for *Jazz Hot*, and his companion, Madeleine Gautier, regularly contributed commentary and translations of blues lyrics into French. Until the 1950s, practically all the French articles devoted to the blues were published in that periodical.

Another development that increased France's blues exposure was linked to the concert activities of Panassié's Hot Club. In 1933, on the occasion of Duke Ellington's concert tour, came Columbia producer John Hammond.

A long-lasting friendship with Panassié ensued. It was probably through that relationship that Bessie Smith, whom Panassié and Madeleine Gautier idolized, saw her records begin to reach the French market in 1936.[16] Just as importantly, in 1939, as a result of interest in Count Basie and his band, the Brunswick label issued several records featuring Jimmy Rushing, among them "Sent for You Yesterday"/"Swingin' the Blues."[17]

On the whole, before World War II, French jazz fans were aware of the existence of a few "classic blues" singers and blues shouters, largely because their music was linked to jazz, but there was no knowledge of traditional blues. Only Hugues Panassié, who had been invited to New York by John Hammond in 1938, had a broader experience, having attended the From Spirituals to Swing concerts at Carnegie Hall just before Christmas, with musicians like Big Bill Broonzy and Sonny Terry, and brought back genuine blues records like those of Little Brother Montgomery.[18] Blues awareness was developing slowly but, if there were French blues fans in the 1930s, they were probably first and foremost jazz fans with a penchant for the blues.

The activities of the Hot Club de France were interrupted during the war but, with the arrival of the first American troops came the V discs which, from 1943 onward, were issued to entertain G.I.s and, fortunately, reached French and European ears. It is clear that a number of those discs were meant for African American soldiers as they contained songs by Jimmy Rushing, but also Big Bill Broonzy, Josh White, Doctor Clayton, and Lil Green, among others.[19]

After the war, France was hit by the "sour-grapes-moldy-figs" controversy over bebop which led Panassié to resign from *Jazz Hot* in 1946 and ban Charles Delaunay and his bebop-loving friends from the Hot Club. His traditionalist views made him return to the roots of jazz and re-emphasize the importance of the blues. In 1949, he launched *La Revue du Jazz*, followed in 1950 by the *Bulletin du Hot Club de France* in which he penned many articles on the blues and its performers and printed the first pictures of blues artistes to appear in France.[20]

Jazz Hot too resumed its activity with, among other things, many articles on the blues artistes French audiences were just discovering: Roosevelt Sykes, Bumble Bee Slim, Peetie Wheatstraw, and Kokomo Arnold, for instance. This is not to say that new records were suddenly available, and it was precisely to pressure record companies into re-releasing their jazz and blues catalogs that the Association Française des Collectionneurs de Disques de Jazz was founded in 1945 by Hugues Panassié and Charles Delaunay. It also did the job itself and reissued a considerable number of jazz and blues classics, including Leroy Carr. It was joined by a few other small labels, among them Jacques Demêtre's own Jazz Document in the 1950s.[21]

Blues Exposure after World War II

By the end of the 1940s, as was happening elsewhere in Europe, blues appreciation in France had begun to sever its previous ties with jazz and to ride on the coat tails of the vogue for rhythm & blues imported from the United States, while true jazz fans tended to look down on the new genre. From 1950 on, the Vogue label bought the distribution rights of several indies like King, Chess, Apollo, Modern, and Peacock and released records by Wynonie Harris, Eddie "Cleanhead" Vinson, Jimmie Witherspoon, but also Lonnie Johnson, Muddy Waters, and John Lee Hooker, to name a few.[22] Other small French labels joined in, but it should be noted that most of these 78s were pressed at no more than five hundred copies. Still, these French reissues, coupled with the early concert activity, led a number of jazz fans who, like future blues researcher Jacques Demêtre, disliked bebop, to see the light.[23] In 1955, he started a monthly blues column in *Jazz Hot*,[24] not without having to endure the frequent taunts of "Demêtre and his primitive music" coming from his jazz colleagues, however.[25]

Jazz and blues presence on the radio increased markedly after 1944, when the American Forces Network (AFN) established itself in Paris and broadcast the whole gamut of the V discs for the benefit of G.I.s and any French household in possession of a radio.[26] An American presenter, Simon "Sim" Copans, was notably instrumental in exposing French listeners to the riches of African American music, including blues. The more than four thousand radio shows he hosted from 1946 to 1973, first on the AFN and The Voice of America (VOA), and soon after on French national radio transmitters, Paris-Inter in particular, were an invaluable pedagogical contribution in an area where little was known in France.[27] Week after week, in "Panorama du jazz américain," "Deep River," "Le jazz en liberté," and other programs, he enlightened generations of French listeners. Willis Connover's nightly "Voice of America Jazz Hour" was equally educational for those of us who did not mind burning the midnight oil. By the turn of the 1950s, exposure to the blues for the general public was at least adequate.

When microgroove vinyl records, lighter, sturdier, and easier to ship, came to France after 1954, blues reissue activity became more sizeable, though, for avid fans, ordering what was unavailable from Switzerland, England, or the United States became indispensable. In the late fifties and early sixties, this activity began to take off among the previously mentioned record labels, particularly Vogue, but also thanks to Columbia and RCA, along with recordings made in France by visiting artistes, though none of the productions sold more than a thousand copies.[28]

The rock 'n' roll boom of the late fifties also helped the blues in France and elsewhere, as did the folk blues vogue of the turn of the sixties. By that time, knowledge of the existence of a local audience of blues lovers had apparently reached beyond the borders of France. In 1960, Chris Strachwitz, chairman of the International Blues Society, even deemed it natural to ask French folk blues fans to contribute financially to his newly-founded Arhoolie label with a view to "recording the great blues specialists in the most relaxed and least commercial atmosphere possible."[29]

In the 1950s and 1960s, two important inlets for African American music in general and blues and rhythm & blues in particular were the English sea-ports and, more relevantly for the Continent, the post-exchanges of American and Canadian military bases in France and in neighboring West Germany from which they trickled into French society. These entry ports made it possible for 45 rpm records to reach the younger generations in Western Europe. After the skiffle movement of the late 1950s in Britain, this early musical dissemination gave birth to the beat groups of the early 1960s whose early hits covered blues and rhythm & blues numbers which had previously been successful among black Americans. The French equivalent were the "yé-yé" groups, so called because they tended to overuse shouts of "yeah yeah" in their songs in imitation of what they were hearing in the original songs they had chosen to adapt in French.

Still, radio programs devoted to the blues remained infrequent. Radio Luxembourg and the American Forces Network had occasionally played rhythm & blues and some blues since the late fifties. From the mid-sixties on, public and private transmitters, followed a few years later by the British pirate stations, Radio London and Radio Caroline, particularly the latter, began to fill part of the vacuum and were audible to French listeners. While in Britain the blues audience was large enough to warrant the existence of highly specialized broadcasts like Mike Raven's on Caroline, monolingual French blues fans still had to make do with the blues sections within jazz programs to satisfy their cravings for music and enlightenment. Frank Ténot and Daniel Filipacchi on Europe N°1 in their nightly "Pour ceux qui aiment le jazz," regularly played blues records, but in small doses only. French television pioneered the first programs devoted to the blues in 1959 and the next few years.[30]

By the late sixties, the British blues boom followed in the footsteps of the beat craze with proponents like John Mayall and Ten Years After, who played an African American blues repertoire with few concessions to other musical genres. France and the rest of the Continent owe an immense debt to this development, as these groups were frequently on tour and also served as accompanying bands to visiting African American blues artistes.[31]

Despite such auspicious circumstances, blues records were still difficult to come by and fans had to be particularly perseverant if they wished to satisfy their musical passion. The blues record market was considered minor by the major companies and, in the absence of much promotional effort, the main spur came from the prospective buyers themselves, who often had to use considerable persuasion to get their local record retailer to order what was not in stock. Fortunately, a few small labels like OJL (Origin Jazz Library) in the United States were soon emulated by others in Europe and filled the need of blues buffs by issuing on LP anthologies of rare 78 rpm recordings which would otherwise have been inaccessible to the vast majority. French label Le Chant du Monde, for one, released the Folkways re-issues of Library of Congress recordings which began to meet the needs of rural blues fans.

But there was nothing like seeing musicians in the flesh, and the first opportunity came in May 1949 with Leadbelly (Huddie Ledbetter), who was brought over by the Hot Club de France. Unfortunately, owing to ill health, he had to return to New York after a few dates and died a few months later.[32] His most acclaimed concert, organized by the Fondation des Etats-Unis, was held in Paris at the Théâtre de l'Université.[33] Though his visit was "too short to make much impact[, . . . it] did sow the seeds of an interest in blues which took root in Europe."[34]

He was followed two years later by Big Bill Broonzy, whose extended tours from 1951 to 1957 hit Paris and the French provinces but also other venues on the Continent, gaining "huge followings."[35] He too, had come under the aegis of the Hot Club, but, on his first tour, again, someone—presumably Hugues Panassié—had felt it necessary to place a small jazz combo on stage next to him for fear that he might not go down well on his own. Fortunately, in 1952, he was accompanied by blues pianist Blind John Davis only.[36] His appearances, which left audiences in awe of his facile instrumental proficiency and thrilled by his stage personality, together with his locally-recorded output were a decisive influence in France. After Bessie Smith, who had been seen as the last of the blues singers, he was touted as the last living traditional blues exponent, a reputation he did his best to cultivate. When he died in 1958, he was all but forgotten in Chicago and the rest of the United States, while the European press eulogized him.[37]

After the initial impetus given by Big Bill Broonzy's concerts, the popularity of the blues on a broader scale must without hesitation be attributed to the German tandem Horst Lippmann and Fritz Rau who, by means of the annual tours of the American Folk Blues Festival (1962–1972), exposed Europe to the blues in all their rich variety. The concerts were very well attended in France and their live recordings were a revelation to a generation of fans. Many of the musicians stayed on, most temporarily, some permanently, and availed themselves of the opportunities to play in France and the rest of Western Europe. In Paul Oliver's view, "by the mid-sixties, incredibly, European blues enthusiasts had heard more blues singers in person than most of their American counterparts had ever done."[38]

Some critics may have deplored the rather stiff format of the concerts which, due to the laudable intention of offering a rich palette of styles before the passing of the last exponents, left each combo or solo artiste just enough time for three pieces. Despite this drawback, to which the language barrier must be added, the musicians appreciated, or indeed were surprised by, the acclaim extended to them at last, but also the artistic competition and the camaraderie that the communal life of a touring show afforded thousands of miles and an ocean away from home.

After hearing the blues performed live in concert, the next step for a few blues connoisseurs was to cross the Atlantic to experience the music in its natural habitat. It must be remembered that Big Bill Broonzy's visits to

Europe had been made possible by the initiative of a Belgian blues enthusiast, Yannick Bruynoghe, who had "rediscovered" him on the occasion of a
trip to Chicago in 1950 and later published a book, *Big Bill Blues*, detailing
the life and times of his protégé.[39] Bruynoghe was soon followed by several
budding European blues researchers who managed to convince other artistes
to visit the Europe, all before the British blues boom, at a time when, in
America, blues and rhythm & blues performers were being pushed offstage
by rock 'n' roll and, later in the fifties, by soul music among black audiences,
leaving them without engagements. Thus, in September and October 1959,
Jacques Demêtre and Marcel Chauvard left France on a trip to document the
blues, meeting and interviewing Champion Jack Dupree and Tarheel Slim in
New York, John Lee Hooker in Detroit, and Elmore James, Memphis Slim,
Muddy Waters, B.B. King, Howlin' Wolf, and Kokomo Arnold, among many
others, in Chicago.[40] Their account of their visit, based on the documentation they had collected, was published in six instalments in *Jazz Hot* almost
immediately on their return and had a considerable impact, with translations
appearing in England, Poland, and even the United States, belying the commonly held assumption in and outside France that the blues was dead.[41] After
their return, Demêtre also kept epistolary contacts with several of the musicians he had met. In November and December, Belgian fan Georges Adins
followed suit, visiting Sam "Lightnin'" Hopkins in Houston, Texas, meeting
Sonny Boy Williamson (Rice Miller) in St. Louis and most of the artistes
Demêtre had seen in Chicago.[42] These two seminal trips preceded that of
English researcher Paul Oliver and his wife Valerie, who crossed the Atlantic
the following summer, encouraged as they were by Demêtre's success.

Blues Appreciation and Reception

The opportunity of prolonging or, more likely in the 1960s and after, restart-
ing a career outside the United States convinced a number of blues expatriates to join writers Richard Wright and James Baldwin and jazz musicians
Sidney Bechet, Bud Powell, and Dexter Gordon in Paris.

Champion Jack Dupree was the first to settle in Europe, moving
from Britain to Switzerland and, finally, Sweden. France's first permanent
blues resident was Memphis Slim (Peter Chatman) who, not without some

justification in his adoptive country, liked to be known as the "Ambassador of the Blues." He had come to Europe in 1960 on a solo tour, and, on his return the following year, decided to settle in Paris; he was for several decades the bluesman in residence at the Trois Mailletz club.

As for Curtis Jones, who was "discovered" in Chicago in 1959 by Demêtre and Chauvard, he first settled in Zürich in January 1962 with the help of Champion Jack but opted for Paris a few months later. He frequently toured the Continent and even spent some years in Morocco, before making Germany his base and dying in Munich in 1973, in total destitution, a sign that a lasting successful career was far from guaranteed to every expatriate.

In the 1970s, pianist Willie Mabon and guitarist Luther Allison also decided to live in Paris. Mabon took the opportunity of a European tour to stay from 1973 to 1976. After returning to Chicago, he was still to be found on and off in Paris where he died in 1986.

It is worth noting that the original blues expatriates to Europe were invariably pianists, while more recent residents have been guitarists. The former could easily find engagements in clubs and restaurants, which is no longer the case today as only rarely do such establishments hire musicians, though it must be added that contemporary blues has lost most of its solo pianists.

The expatriates with the longest European careers were, quite logically, those who had married locally. This situation probably motivated their final decision though, initially, they had sought to pursue a musician's career away from Jim Crow and related unpleasantness. On this particular point, the musicians' testimonies are concordant: " . . . I went to Europe and I don't have to crawl. I'm respected as a man and nobody bothers me. . . . I'm no special target. . . . I live better than I ever lived in my life. . . . Europe has been a real conversion for me. . . . I mean, I live SO peaceful," said Eddie Boyd in 1977.[43] Things were far from perfect, though. The same artiste, in the same interview, mentioned an experience in Switzerland when neighbors of the producer he was staying with sent a petition to the real estate agency demanding his removal from the building,[44] a mishap similar to that suffered by Leadbelly with Alan Lomax in Washington in 1937 which gave birth to the famous "Bourgeois Blues."[45] Still, the disease, in the eyes of African Americans, seemed less ingrained and one might have perceived, in France if not elsewhere, a hidden intention to show the United States a more open-minded attitude after the events at Little Rock, Arkansas, and the civil rights struggle. But the difference in treatment may also have been partly due to the fact that blues and jazz musicians, contrary to other immigrants of color, brought in their baggage an attractive music that thrilled audiences wherever they performed.

Unanimously, blues performers have admitted that the vogue of the blues in France and the rest of the Continent in the 1960s provided them with opportunities to perform and record which they had seldom had before. However, after the early years of near adulation when they were still a novelty, they often deplored that, once the blues boom had worn off, they no longer received the same treatment and, among other things, frequently had to travel by themselves from one venue to the next, a situation which could easily lead to problems but was the result of the tight budgets of tour and concert promoters due to shrinking audiences. Indeed, in Britain as elsewhere, not infrequently, the musicians of the pick-up bands recruited to accompany black blues artistes were often expected to provide them with room and board.[46]

According to the musicians, French and European blues audiences are more receptive and knowledgeable about their favorite music than their American counterparts. This is probably partly due to the relative rarity of the "product," which has tended to whet the fans' appetite and which, in most European countries, led to the birth of an important blues literature in the form of specialized books and magazines which, for the past five decades, have pursued their patient, painstaking task of researching and documenting the blues. In 1959, to satisfy the thirst for discographical knowledge of the emerging blues and rhythm & blues audience, a Belgian, Serge Tonneau, published the mythical, yet intermittent, first periodical devoted to African American popular music, *Rhythm and Blues Panorama*, in which the blues had pride of place with contributions by Jacques Demêtre. Today, a sign that blues interest endures is the continued activity of *Soul Bag*, originally founded by fans of soul and rhythm & blues in 1968, which remains France's oldest blues publication, available only by subscription, but recently joined by the glossier *Blues Magazine* and *Blues Again*.

Though blues performers may have found French and European audiences rather lukewarm, especially in the early days of the AFBF, this was probably due to the concert format and the absence of a participatory culture, applause being customarily extended at the end of numbers only. But, after their initial surprise or disappointment, musicians recognized a form of respect in this reception and some even came to prefer playing in concert as they felt the environment was more conducive to musical appreciation. The return home to playing in bars and clubs to scarce audiences could then be something of a disappointment/let down in reverse.

Continental audiences have also been perceived as more respectful to the genre itself. John Lee Hooker, for one, was grateful to be able to play other fare than the protracted boogies that had made his reputation and that American audiences seemed never to get enough of.[47] American audiences, it was perceived, were excessively influenced by fashion. Although they had the blues within earshot, they had scarcely paid attention to the music before the blues boom of the sixties propelled by the British beat groups. Once the excitement was over, they moved on to other fads, whereas Europe has always retained a small but faithful blues audience and, today, 70 percent of blues records are sold in Europe.

Collectively, blues musicians came off from their performances on the Continent with the feeling of having established a rapport that transcended language and cultural barriers and that some thought was linked, on the one hand, to the familiarity of Europeans with oppression, largely due to World War II, and, on the other hand, with a consumer culture that was less ostentatious than in the United States.[48] It is significant, in my view, that African American blues exponents, particularly when in France, often felt they were among kindred souls in suffering and found similarities to their own experience in the history of occupied France when a tyrannical power imposed censorship of ideas and artistic expression and used the most extreme forms of violence on a daily basis. It is also likely that French and European audiences were capable of a purely musical appreciation generally untouched by the racial prejudices which, initially, had hampered American audiences on the whole and later often confined the genre to the role of "feel good" music.

Lastly, in France and in Europe, interest in the lived experiences of African Americans that lay behind the music often followed close behind an aesthetic appreciation of the blues. As I have suggested elsewhere, contrary to the "common assumption among music historians and sociologists that, in the 1960s, embracing the blues was for white fans a form of slumming or a way of expressing feelings of generational oppression by proxy," in countries where the mother tongue is not English, the immediate attraction, except for a minority, "was to the sound of the music rather than the result of instant comprehension of the lyrics and identification with the racial group from which they emanated."[49]

In France and other European countries where the command of English has not significantly improved in recent decades, audiences have generally been attracted to the blues by its sound ("the instrumental devices still have power to trigger responses," Paul Oliver observed almost four decades ago[50]) and its sincerity, and have compensated for their lack of comprehension of the lyrics by being more knowledgeable about the artistes and their backgrounds.

Lack of familiarity with the English language did not mean that French blues (and jazz) audiences were unaware of the second-class citizenship that the musicians they loved had to accept back home. In 1963, for instance, readers of the communist daily *L'Humanité* were reminded that "it goes without saying that the blues, just like the spirituals, are a means for black Americans to struggle against oppression."[51]

To conclude, the development of blues appreciation in France has been marked by the influence of a few personalities like Hugues Panassié, Jacques Demêtre, and Sim Copans. In a way, they were instrumental in stimulating, escorting and, at times, rekindling the French part of the European demand, which, since the 1950s, after the first blues records were imported, made it possible for the genre, by means of the concert tours and the presence of bluesmen in residence in Paris or elsewhere, to avoid falling into oblivion. Such a fate, in retrospect, would have been all but inevitable at a time when its decline among Blacks was undeniable and when the interest evinced by Whites in the United States was embryonic at best. In return, the blues irreversibly transformed contemporary popular music on both sides of the Atlantic.

Over the last couple of decades or so, with the advent of other musical genres popular with French and European youth, the situation has undergone further changes. The blues today is a marginal genre whose presence on the air waves and on television is rare. The French audience of faithful fans has been weaned off authentic blues artistes, whose ranks are steadily depleted by the passage of time, and is ready to give those who will visit a welcome that can sometimes compare with that of the 1960s. The current success in

Paris of the blues and gospel show *Wild Women Blues* may be a hopeful indication that there is a broader potential audience for the blues "out there."

NOTES

1. See William A. Shack, *Harlem in Montmartre: a Paris Jazz Story between the Great Wars* (Berkeley: University of California Press, 2001), 4.

2. See ibid., 66, 105, and 125 for other aspects of this apparent lack of racial prejudice.

3. Ibid., xvi–xvii. The Harlem Hellfighters, with other black units, saw action after having been placed under French command by General Pershing to circumvent rules that prevented then "from engaging in combat against the white enemy (Shack, *Harlem in Montmartre*, 19). Blues musicians like Big Bill Broonzy and Henry Sims were stationed in France during World War I, though it is not known whether they took part in combat. The majority of African American troops served in non–combat roles.

4. In what follows, the reader will realize that it is not always easy to separate the French evolution from that of other European countries and that, more specifically, the debt owed to Britain is considerable. The choices I have had to make should in no way be interpreted as a belittling of the contributions of the rest of Europe.

5. Sheldon Harris, *Blues Who's Who* (New Rochelle, N.Y.: Arlington House, 1979), 279.

6. Philippe Sauret in "Et la France découvrit le blues : 1917 à 1962," (Master's dissertation, Université de Paris I, n.d.), chap. I, 3 (available at: http://www.gazettegreenwood.net/doc/blues-france.htm) indicates that Hunter first traveled to Europe in 1925 but other sources fail to confirm this. This master's thesis has been an invaluable source and has been used extensively as its author apparently had access to a complete collection of *Jazz Hot* and the *Bulletin du Hot Club de France* for the periods 1935–1962 and 1950–1962, respectively.

7. Details compiled from Harris, *Blues Who's Who*, 256, and Shack, *Harlem in Montmartre*, 43.

8. Shack, *Harlem in Montmartre*, 43–44.

9. From: www.ketupa.net/emi2.htm

10. Sauret, chap. II, 6.

11. Ernest Ansermet, "Sur un orchestre Nègre," *La Revue Romande*, series 3, no. 10 (October 15, 1919): 10–13. Reprinted in *Jazz Hot* 28 (November–December 1938): 4; *Jazz Magazine* 325 (January 1984): 32–33, 83; Anette Hauber, Ekkehard Jost, Klaus Wolbert, eds., *That's Jazz. Der Sound des 20. Jahrhunderts* (Catalog of the Jazz exhibition, Matildenhöhe, Darmstadt, May 29–August 28, 1988), my translation.

12. André Schaeffner and André Coeuroy, *Le Jazz* (Paris: Jean-Michel Place, 1988; first edition, Paris, 1926), 93–94.

13. Denis-Constant Martin and Olivier Roueff, *La France du jazz: Musique, modernité et identité dans la première moitié du XXe siècle* (Marseille: Parenthèses, 2002), 47.

14. Sauret, chap. II, 4.

15. Ludovic Tournès, "La reinterpretation du jazz: un phénomène de contre-américanisation dans la France d'après-guerre (1945–1960)," *Revue Française d'Etudes Américaines*, hors-série (December 2001), 73.

16. Sauret, chap. III, 2.

17. Ibid., chap. III, 4, 7.

18. Ibid., chap. III, 6.

19. Ibid., chap. V, 2.

20. Ibid., chap. VI, 3.

21. Ibid., chap. V, 4–5.

22. Ibid., chap. VII, 1–2.

23. Ibid., chap. VII, 3.

24. Ibid., chap. IX, 1–2.

25. Sebastian Danchin, 19.

26. Sim Copans, "Play it again, Sim," *Revue Française d'Etudes Américaines*, op. cit., 8.

27. Bernard Vincent, "Avant-propos," *Revue Française d'Etudes Américaines*, op. cit., 3.

28. Philippe Sauret, chap. XI, 1.

29. Quoted in Philippe Sauret, chap. XIII, 1 (my translation).

30. Jean-Christophe Averty's *Way down the Mississippi* on December 19, 1959, *Hommage à Bessie Smith* on February 20, 1960, *Singing the blues* on May 19, 1962, and *Memphis Slim on the road* on August 18, 1962. From Philippe Sauret, chap. XI, 1, 3–4, and chap. XIII, 5.

31. Bob Brunning, *Blues: the British Connection* (Poole: Dorset: Blandford Press), 166 passim.

32. Bob Groom, *The Blues Revival* (London: Studio Vista, 1971), 11

33. Jean-Claude Arnaudon, *Dictionnaire du blues* (Paris: Filipacchi, 1977), 155; Sheldon Harris, 318.

34. Paul Oliver, *The Story of the Blues* (London: Barrie and Jenkins, 1970), 163.

35. Ibid.

36. Philippe Sauret, chap. VIII, 1.

37. Gérard Herzhaft, *L'Encyclopédie du blues* (Lyon: Fédérop, 1979), 55.

38. Paul Oliver, *The Story of the Blues*, 167.

39. Big Bill Broonzy and Yannick Bruynoghe, *Big Bill Blues* (Brussels: Editions des Artistes, 1955; reprint Paris: Ludd, 1987. English version New York: Oak, 1964).

40. Bob Groom, *The Blues Revival*, 35–36, Philippe Sauret, chap. XI, 2.

41. Philippe Sauret, chap. XI, 2–3. These articles, originally published in *Jazz Hot*, nos. 149–54 (December 1959 through May 1960), are now available in Jacques Demêtre and Marcel Chauvard, *Voyage au pays du blues* (Levallois-Perret : CLARB, 1994).

42. Philippe Sauret, chap. XI, 3.

43. Eddie Boyd, "Interview," *Living Blues* 37 (March/April 1978): 14.

44. Ibid., 13–14.

45. Charles Wolfe and Kip Lornell, *The Life and Legend of Leadbelly* (New York: Da Capo, 1994), 206–9.

46. Brunning, *Blues: the British Connection*, 188.

47. John Lee Hooker, "Interview," *Living Blues* 44 (Autumn 1979): 20.

48. Isaiah "Doctor" Ross, personal unpublished interview, Nancy, France, October 17, 1975.

49. Robert Springer, ed., *The Lyrics in African American Popular Music* (Bern and New York: Peter Lang, 2001), 1.

50. Paul Oliver, *The Story of the Blues*, 168.

51. Alain Guérin, *L'Humanité* (July 6, 1963), quoted by Ludovic Tournès, 81 (my translation).

15

Cultural Displacement, Cultural Creation

AFRICAN AMERICAN JAZZ MUSICIANS IN
EUROPE FROM BECHET TO BRAXTON[1]

—CHRISTOPHER G. BAKRIGES

A number of contemporary African American artists have spoken musically and extra-musically about how they both use "the tradition" and add to its further evolution. If tradition means the continuity of culture, then these artists deliberately muddy the definition. For example, they dislike the word *jazz*, a term they feel is ambiguous, a misnomer and, by some definitions, demeaning, to describe their work yet they insist they come from a black music tradition that informs them. Moreover, the vanguard have a heightened sense of aesthetics developed in various formats, including published treatises, essays, interviews, record liner notes, scores, poetry, painting, and dance, that are not often considered in black music criticism or jazz discourse. In fact, most jazz histories interpret the notion of avant-gardism as a culturally monolithic and politically militant musical style of the turbulent sixties rather than as an enduring ideological feature of black intellectual thought.[2] African American artists who exist in this *high* rather than *popular* art category have created a variety of names for their work that veer away from the all-encompassing term jazz and include the following[3]:

- Yusef Lateef's *Autophysiopsychic Music*
- Anthony Braxton's *Tri-axium Writings*
- Ornette Coleman's *Harmolodic Theory*
- William "Butch" Morris's *Theory of Conduction*
- George Russell's *Chromatic Lydian Concept of Tonal Organization*
- Wadada Leo Smith's theories of *Ankhrasmation and A New World Music*
- Rachied Ali's *prima materia*
- Jack DeJohnette's *omnidirectional music*
- Oliver Lake's *expandable language*
- Joe McPhee's *lateral composition*
- Roscoe Mitchell's *Scissors Music*
- Bill Dixon's, Leroy Jenkins's, Marion Brown's, Muhal Richard Abrams's, George Lewis's, Bobby Bradford's, John Carter's, Sam Rivers's, and William Parker's take on *creative music*
- Cecil Taylor's *constructivism*
- Glenn Spearman's *alternative auditory architecture*
- Sun Ra's transcendent aesthetics privately published as *The Immeasurable Equation*
- Max Roach's, Rahsaan Roland Kirk's, Art Ensemble of Chicago's, Archie Shepp's, Horace Tapscott's, Randy Weston's, and William Shadrack Cole's *Black Classical Music* and Africacentric assessments

Each one of these artists had close ties to blues and rhythm & blues groups in regions around the United States in their earlier careers. Many of these artists left their towns and moved to New York City, the site where previous generations of creative black artists, especially in jazz, had gone. The majority of these "free" artists, however, were denied full entrée into both the city and the jazz tradition because of the obdurate belief by those who broker musical "high" culture that avant-gardism is a private citadel of white privilege.[4] The attempt to contain or narrowly limit artistic range and activity has forced scores of African American artists to move between two or more national spaces in order to continue to create and work as equals. This article considers three levels of cultural displacement that have affected many African Americans operating in jazz throughout the twentieth century and into the present. The artists named here are among those critical thinkers who had, by necessity, to transform their cultural space as well as their range of experience beyond the borders of America in order to create art. These levels of displacement can be called 1) chosen exile, 2) expatriation, and 3) transculturation. Each of these terms, although they overlap, can be viewed separately not only as states of mind as to how people feel about what they do and where they do it but also as musical ideas, that is, the methods and materials they use to create.

Chosen Exile

Chosen exile is a state of self-imposed banishment for significant periods of time from one's place of birth in order to accomplish a certain task or to complete a mission. For example, dozens of African American painters went to Paris during the interwar years in order to produce some of the most indelible images of the New Negro movement, such as Archibald Motley's *Blues* ca. 1929, Elizabeth Prophet's *Congolais* ca. 1931, and Palmer Hayden's *Fetiche et Fleurs* ca. 1931–32. These and many other artists were able to study and create in France and in other countries, where they also won fellowships, grants, and awards.[5] Study abroad won these artists the critical acclaim that established their reputations as some of the most significant leaders of the international Black Atlantic movement in the visual arts.

African American blues musicians have been performing in Europe for over fifty years. Eileen Southern cites Big Bill Broonzy as the first person to take the Chicago-Delta blues to Europe as early as 1951.[6] Having been dropped by Mercury records that same year, Broonzy found a new audience in Europe. According to Bruce Eder, Broonzy led the way to Europe for a generation of elder statesmen of the blues, and his performances were so well-received that for fifteen years after he first went over, American bluesmen like Memphis Slim (a.k.a. Peter Chatman, Jr.), Broonzy's friend and accompanist since the late 1930s, were able to follow his path across the Atlantic, to bigger, more enthusiastic audiences and better paying engagements than they'd ever known in their native United States.[7] Moreover, Bill Broonzy's book *Big Bill Blues*, one of the first autobiographies of a blues man, was originally published not on his home soil but in London.[8] The original 1955 publication, compiled by Yannick Bruynoghe from Broonzy's letters is significant in that Broonzy had learned to write only five years before, having been taught by students at Iowa State University, where he worked as a janitor.

The influence exerted by the blues on the development of rock groups in England and elsewhere cannot be denied and is discussed elsewhere in this volume. By the early sixties Europe heard scores of blues greats through the auspices of the American Folk Blues Festivals.[9] It is ironic that the American Folk Blues Festivals were never held in America. Established in 1962 and lasting through 1972, these festivals toured throughout Europe and lasted anywhere from three to six weeks and were made up by groups of blues artists thankful to get consistent work ranging from Willie Dixon to T-Bone Walker, Doctor Ross, Sonny Boy Williamson, and Big Mama Thornton. One could argue the point, albeit somewhat vicariously as the claim has never been articulated by the artists themselves, that Europe was to hear the more modern-electric, city blues as a musical force before the white public in America.

Jazz musicians also experienced exile during the early twentieth century. Phonograph recordings by the Original Dixieland Jazz Band did bring jazz to Great Britain in 1917, but it was James Reese Europe and his assistant Gene Mikell's arrangements of American popular songs, marches, ragtime, and blues that brought the sound of live jazz to Europe less than a year later.[10] In 1910, Europe helped create a musician's union and booking agency called the Clef Club, making it the premiere African American musical organization in the United States during his presidency. In 1913 his band became one of the first black groups ever to make recordings. Along with Irene and Vernon Castle, Europe developed the foxtrot and other African American derived dances disseminated to the white middle class. James Reese Europe was the first African American officer to lead men into conflict during World War I and was leader of the 369th Infantry regimental Band which took France by storm with the new sounds of jazz. Mr. Europe stated that he returned to America "more firmly convinced than ever that Negroes should write Negro music."[11]

Sidney Bechet left with Will Marion Cook, John Payne, and the Southern Syncopated Orchestra (initially called the New York Syncopated Orchestra) for London in the summer of 1919 as a star improviser and concert artist. Arguably the first legitimate saxophone soloist in jazz, Bechet's microtonal playing, alternative (false) fingering techniques, and distinctive tonality are still being emulated today. Yet Bechet's first records were not made in America but with Benny Peyton's Jazz Kings in London for English Columbia, probably in 1921, and never issued.[12] Moreover, he bought his first soprano saxophone in the West End of London and also taught his first pupils there. He rekindled his French roots while in Paris beginning in Fall 1925, first with Josephine Baker and *The Black Revue* (*La Revue Nègre*), then as an outright star and adopted son of the Parisians. There he began working on an extended composition, *The Negro Rhapsody*, subtitled the *Voice of Slaves*, in 1928. He wrote his book *Treat it Gentle* in Paris in 1951, and he premiered his ballet suite there in spring 1953. He was quick to tell people how much he loved America, but just as quick to defend France because that, he said, is the place that loved him and, further, that French descent was inextricably tied to being Creole in New Orleans, Bechet's place of birth and ancestry.[13]

Thus, while "chosen" exile deals with official or functional reasons to depart from home, there is also this idea that artists can, over time, become almost biologically attached to another place. Josephine Baker, who left the United States for Paris in 1924, told Henry Louis Gates, Jr., that she felt liberated in France: "At first, I wondered if [leaving America] was cowardice, wondered whether I should have stayed to fight. But I couldn't have done anything. I would have been thwarted in ways in which I was free in France. I probably would have been killed. . . . I belong to the world now. . . . America represented that: people coming from all over to make a nation. But America has forgotten that. . . . It's ironic: people ran from slavery in Europe to find freedom in America and now. . . ."[14]

In short, American artists became as did Josephine Baker or Sidney Bechet, translocated, genetically or spiritually windswept to distant shores. Their art, as a result, becomes diffracted, radiated in all directions across Europe and beyond—jazz, in essence, is seen as a behavior, something one does, and the Jazz Age reaches Europe in this light. The point is that jazz became not just American, but an international music shaped and formed beyond the shores of the United States. Jazz is part of the transatlantic culture in which African Americans have played a major role.

Expatriation

As used here expatriation means one's exile from America for decidedly extra-musical reasons, at least at first. Just as writers such as Richard Wright,

James Baldwin, and John A. Williams sought refuge from their constant confrontation with the "Negro Problem" and higher ground for their protracted battle against racism and oppression, jazz artists sought similar sanctuary while gaining international reputations as serious artists. These intellectuals agree that African American expression is normally only seen through the lens of popular culture, either as a static folk tradition or else depicted only in consumer culture. Moreover, they see Black aesthetics grounded solely in a vernacular full of racial stereotypes. For example, the composer and saxophonist Anthony Braxton, who has left a lasting impression on the jazz scene ever since his arrival in Paris in the late sixties along with members of the Chicago-based Association for the Advancement of Creative Musicians, remarks that the "history of the music is a history of tampering. What offends me has been the American marketplace's attempts to redefine the aesthetic of the music."[15]

In 1933 saxophonist Coleman Hawkins, amidst the swing dance craze in the States, set sail from New York to London on the *Ile de France* at the behest of British bandleader Jack Hylton.[16] Many artists followed in Hawkins's wake, for example Kenny "Klook" Clarke and Bud Powell, the virtual inventors of the modern drum and piano language called bebop. Saxophonists Don Byas and Dexter Gordon, whose first engagements as an expatriate were at London's famous Ronnie Scott Club in 1962, had styles of playing which earned them cult followings in Europe prompting them to drop anchor. These and many other artists, among them, Art Taylor, Ben Webster, Kenny Drew, Idrees Sulieman, Sahib Shihab, and Nathan Davis, settled into nomadic routines—shuttling between engagements in England, France, Belgium, Holland, Denmark, and Switzerland.[17] Other musicians felt the snubbing from American record labels whose executives viewed certain artists as non-saleable, unpopular, or as grade "b" players, as Orrin Keepnews of Riverside and, later, Fantasy Records expressed towards Johnny Griffin, prompting the saxophonist's departure to Holland and, later, France.[18] These artists garnered top billing all over Europe and enjoyed the benefits of numerous recordings, artist subsidies, commissions, and representation that they probably never would have had in America.

Mal Waldron, who had worked with Charles Mingus's Jazz Workshop from 1954 to 1957 and who became Billie Holiday's last regular piano accompanist, had made Europe his home from the early sixties up to his death in

2003. Waldron, who studied composition at Queens College in New York under Karl Rathaus and who wrote modern ballet scores for the Henry Street dance group and others before his expatriation related that, "When I left America, I was thought of as the lowest man on the totem poll because I was a jazz musician. In the status structure of America I was considered to be the lowest one because I was a jazz musician, while in Europe when I got there, it was just the opposite. I was considered to be the top, the best one they could find. It was such a revelation. I decided why should I settle for that when I can have something like this."[19]

From 1961 on dozens of articles appeared in jazz magazines around the world on or by saxophonist Archie Shepp, a long-time Paris resident, relating his feelings on how the social situation is implicit in the music of the Black musician. His language exhibited strong condemnation of the aesthetic and social position of the jazz musician:

> There are limitations, especially in intense political times. Some people may
> call them revolutionary times. At times simply to play is not enough; but that's
> a person's judgment. At times we must do more than play. Because, I think,
> whites in America have allowed themselves the luxury . . . we have been
> reluctantly forced to give that luxury . . . of interpreting our music anyway
> they see fit. . . . Those people who went to the red light district in New Orleans.
> What did they hear? What did they see? What did they choose to hear? It is a
> question of what they choose, not what [we] intended.[20]

The impact of the 1960s black nationalist movement lessened because of the passing of hard-fought equal rights legislation in America. As a result, the musical genius of many expatriates who were seen as somehow tied to this nationalism receded further into the new cultural current of America which has led to another kind of displacement, one based as much on contact as exile.

Musical Transculturation

In trying to account for a dynamic process involving culture contact, Margaret Kartomi uses the term musical transculturation. This term tries to explain how the tension between two or more musical cultures can create a new, independent style or genre complete with its own musical identity.[21] Musical transculturation is cultural contact that has the following characteristics:

a. a group of people select and use new musical principles and concepts from a different musical culture;
b. the cause that produces and preserves the process of musical trans-culturation is principally extra-musical;
c. the process produces a new musical style or genre accepted from a relevant number of people as representative of their own musical identity.

African American avant-garde musicians are involved with creating a music that is considered at best distanced from jazz practice. Historically, these musicians were forced to make their art in lofts, cold water flats, churches, galleries, coffeehouses, dance spaces, and even the outdoors. Over time, vanguard musicians became merely interlopers within America's urban communities, unlike previous generations of artists and intellectuals. Over time, these artists exerted influence on European jazz practitioners and gained acceptance in certain European cultural niches. Today, artists like Archie Shepp, Bill Dixon, Cecil Taylor, Makanda Ken McIntryre, Milford Graves, George Russell, Steve Lacy, Andrew Cyrille, Wadada Leo Smith, Bobby Bradford, John Carter, Anthony Braxton, Yusef Lateef, Sam Rivers, Reginald Workman, William Shadrack Cole, George Lewis, John Handy, Charles Gayle, and Raphe Malik have become transnational figures. They lead or have led academic lives in the United States while conducting their recording and performing careers almost exclusively in Europe.[22] This process of transnational and transcultural dialogue between African American and European artists and other culture producers has become a separate genre created in Europe under the banner of "creative improvisational music."[23]

Between 1966 and 1981 nearly ninety recording companies originated in Europe to document an increasing presence on those shores of predominantly African American musicians who were playing the new music, a music known by a variety of names, e.g., new jazz, "the" music, "out" music, free jazz, energy music, black music, Great Black music, and the "new thing." Mal Waldron's recording of *La Gloire Du Noir* ("Black Glory") made live at the

Munich jazz club Domicile in 1971 which featured another African American émigré, the late bassist Jimmy Woode, was the inaugural album for Horst Weber's and Matthias Winckelmann's European New Jazz Association label (ENJA 2004ST). Other African American avant-garde artists whose works served as the debut or seminal release for one or another European label include Marion Brown, Billy Harper, and Joe McPhee. Brown went to Europe in 1967, and from 1968–1969 was an American Fellow in Music Composition and Performance at the Cite Internationale Des Artistes in Paris. His critically acclaimed album *Afternoon of a Georgia Faun* (ECM 1004ST), a self-described tone poem depicting the "nature and environment in Atlanta," was produced in 1970 by the German entrepreneur Manfred Eicher for his Edition of Contemporary Music label (ECM). Up to this point, ECM had primarily been a basement industry in Munich operating as Jazz by Post, or JAPO.[24] In addition, Brown's 1966 *Capricorn Moon* (Fontana ESP-Disk SFJL930) initiated the jazz catalog for the Dutch company Fontana, based in Baarn. In 1971 Texas-born tenor saxophonist Billy Harper, who refers to jazz as Black creative music, released *On Tour in Europe* (BSR 0001), the first album for Italian Giovanni Bonandrini's Black Saint label and its affiliate Soul Note Records in Milan. Joe McPhee was the initial artist for Swiss pharmaceutical executive Werner Uehlinger's "hat Hut" label of Basle ("hat Art" was subsequently founded in 1980) with *Underground Railroad* (hat A) around 1970. Uehlinger's company, formed in West Park, New York, became a transnational enterprise with the opening of offices in Switzerland in 1981. Alan Bates's Black Lion Records originated in 1968 in the United Kingdom with initial productions as diversified as Mississippi Fred McDowell's *Mississippi Blues* (BLCD760179-1992) and Sun Ra's *Pictures of Infinity*, later re-titled *Outer Spaceways Incorporated* (BLCD760191).

The following table lists the proliferation of European record companies started between 1969 and 1981 to document African American new music performers who descended on the continent:

ITALY: Black Saint, Soul Note, Fore, Horo, Ingo, Jazz, Oxford, Ferrari

GERMANY: Birth, Ring/Moers Music, Free Music Productions, New Artists Guild(precursor to FMP), Po Torch, Mood, MPS, Futura GER, Mouloudji, Sound Aspects, Saba, Calig Verlag,

	Praxis, Konnex, Sandra, European New Jazz Association (ENJA), ECM/Japo
SWEDEN:	Jazz Society
ENGLAND:	Incus, Leo (2), Ogun, Bead, Matchless, Black Lion, A Records (later called Arc), Rough Trade, Emanem
DENMARK:	Steeplechase, Dane, Brazillus
SWITZERLAND:	GNM, *hat Art* United Composers and Artists/*hat Hut*
AUSTRIA:	Reform Art Unit, Pipe
HOLLAND:	Instant Composers Pool (ICP), BvHaast, Claxon, Attacca, Broken Records, Coreco, Hummeloord, Kloet Muziek, Ooyevaar Disk, Catfish, Waterland, Timeless, Criss-Cross, Circle, KGB/Snipe Sound, Peace, Altsax, Osmosis, Fontana, Relax, Renais Sense, Elf Provincien, Intercord Freedom, Artone, Vara
FINLAND:	Leo (1)
FRANCE:	BYG Actuel, Freedom/Intercord ITC, Affinity, Toho, Pathe, America, Futura, Black & Blue, Calumet, Free Lance, Red, Palm, Blue Marge, Shandor, Sun, Calumet, Fractal, Center of the World and Goody/Gravure Universelle

The vast majority of the New York-born innovative pianist Cecil Taylor's recorded output since late 1966, nearly one hundred records, has been made in Europe. This prodigious output includes Germany's Free Music Productions' (FMP) eleven-CD documentation of a month-long series of 1988 concerts in Berlin, with Taylor performing alongside many of the leading creative musicians in Europe, including a duet with South African expatriate drummer Louis Moholo. The table below chronicles Taylor's discographical movement out of America by decade.

Taylor's first recording, *Jazz Advance*, made for American Tom Wilson's Transition label in 1955 has been called "the earliest example of the new music to find its way on record" by the pioneering British new music writer Valerie Wilmer.[25] Other early American efforts had titles like *Looking Ahead!* (Contemporary) and *Nefertiti, The Beautiful One Has Come* (Debut). While

Cecil Taylor's Label Movement

1950s	1960s	1970s	1980s	1990s
Blue Note (US)	Candid (US)	Jazz (IT)	Hat Art (SW)	FMP (GR)
Verve (US)	Impulse (US)	Unit Core+** (US)	MPS (GR)	Musica (IT)
Contemporary (US)	Debut (US)	Trio (JP)	Hat Musics (SW)	Cadence (US)
United Artists (US)	Ingo (IT)	Arista-Freedom (US)	Philips (NL)	Verve* (US)
Transition (US)	Fantana (NL)	[licensed by FR]	Soul Note (IT)	
	Blue Note (US)	ENJA (GR)	Blue Note (US)	
	Freedom (FR)	Shandor (FR)	Sound Hills (IT/JP)	
	BYG (FR)	Brain (A)	Leo (UK)	
	Pablo (US)	Free Music Prod. (GR)	A&M (US)	
	JCOA+/++ (US)	New World (US)		
	Praxis (G)	MPS (GR)		
		Hat Art (SW)		
		Columbia* (US)		
		Soul Note (IT)		

*side-person; all other listings are as leader or co-leader
**self-produced session; +American artist-driven label; ++European artist-driven label;
US = United States; NL = Netherlands; GR = Germany; G = Greece; FR = France; JP = Japan; IT = Italy;
UK = United Kingdom; A = Austria; SW = Switzerland
Table indicates label movement, not recording activity.

in Europe for six months in 1962 Taylor recorded *At the Golden Circle in Stockholm,* released by the Italian Ingo label and *At the Café Montmartre,* for Holland's Fantana Records that featured the expatriate tenor saxophonist Albert Ayler. By the mid-1960s Taylor was recognized by critic Leonard Feather as one of the avant-garde's "most important teachers and influences, while other pianists had begun to emulate his playing."[26] However, there was not a market in the United States that could accommodate the African American musical avant-garde. Despite his increasing notoriety, Taylor's records after his 1966 Blue Note release *Unit Structures* have been produced by companies throughout Europe, not the United States. There were artists and critics at that time who described Taylor's music as European derived or overly literate and inquired as to whether the music warranted inclusion in the jazz idiom. He defended his music to an audience attending a 1964 panel discussion at Bennington College on the topic "The Shape of Jazz to Come":

> I'm not interested in becoming integrated on the terms that are currently in vogue. I want to know who I am and what I am and historical books do not tell you so you cannot know that . . . there is a blind in America. . . .
>
> I'm asking you to accept me on my terms because I am standing and I have experienced certain things that I want to be evaluated on historical facts. I say that as long as history books in America don't give us that historical fact . . . my life is not a matter of theory. My life is a matter of existence. Nothing is granted me. The only thing that is granted is that which I work for, and they don't grant me anything. I take it. I make it. That's the whole point. The jazz musician has taken Western music and made of it what we wanted to make of it.[27]

The distancing of Taylor from the jazz category persists today and it is little wonder that his career for the last forty years almost exclusively resides in Europe except in self-produced circumstances or else as a side-person in rare special appearances. Rob Gibson, former director of the Lincoln Center jazz project, which grew out of the success of the summer Classical Jazz series produced in 1987 by Alina Bloomgarden along with consultant Stanley Crouch and artistic director Wynton Marsalis, cannot validate the music of Taylor as being worthy of a Lincoln Center audience, despite Taylor's curriculum vitae: "I buy his records. I listen to them at home, but I hear so much of Western European classicism in his music. I don't know if I'd call that jazz. And presenting jazz from a broad perspective is my mission at Lincoln Center."[28]

Certain European creative arts institutions have internalized the world-view of the African American vanguard by acknowledging that place, that is, locality or local factors, shapes the production and consumption of music. The European Jazz Federation was founded in 1964 in Warsaw, Poland, and eventually established its headquarters in Vienna, Austria, to promote cooperation between all European countries in the field of jazz. The development of European "national schools" of jazz, an outcome of African American penetration across the Atlantic, was as much an ideological marker as a musicological one. These schools based their distinctiveness on the assumption that sound and location is connected to identity. "Muse" is a music institute and independent record label established in Athens, Greece, by guitarist Vasilis Rakopoulos and saxophonist Antonis Ladopoulos. Their mission is to focus mainly on jazz and Mediterranean music in "an amalgam of Eastern traditions and Western practices, influenced by the Arab culture and inspired by the colorful Aegean sunset...."[29] Manfred Eicher's aforementioned ECM label established in Munich, Germany, in 1969, states that the music he records, his company's engineering and production values, and even its record covers, reflect a "new ecology of catching sound" and are evocative of northern European spaces, "of a certain quality of light and air in that region."[30]

Music training in schools such as the Swiss Jazz School in Berne, Koninklijk Conservatory in The Hague, or Siena Jazz Workshops in Italy enables players to sometimes say that the music they play has a distinct national character derived from their individual folk expressions or else influenced by climate or geography.[31] By contrast, African American creative artists tend either to defy place in order to lead successful artistic lifestyles or else relocate cultural, even ethnic roots. The increased opportunities for cultural contacts between African Americans and European producers, musicians, and endearing fans has had a profound influence on the transformation of black music or free music to European creative improvisational music, literally a new musical genre which this author conservatively estimates numbers over twelve thousand albums.

This article states that looking at music as an aspect of intellectual history can contribute to new cultural complexities derived from African American dispersal and exile, in which several generations of forward-looking jazz artists operating outside the realm of the popular entertainment industry are forgotten protagonists. Not only is music, and art in general, the principal way in which these forward-looking thinkers express themselves, but it is also a medium in which culture, identity, selfhood, and social reality are mixed together in an attempt to move the world. The notion of displacement can also be a place of identity. Expanding the geo-cultural setting of the jazz historical narrative better situates African American creative genius and helps us reshape our notions of what jazz really is. Jazz has become not just American, but an international music shaped and formed beyond the shores of the United States. Viewing the travel, movement, and displacement of several generations of African American artists offers powerful testimony to the intellectual and aesthetic benefits of scrutinizing jazz beyond the borders of its birthplace.

NOTES

1. This is an extended version of the paper given at the "Overseas Blues" conference, University of Gloucestershire, July 2004, and entitled, "Expatriation, Chosen Exile, and Musical Transculturation: African American Jazz Musicians in Europe from Bechet to Braxton."

2. Christopher Bakriges, "African American Avant-Gardism and New Jazz Criticism," in *Jazz Research Proceedings Yearbook*, #24 (Manhattan, Kans.: International Association of Jazz Educators, 2004), n.p.

3. A sampling of these avant-garde manifestoes include, Yusef A. Lateef, *Method on How to Perform Autophysiopsychic Music* (Amherst, MA: Fana Music, 1995); Anthony Braxton, *Tri-Axium Writings*, volumes 1– (New Hampshire: Frog Hollow Press, 1985); Ornette Coleman, "Harmolodics," *Musician* 12 (May 1–June 15, 1978): 8–10, and *Harmolodic Theory* web site (New York: Harmolodic, Inc., 1995); George Russell and Martin Williams, "Ornette Coleman and Tonality," *Jazz Review*, vol. 3 (June 1960): 6–10; George Russell, *Chromatic Lydian Concept of Tonal Organization* (New York: Concept Publishers, 1959, 1953); George Russell, "Where Do We Go From Here?" in Don Cerulli Burt Korall, and Mort L. Nasatir, *The Jazz Word* (New York: Da Capo, 1987, 1960), 238–39; Wadada Leo Smith, Liner Notes, *New Dalta Ahkri: Reflectivity*. Kaball (2, 1975); Peter Bull and Alex Gibney, *John Carter and Bobby Bradford: The New Music* (Rhapsody Films, 1986); William Parker, *Sound Journal* (New York: Centering Music, 1998); Lawrence D. "Butch" Morris, Liner Notes, *Testament: A Conduction Collection*. New World (80478-2, 1995), and Suzanne McElfresh, "Butch Morris' Conduction—Improvisation with a Wave of the Hand," *Down Beat*, September 1992, 64–65; George Lewis, *A Power Greater Than Itself: The Association for the Advancement of Creative Musicians* (Chicago: University of Chicago, forthcoming); Bill Dixon, *L'Opera: A Collection of Letters, Writings, Musical Scores, Drawings, and Photographs, 1967–1986*, Vol. 1 (North Bennington:, VT: Metamorphosis Music, BMI, 1986); Sun Ra, *The Immeasurable Equation* (Chicago, 1980), and "The Possibility of Altered Destiny," DIW Records (DIW388B, 1994); Glenn Spearman, *The Musa-Physics: Myth, Science, Poetics* (Berkeley, CA: Ascension Publication, 1996); Marion Brown, *Recollections* (Frankfurt: JAS Publications, 1984), and *Faces and Places: The Music and Travels of a Contemporary Jazz Musician*, Masters Thesis (Wesleyan University, 1976), and "Improvisation and the Aural

Tradition in Afro-American Music," *Black World*, November 1973; Randy Weston Interview, African American Oral History Collection (Smithsonian Institution, 1995).

4. This is detailed in Christopher Bakriges, *African American Musical Avant-Gardism*, Dissertation (York University, 2001).

5. See Theresa Leininger-Mill, *African-American Artists in Paris, 1922–34*, Dissertation (Yale University, 1995).

6. Eileen Southern, *The Music Of Black Americans: A History* (New York: W. W. Norton and Company, 1983, 1971), 494. Although three other blues artists preceded Broonzy to Europe, they did so in other capacities. Alberta Hunter left for Europe in 1927 for primarily theatrical reasons, eventually appearing in the 1928 London production of *Showboat* with Paul Robeson. Josh White's popularity in Britain first occurred as a folk singer during the Second World War when the BBC began broadcasting his performances for the U.S. Office of War Information. Blacklisted by the House Un-American Activities Commission for his association with Robeson's communist-backed charity performances, White's career veered to Europe in late 1950 where he recorded for both Vogue in France and EMI in Britain. Huddie Ledbetter (a.k.a. Leadbelly) first traveled to Europe in 1949, where he appeared in jazz events in Paris, only six weeks before succumbing to amyotrophic lateral sclerosis.

7. Bruce Eder, Album review of *Amsterdam Live Concerts 1953* on the Munich label, released June 2006. All Music Guide. AEC One-Stop Group, Inc. www.billboard.com/bbcom/discography/index.

8. William Broonzy, *Big Bill Blues: William Broonzy's Story as told to Yannick Bruynoghe* (New York: Da Capo Press, 1995; New York: Oak Publications, 1964. Originally published by Grove Press in 1955).

9. These festivals have been documented in both CD and DVD collections entitled *The American Folk Blues Festival* and are available from Universal Music and Reelin' in the Years Productions, reelinintheyears.com. A five-CD box set from 1962–1965 concerts is available from Evidence Music (ECD-26100).

10. Reid Badger, *A Life in Ragtime: A Biography of James Reese Europe* (New York and Oxford: Oxford University Press, 1995), 7.

11. James Reese Europe, "A Negro Explains 'Jazz,'" *The Literary Digest*, April 26, 1919, 29, reprinted in Robert Walser, ed., *Keeping Time: Readings in Jazz History* (Oxford and New York: Oxford University Press, 1999), 14.

12. See Mal Collings's discography on the Sidney Bechet Society, Ltd. Web Site, www.sidneybechet.org.

13. John Chilton, *Sidney Bechet: The Wizard of Jazz* (New York: Da Capo Press, 1996, 1987), 284–85.

14. Henry Louis Gates, Jr., "An Interview With Josephine Baker and James Baldwin," in Quincy Troupe, ed. *James Baldwin: The Legacy* (New York: Simon and Schuster/Touchstone, 1973, 1989), 166.

15. Joe Roseburg. "Anthony Braxton," *Windplayer* 10/5 (1993): 50.

16. Scott DeVeaux, *The Birth of Bebop: A Social and Musical History* (Los Angeles: University of California Press, 1997), 87. The *Ile de France* was also the vessel that carried Teddy Hill's Savoy Review to Europe in 1937. The sixty-two-person troupe, made up of chorus girls, dance teams, and a tramp band, also included a big band which introduced audiences to a young John Birks "Dizzy" Gillespie's playing the new jazz conceptions later dubbed Be-bop. See John Birks

Gillespie with Wilmot Alfred Fraser, *To Be or Not . . . To Bop* (Garden City, N.Y.: Doubleday and Company, Inc., 1979), 74.

17. Stan Britt, *Dexter Gordon: A Musical Biography* (New York: Da Capo Press, 1989), 84.

18. Orrin Keepnews, *The View From Within: Jazz Writings, 1948–1987* (New York and Oxford: Oxford University Press, 1988), 195.

19. Quoted in Chuck France's video, *Jazz in Exile* (Rhapsody Films, 1986). Also see Nathaniel Mackey and Herman Gray, "Notes from an Expatriate: A Conversation with Pianist/Composer Mal Waldron," *Jazz Spotlite News*, 1981, 18–21.

20. Lawrence Neal, "A Conversation with Archie Shepp," *Liberator* 15 (November 1961): 11. Avant-garde artists, events, and organizations are part of a discourse concerning jazz criticism considered in Bakriges, "African American Avant-Gardism and New Jazz Criticism," *Jazz Research Proceedings Yearbook*, #24, 2004.

21. Margaret Kartomi, "The Process and Results of Musical Culture Contact: A Discussion of Terminology and Concepts," *Ethnomusicology* 25 (1981): 234.

22. Bill Dixon, Arthur Brooks, Milford Graves, Charles Gayle, Raphe Malik (Bennington College), George Russell and Steve Lacy (New England Conservatory), Charlie Haden (Cal Arts), Bobby Bradford (Pomona College and UCLA), Archie Shepp, Yusef Lateef (UMass, Amherst), Wadada Leo Smith (Cal Arts, Bard College), Makanda Ken McIntyre (CUNY), Bill Cole (Dartmouth), Cecil Taylor, Andrew Cyrille (Antioch College, Glassboro State College, U Wisconsin Madison), George Lewis (Cal Arts, New York University), Anthony Braxton (Wesleyan, Mills College), Reggie Workman (New School for Social Research).

23. Christopher Bakriges, "Musical Transculturation: From African American Avant-Garde Jazz to European Creative Improvisation, 1962–81," in E. Taylor Atkins, ed., *Jazz Planet* (Jackson, Miss.: University Press of Mississippi), 103.

24. Technically, Eicher's first release was *Free at Last* (ECM 1001) by pianist Mal Waldron, recorded in November 1969 in a limited edition.

25. Valerie Wilmer, *As Serious As Your Life: The Story of the New Jazz* (Westport, Conn.: Lawrence Hall, 1980, 1977), 55.

26. Leonard Feather, *The Encyclopedia of Jazz in the Sixties* (New York: Horizon Press, 1966), 271.

27. Cecil Taylor interview. New York City, May 1999.

28. Howard Mandel, "Questions, Questions, Questions: Answers in the Works?" *Ear: Magazine of New Music* 15 (March 1991): 44–45.

29. Muse is operated through their web site Muse.gr.com/

30. Frank Bergerot and Arnaud Merlin, *The Story of Jazz: Bop and Beyond* (New York: Harry N. Abrams, Inc., 1993, 1991), 97.

31. *Jazz Education Journal*, an on-line publication by the International Association of Jazz Educators reproduced fascinating results of a survey conducted by saxophonist David Liebman at his annual International Saxophone Master Class at East Stroudsburg University of Pennsylvania. See "Thoughts from Jazz Students Around the World," by Patrick Dorian and Dr. Terry Giffel, May 2001 issue. See www.iaje.org/article.asp?ArticleID=33

Contributors

Pianist and composer **Christopher G. Bakriges** is lecturer and artist-in-residence at Elms College in Massachusetts and has written on jazz and world culture. His recent publications appear in *The Source: Challenging Jazz Criticism*, published by Leeds College of Music; *Jazz Research Proceedings Yearbook*, produced by the International Association of Jazz Educators; *2006 Proceedings of the Twentieth Annual National Conference on Liberal Arts and the Education of Artists* published by New York's School of Visual Arts; and *Jazz Planet*, by University Press of Mississippi. Bakriges has a Ph.D. in musicology/ethnomusicology from York University in Toronto and M.A.s in world music from Wesleyan University in Connecticut and in International Politics and Economics from the University of Detroit.

Sean Creighton works for community and voluntary sector organizations and is active in a number of historical fields, including UK black history (see www.seancreighton.co.uk). His contribution builds on his talk "Politics and Culture: Paul Robeson in the UK" at the 100th Robeson Birth Anniversary Conference held in 1998 at the School of Oriental and African Studies, subsequently published by Agenda Services in 1999.

Independent historian, broadcaster, and author **Jeffrey Green** has written *Edmund Thornton Jenkins: The Life and Times of an American Black Composer,*

1894–1926 (Greenwood Press, 1982) and *Black Edwardians: Black People in Britain, 1901–1914* (Frank Cass, 1998), contributed essays to several collections, and had multiple articles published in *Immigrants and Minorities, New Community, Storyville, The Black Perspective in Music* (New York), and the *Black Music Research Journal* (Chicago). He is currently working on the biography of composer Samuel Coleridge-Taylor (1875–1912), the London-born son of an African. He edited the Coleridge-Taylor edition of the *Black Music Research Journal* (Fall 2001: published in 2003).

Leighton Grist is senior lecturer in Media and Film Studies at the University of Winchester where he is programs director for the MA in Film. The writer of numerous articles published in edited collections and journals, his work centers predominantly upon the intersection of film, theory, and culture. He is the author of *The Films of Martin Scorsese 1963–77* (Macmillan/ St. Martin's Press, 2000) and is presently working on a follow-up volume.

Bob Groom is a music historian, writer, reviewer, and broadcaster. He is probably best known as the one-time editor and publisher of *Blues World* and for his book *The Blues Revival* (Studio Vista, 1971). He has written Blues World Booklets on Robert Johnson (1967), Charlie Patton (1969), and Blind Lemon Jefferson (1970). In addition he has written numerous CD notes for Document Records and contributed to *The Blackwell Guide to Recorded Blues* (1996), *Aspects of Elvis: Tryin' to Get You* (1994), and to various magazines including *Blues & Rhythm, Juke Blues, Living Blues,* and *American Music Magazine.*

Rainer E. Lotz, an economist and mechanical engineer by education, is a retired civil servant (development aid) and lecturer in political science who has compiled more than fifty LP and CD anthologies of historic recordings and authored over 160 articles in scholarly journals and more than eighty monographs, including *German Ragtime and Pre-History of Jazz* (1985), *The AFRS Jubilee Radio Transcription Service* (1985), *Under the Imperial Carpet— Essays in Black History* (1987), *The Banjo on Record* (1993), *Hitler's Airwaves* (1997), *Black People—Entertainers of African Descent* (1997), *Beyond Recall— A Documentation of Jewish Musical Life in Nazi Berlin, 1933–1938* (2001), and *Live from the Cotton Club* (2003). His current projects include the

German National Discography (twenty-one volumes published to date) and a Biographical Dictionary of Entertainment in Germany.

Paul Oliver is an international scholar, reviewer, broadcaster, and musicologist whose influence has been enormous in two areas—vernacular architecture and African American music. He has written numerous publications in both areas, including the award-winning book *Blues Fell This Morning*, and is the winner of a Sony Radio Award and the Grand Prix du Disque for his programs on blues music. His many other publications include: *Savannah Syncopators, Yonder Come the Blues, Screening the Blues*, and editing the *Blackwell Guide to Blues Records*. He is the editor of the four-volume *Encyclopedia of Vernacular Architecture of the World* (which was published by Cambridge University Press in 1997). Oliver has been connected with Oxford Brookes University for many years, and was associate head of the School of Architecture between 1978 and 1988. Among his many honors is the MBE awarded by the Queen in 2003 in recognition of his contribution to architectural education.

Catherine Parsonage is head of the Centre for Jazz Studies at Leeds College of Music. She completed a Ph.D. on early jazz in Britain at City University, London, and her book, *The Evolution of Jazz in Britain 1880–1935*, was published by Ashgate in 2005. Parsonage was awarded a prestigious Edison Fellowship at the British Library for 2006–7.

Roberta Freund Schwartz is assistant professor at University of Kansas in Lawrence, Kansas. Her interests include the music of the Renaissance, Spanish music, and African American urban popular music. Among her publications are "To Get My Hambone Boiled: Food as Sexual Euphemism in the Blues," *Journal of Popular Culture* (forthcoming), a review-essay, "*Cambridge Companion to Jazz, Jazz and the Germans*, and *The New Grove Dictionary of Jazz*, 2d ed.," in *College Music Symposium* 43 (2003), and "From Criado to Canonization: Music in the Life of Saint Francis of Borja," in *Essays on Music and Culture in Honor of Herbert Kellman*, ed. Barbara Haggh (Klincksieck, 2001).

Iris Schmeisser completed an internship at the Museum of Modern Art, New York, in 2005 and is now an assistant professor of American cultural history at the University of Erlangen, Germany. Her book *Transatlantic*

Crossings between Paris and New York: Pan-Africanism, Cultural Difference and the Arts is forthcoming.

Robert Springer is emeritus professor of American civilization at the University of Metz, France. He has contributed articles, interviews with blues performers, and reviews to such specialist magazines as *Blues Unlimited, Living Blues*, and *Jefferson*. He is the author of various scholarly articles and of *Le Blues authentique, son histoire et ses thèmes* (1985), whose English translation, with André Prévos, appeared as *Authentic Blues: Its History and Its Themes* (1995), and of *Fonctions sociales du blues* (1999). He convened the 2000 and 2002 conferences on "The Lyrics in African American Popular Music" at the University of Metz. The proceedings of the former were edited under the same title (2001), while selected contributions to the latter were published as *Nobody Knows Where the Blues Come From: Lyrics and History* (2006).

Rupert Till is a senior lecturer in music at the University of Huddersfield, teaching in the areas of composition, popular music, and music technology. His most recent publication focused on electronic dance music and Christianity in a special edition of the *Culture and Religion Journal* (Routledge, March 2006). He has also written about popular iconography and the star system, Britpop, and music production techniques. He is an active composer and performer, having studied with composers Gavin Bryars, Christopher Hobbs, and Katharine Norman. He founded electronica group Chillage People, whose music is distributed online through i-tunes and on CD by Liquid Sound Design and Vagalume/Ultimae records.

Guido van Rijn received his Ph.D. from Leiden University (1995) and teaches English at Kennemer Lyceum in Overveen, the Netherlands. His previous award-winning book *Roosevelt's Blues: African-American Blues and Gospel Songs on FDR* (University Press of Mississippi, 1997) is a companion volume to *The Truman and Eisenhower Blues: African-American Blues and Gospel Songs, 1945–1960* (Continuum, 2004). A freelance writer and blues historian, he has published articles in *Blues Unlimited, Blues & Rhythm, Juke Blues, Living Blues* and *78 Quarterly*. He has also produced eighteen LPs and CDs for his own Agram label and, in 1970, co-founded the Netherlands Blues and Boogie Organization which culminated in the annual Utrecht Blues Estafette.

David Webster is senior lecturer in religion, philosophy, and ethics at the University of Gloucestershire. His main research interests are in Buddhist studies, the philosophy of desire, and issues of aging, sickness, and death in philosophy and religion. He has written several articles and his first book, *The Philosophy of Desire in the Buddhist Pali Canon*, was published by Routledge Curzon in 2005.

Neil A. Wynn is professor of twentieth-century American history at the University of Gloucestershire. He has published several works on African American and American history, most notably *The Afro-American and the Second World War* (Paul Elek, 1976; Holmes & Meier, 1976, paperback 1993), *From Progressivism to Prosperity: American Society and the First World War* (Holmes & Meier, 1986), and a *Historical Dictionary from Great War to Great Depression* (Scarecrow Press, 2003). He has also written numerous articles and reviews including pieces on American society and World War II, trans-atlantic race relations, Mike Tyson, and *The Sopranos*.

Index